SWITZERLAND UNDER SIEGE

1939 – 1945

A Neutral Nation's Struggle for Survival

Edited by

Leo Schelbert

Foreword by

Faith Whittlesey

PICTON PRESS
ROCKPORT, MAINE

Published under the auspices of the *American Swiss Foundation* and the *Swiss
American Historical Society*. This book is *Swiss American Historical Society
Special Publication No. 18*

First Printing December 2000

This book is available from:

Picton Press
PO Box 250
Rockport, ME 04856-0250

Visa/MasterCard orders:
1-207-236-6565
FAX orders: 1-207-236-6713
e-mail: sales@pictonpress.com
Internet secure credit card orders: www.pictonpress.com
Web site: www.pictonpress.com

Manufactured in the United States of America
Printed on 60# acid-free paper

TABLE OF CONTENTS

LIST OF ILLUSTRATIONS

FOREWORD

Switzerland is one of the oldest constitutional republics in the world. Having few natural resources, the Swiss, relying principally on ingenuity and exceptionally sound governing arrangements, nevertheless built a stable, prosperous society based on the rule of law and stout protections of individual liberties. The original 1848 Swiss constitution establishing the modern Swiss state, fashioned in some respects after the U. S. Constitution, has frequently been cited as a model of wisdom and forethought. And with a longstanding policy of active, armed neutrality, the Swiss have ensured the safety of their state and their citizens in an uncertain world, without compromising individual freedoms.

The short version of the Swiss and World War II history is this:

- A landlocked democratic country with an ancient history of neutrality, Switzerland prepared to defend herself as fascism engulfed Europe and the continental democracies collapsed in the face of superior power.
- Switzerland's serious preparations for war made invasion more costly to a prospective aggressor.
- She banned the Nazi party, shot German spies, and maintained her federal and democratic institutions, including a free press, free universities, and even free theater.
- Encircled and neutral, she traded with Germany and with the Allies alike for food and fuel to maintain a bare-subsistence standard of living during the war.
- She accepted and protected 230,000 refugees, Jewish and non-Jewish, from 1933 to 1945 — a number which in proportion to population was by far the highest accepted and protected by any country during World War II.
- Short of food and fuel and facing unemployment, she also, and most regrettably, turned back 25,000 refugees, a national policy decision which was not consistently enforced and which Switzerland acknowledged long ago as a grave moral lapse.

- She treated the nearly 1,700 American servicemen interned in Switzerland during the war no worse than her own citizens, saving the Americans from Axis stalags or death.
- The International Committee of the Red Cross, a Swiss institution, and Switzerland's service as "Protecting Power" ameliorated the suffering of prisoners of war on all sides.

I am one who believes that had other European countries reacted to the Nazi expansion and aggression as did the Swiss, the spiral into the inferno might have been halted. This is, I acknowledge, an unprovable claim. Yet it is more plausible than any other claim — in recent years presented in the U.S. press and set forth by the Department of State Report, the so-called Eizenstadt Report — that the small country Switzerland, which did so much to ensure the safety of her very sound institutions and to protect victims of war, should be held accountable for the duration of a war she could not prevent and, once it was unleashed, was in no position to influence.

It was also important to consider that the decentralized and open Swiss political system, with its provisions for direct democracy and its capacity to ensure the full flowering of individual ability, proved barren ground for the seeds of hate and passion that sprouted in Germany and much of Europe.

Americans might do well to reflect soberly about the world we live in. It is not such a safe place for constitutional democracies. American and Swiss institutions, similar in many respects, have worked well and, in the main, made possible levels of human fulfillment that could once only have been imagined. Even if one were to ignore Switzerland's long history of stability and individual liberty, or her history in World War II, it is worth noting that for the roughly fifty years of the Cold War, Switzerland, while retaining her formal neutrality, stood as a stoutly defended example of political and economic liberty. There was never any ambiguity in Swiss foreign policy or defense planning about what values she cherished and defended.

America has had friends and allies markedly less conscientious than Switzerland about protecting individual liberties and offering genuine prospects for individual fulfillment and advancement. Whether or not Switzerland could be counted for reasons of interest or sentiment to be a friend or ally, formal or informal, of the United States, is, ultimately, less important than the fact that Switzerland is a constitutional democracy which offers her own citizens exceptionally good circumstances in which to live meaningful lives. And Switzerland is a nation which, in turbulent times, has looked to her own defenses. Such a nation, whether large or small and whether or not bound to the United States by historical or emotional ties, should invariably receive fair and respectful treatment from the United States. Democracies face enough threats and dangers in the world, and there are still too few of them.

This book is a valuable contribution to the body of literature that can instruct and illuminate English-speaking readers about Switzerland's situation and actions during the dark and turbulent years of World War II. Americans and others who wish to know about this period deserve serious, truthful accounts. Because Switzerland is small and neutral, she attracts far too little interest in the United States. Because Switzerland protects and defends democratic virtues, she should always be regarded, however, as a true and valued friend of the United States. In this context, the American-Swiss relationship, until the late 1990s so rock solid, is a relationship that needs and deserves thoughtful care and understanding in the future. The essays contained in this volume are a most welcome addition to the literature about Switzerland in World War II available in English.

Faith Whittlesey, former U.S. Ambassador to Switzerland

INTRODUCTION

Like other countries of the Western World which struggled through the Second World War,[1] Switzerland too has come under severe criticism from within as well as from without its borders.[2] Whereas members of a previous generation, especially those who endured those years of trial, acknowledged, admired and perhaps unduly idealized the foresight, dedication, and courage of those in decision-making positions as well as of the people at large,[3] scholarly and journalistic utterances of recent years seem to vie with each other to find fault, to criticize, and to condemn.[4] Too often, it seems,

---

[1] Of the extensive literature see for instance Yoav Gelber, "Moralist and Realistic Approaches in the Study of the Allies' Attitude to the Holocaust," in: *Comprehending the Holocaust. Historical and Literary Research*. Edited by Asher Cohen, Yoav Gelber, and Charlotte Wardi (Frankfurt a. M.: Peter Lang, 1988): 107–123. Gelber, 107 refers to the "Allies, the neutral states, international agencies such as the Church or the International [Committee of the] Red Cross and the Jews outside occupied Europe" being labeled by the critics as "Bystanders." For a critical review of the various positions see William D. Rubinstein, *The Myth of Rescue. Why the Democracies Could Not Have Saved More Jews from the Nazis* (London: Routledge, 1997): 1–14. Peter Novick, *The Holocaust in American Life* (Boston: Houghton Mifflin, 1999): 47–59 also dismisses much of the criticism, stresses unemployment in the United States as an understandable barrier to admission of large numbers of refugees, and refers to the accusations against the Swiss banks as self-serving "exploitation by politicians" (230).

[2] The extensive literature is reviewed by Georg Kreis, "Neue Forschungen zum Zweiten Weltkrieg in der Schweiz", in: *Neue Forschungen zum Zweiten Weltkrieg. Literaturberichte und Bibliographien*. Herausgegeben von Jürgen Rohwer und Hildegard Müller (Koblenz: Bernard & Graefe, 1990): 418–426; also in "Vier Debatten und wenig Dissens," *Schweizerische Zeitschrift für Geschichte* 47 (1997): 451–476; the whole issue is devoted to the subject of Switzerland in World War II, pp. 449–808; the footnotes represent a veritable compendium of relevant references to the themes covered to 1997.

[3] See for instance Urs Schwarz, *The Eye of the Hurricane. Switzerland in World War Two*. Boulder, CO: Westview Press, 1980; also Werner Rings, *Schweiz im Krieg 1933–1945. Ein Bericht*. 2. Auflage. Zürich: Ex Libris, 1974; Rings questions only aspects of the refugee policies.

[4] See for instance Jean Ziegler, *The Swiss, the Gold, and the Dead*. Translated by John Brownjohn. New York: Harcourt Brace, 1997, paperback 1999 ; Peter F. Koch, *Geheim-Depot Schweiz. Wie Banken am Holocaust verdienen*. Mit einem Kapitel von Richard Chaim Schneider. München: List Verlag, 1997. A typical summary comment is that of Hans Ulrich Jost: "The main concern of official Switzerland did not relate to the war and its moral tragedy, but the optimal preservation of a highly developed economy based on private

commentators—safe at their desks, facing neither possible invasions, bombings, and blockades, nor increasing unemployment nor looming scarcity of food and heating materials—forget "the scorching winds of mortal danger that swept across the borders of Switzerland in those years."[5] They also appear to ignore the immense difficulties involved in understanding events in the midst of the war's turbulence and struggle for survival in contrast to the benefit of hindsight they enjoy.[6] To these conditions may be added the daunting task of finding places for thousands of refugees in a country marked by scarcity of space, food, and places to work. Unemployment resulting from the 1930s Great Depression still had not been fully vanquished.[7]

This work, however, does not intend to enter the controversies aired in scholarly or public debate but, like other publications, hopes principally to *inform* about some of the significant aspects of the years 1939 to 1945. During those years the neutral country of Switzerland, then numbering some 4.2 million residents, gave refuge to some 300,000 people and struggled to find its way in the face of overwhelming military, economic, and ideological perils.[8]

---

property;" see *Politik und Wirtschaft im Krieg. Die Schweiz 1938–1948* (Zürich: Chronos Verlag, 1998): 27. Four accusatory titles appeared in 1998, eight in 1999; three of the latter were paperback editions of previously published works.

[5] Urs Schwarz, *Hurricane*, p. xv.

[6] Yoav Gelber, in "Moralist and Realistic Approaches," *Comprehending the Holocaust*, 120, referring to the "Gentile free world" and to leaders such as the Pope, W. Churchill, and F. D. Roosevelt, observes: "The principal issue in the eyes of all these persons, both temporal and spiritual, was, of course, the war. In its early years it was a war for survival, and in its later stages, too, it was still everywhere the greatest national effort that had ever been mobilized to achieve national goals."

[7] Novick, *Holocaust*, 48, claims "that the 'comfortable morality tale' ... is simply bad history" and "ignores real constraints at the time." See also Carl Ludwig, *Die Flüchtlingspolitik der Schweiz seit 1933 bis zur Gegenwart (1957). Bericht* (Bern: Herbert Lang, 1966): 89 and E. von Steiger's comment, 380: "... that it was practically impossible to accept a still larger number [of refugees] since it could be neither technically nor financially mastered" and that "the leaders of the Swiss Jewry had declared that the task was overwhelming them." Pertinent is also Helmut F. Pfanner's comment: "No other country has given such an open account [already in 1957!] of its refugee policy, and no other country has been more severely criticized... ;" see "The Role of Switzerland for the Refugees" in" *The Muses Flee Hitler. Cultural Transfer and Adaptation 1930–1945*. Edited by Jarrell C. Jackman and Carla M. Borden (Washington, D. C.: Smithsonian Institution Press, 1983): 235-248; quotation p. 235.

[8] This work follows Yoav Gelber's view that applies also to Neutrals such as Switzerland: "The Second World War should therefore be a principal parameter for the examination of the Allies' responses;" see "Moralist and Realistic Responses", in *Comprehending the Holocaust*, p.110.

This book has three segments. Essays in Part One are essentially about the calamities of war that led to a mobilization for a vigorously publicized and comprehensive armed resistance in the hope of sparing the people of Switzerland the orgy of repression, violence, and destruction that had been unleashed on the peoples surrounding the country. The studies of Part Two explore the demands which perpetual neutrality imposed on the Swiss nation in the domain of foreign policy, trade, and finance as well as on the services Switzerland provided as a Protecting Power to the belligerents and which represented an integral aspect of 'active' Swiss neutrality. At the same time neutrality meant being vigorously non-neutral in the ideological struggle against totalitarianism, racist violence, and politically sanctioned murder. Part Three consists of an appendix with some texts that highlight, first, the often overlooked dangers deriving from demoralization, since during the long war years the people did not have the benefit of hindsight now given; second, the understanding of Swiss neutrality as forcefully outlined in the midst of the conflagration by one of its foremost students; third an unsolicited retrospective view of Swiss 'benevolent neutrality' by an American who spent three years in the heat of battle for accurate news about the enemy's designs in Bern, the capital of Switzerland. A chronology covering the years 1938 to 1945 then provides a brief overview of the main events relevant to those turbulent years.

In the first essay of Part One Hans Senn, a scholar and former Chief of General Staff of the Swiss Armed Forces, sketches the ebb and flow of the Axis powers' threats of invasion which Switzerland faced during World War II. He shows, further, how the army leadership, especially its commander-in-chief General Henri Guisan, constantly adjusted its planning for a determined and elastic resistance to all forms of possible Axis designs. It was often difficult, Hans Senn insists, to ascertain in those turbulent months what was simply posturing by the Axis leadership and what were truly serious threats, especially considering Hitler's quick abandonment of most solemn assurances, the fast conquests of countries such as Belgium and Norway, and the shockingly swift fall of a presumably invincible France. The analysis of the still extant plans of invasion demonstrate that Hitler's comments were more than mere verbiage when he stated: "The Swiss are nothing but an aberrant branch of our people" and: "A State such as Switzerland, which is nothing but a puss-filled sore of Europe, such a thing is simply intolerable!"[9] The article further illustrates that the plan of an Alpine redoubt was in no way a "submissive gesture" as has been claimed, but a potentially effective strategy of deterrence that certainly did not mean a heartless abandonment of the people of the Swiss lowlands. The author concludes by challenging the claim that the armed neutrality observed towards the Allies as well as the Axis had been immoral and had unnecessarily prolonged the war.

In the second essay the historian Jürg Stüssi-Lauterburg expands the discussion by setting the military and diplomatic threats against Switzerland's very existence into the context of the three totalitarian regimes—Fascist Italy, National Socialist Germany, and Soviet Russia. The author explains why Stalin hated "the swine" as he called the Swiss nation, why Mussolini hoped to dismember it and wanted to use its Alpine region or a truncated form of its territory as a buffer against an overbearing German Third Reich, and why in Hitler's circles the country was simply the nasty porcupine, the "Stachelschwein" (i. e. the "barbed *swine*"). Calls for unconditional resistance, Jürg Stüssi-Lauterburg demonstrates, publicly and loudly issued especially by General Henri Guisan, as well as the bitter invective of much of the Swiss press against National Socialist ideology and the regime's infamous policies, were viewed by Hitler's regime as irresponsible and irritating provocation.[10] The author also stresses that the preparedness and determination of the Swiss militia army was fully acknowledged by German military circles as being formidable and, in the event of an attempted conquest, would tie down numerous divisions and, after victory, demand a sustained military presence that the Axis powers simply could not spare from other fronts.

The mobilization of women for the Swiss armed forces was, as Thomas Maissen shows, mainly complementary and excluded women from potential combat, which was then viewed as irreconcilable with a woman's true nature. The women's accomplishments, however, as heads of families or as managers of businesses or farms coping with the absence of husbands on active duty, were highly prized and readily acknowledged during the war years as a vital and indispensable part of military preparedness. The

---

[9] Werner Jochman, ed., *Adolf Hitler Monologe im Führer-Hauptquartier, 1941–1944. Die Aufzeichnungen Heinrich Heims* (Hamburg: Albrecht Knaus, 1980): 217 and 365; the statements were made in January and August 1942.

[10] Jürg Fink, *Die Schweiz aus der Sicht des Dritten Reiches 1933–1945*. Zürich: Schulthess Polygraphischer Verlag, 1985, is a detailed study of how Switzerland was perceived from numerous perspectives by the Third Reich; see however Klaus Urner, *"Die Schweiz muss noch geschluckt werden!" Hitler's Aktionspläne gegen die Schweiz Überarbeitete und aktualisierte Neuausgabe* (Zürich: Pendo, 1998), 21-23, for a critique of Fink's study.

women's experience in the armed forces, the author holds, as well as their managerial independence during World War Two, prepared the ground for the women to strive for eventual full parity with men also in the public domain of Swiss life. The 'Defense Letter' No. 9, issued after mid-1940 by the branch of the Swiss Army called 'Army and Home' to combat demoralization—it is reproduced below in the Appendix—provides some telling insight into the situation of ordinary Swiss women and men.

American scholar James H. Hutson turns to a quite different military facet of the Second World War by offering a study of the mistaken bombing of Switzerland by the Allied Air Force and the complex reactions to the events in Switzerland and the United States. He sketches not only the actual events as experienced and as reported in the Swiss and American press, but also explores the views expressed in official communiqués of the respective governments and of the Air Force, and he contrasts those reports with an analysis of the actual happenings. James H. Hutson empathetically features the nearly insurmountable obstacles faced by the pilots due to weather conditions and a radar technology still in its early stages of development. In his view the ideological bond between the United States and Switzerland as 'Sister Republics' proved to be an invaluable asset at a time when fatal bombing errors meant deadly destruction and strained the relations between the two nations.[11]

While the essays of Part One of this book explore aspects connected with warfare, Part Two is about a peculiarly Swiss problem, Switzerland's stance of perpetual, unconditional, and active neutrality as a principle of foreign policy in peace as well as in war. Edgar Bonjour, one of the foremost scholars of this subject, offers a detached survey of how this attitude was translated into complex decisions during both World Wars which were marked by incredible violence and a collapse of the traditional distinction between the military and civilians. The essay receives added force if read in combination with Edgar Bonjour's analysis, reproduced in the Appendix, of what he considered to be the true meaning of Swiss neutrality. Bonjour quotes approvingly the Swiss writer Heinrich Federer:

---

[11] The theme of the 'Sister Republics' is featured by James H. Hutson, *The Sister Republics. Switzerland and the United States from 1776 to the Present.* Washington, D. C.: Library of Congress, 1991; second expanded edition 1992.—George Gyssler, then a teenager volunteering in the Aircraft Observation and Reporting Services of the Swiss Air Force, comments as follows in a private communication of 5/5/2000 to the editor concerning the 1944/45 bombing: "We felt sorry for the crews who dropped their bombs in the wrong place. We thought they must have felt horrible when they realized their mistakes. We were in no way angry at the Americans, on the contrary, we had pity on them. The thought of blaming them for the damage of the bombing did not enter our minds."

"It does not only take courage to be in the storm, it also takes courage to be the island in the storm."[12]

In "Between Hammer and Anvil" Heinz K. Meier explores the burdensome dilemma for the Swiss nation, that in order to survive as a country—economically, militarily, and politically—it had to rely in part on a regime whose aims, policies, and criminal misdeeds a majority of Swiss people abhorred. With the entry of the United States into the war, Switzerland faced both the 'anvil' of extensive Axis demands and the 'hammer' of the demands of the Allies, enforced by their freezing of Switzerland's assets, their blockade of its desperately needed imports, and the blacklisting of Swiss firms supplying Germany with goods in return for vital supplies, especially coal. What enabled the nation to get by was patient negotiating and a constant re-balancing of the contradictory demands of necessity and policy. Also significant were, as Heinz K. Meier shows, a certain negligence of the Axis powers in using their economic weapons, and the understanding which many Allied negotiators displayed for the dilemma the Swiss faced in their struggle for survival. The rationing of goods and a massive expansion of plowland under governmental direction within the framework of the Wahlen plan vitally supplemented the efforts concerning exports and imports and spared Switzerland the perils of hunger.[13]

Little known and somewhat ignored by the critics of Switzerland's actions in World War II is Switzerland's provision of the 'good offices' that, as a chosen 'Protecting Power' for the belligerents, the neutral nation of Switzerland was called upon to undertake. Leo Schelbert's essay summarizes some of the main studies that have explored these activities. These included numerous attempts to get the warring parties to the negotiating table, to provide meeting places acceptable to both sides in the conflict, to protect a belligerent's property in enemy country, to look after prisoners of war and interned civilians, and to insist on the implementation of international conventions concerning the treatment of soldiers and captives. It is an astonishing story that happened largely in secrecy and remained hidden from public view. It involved actions that at times

---

[12] See Walther Hofer, "Neutralität im totalen Krieg" in: *Einblick in die schweizerische Aussenpolitik. Zum 65. Geburtstag von Raymond Probst.* Herausgegeben von Edouard Brunner et al. (Zürich: Verlag Neue Zürcher Zeitung, 1984): 171-200, for an incisive survey of "how badly neutral states fared in the Second World War, the first truly total war" (171).

[13] Josef Rosen, *Wartime Food Developments in Switzerland.* War-Peace Pamphlets, No. 9 (Stanford, CA: Stanford University, Food Research Institute, 1947): 104; the study presents a fact-filled and illuminating analysis of the subject; see especially Chapter V: "Wartime Expansion of Arable Farming", 38-48.

demanded undaunting courage, imaginative use of available means, and selfless dedication. Those who are inclined to reduce Swiss official actions during World War II to heartless xenophobia and selfish exploitation should ponder these worldwide efforts of Swiss diplomats and of the delegates of the International Committee of the Red Cross, a private Swiss organization, to mitigate the heartbreak and hatreds caused by war.

The final essay of Part Two illustrates that, as Edgar Bonjour succinctly put it, "Neutrality is a principle of foreign policy, not of ethics. . . . In the moral domain Swiss know no neutrality." The Swiss *Wochenschau* and the *Armeefilmdienst* featured by Stephen Halbrook document the intense involvement of Swiss in the ideological struggle during the Second World War. While some Swiss 'Frontists' saw in Hitler's goals the dawn of a new European, if not global, order and supported the intensive German propaganda effort; while some other Swiss groups perceived the future in Communism and looked to Moscow to slay the National Socialist dragon as well as the Capitalist beast; the vast majority of Swiss supported unconditional military and ideological resistance to all threats of invasion and subversion as dramatically documented in the film media analyzed by Stephen P. Halbrook. These helped significantly to strengthen the will to endure and to safeguard the country's semi-direct democracy, free enterprise system, and the ethical core of its culture.[14]

Several important aspects of Switzerland in World War Two have not been dealt with in this book. The astonishing expansion of the production of crops as envisioned and partially implemented by the Wahlen plan—it was to be a general guide to the vitally important expansion of agricultural production and to be fully implemented only if Switzerland should become completely isolated—deserves a detailed and separate description. Also the battle against accommodationists, traitors, collaborators, and sympathizers with 'the enemy' provides a significant story that needs to be considered in order to achieve a fuller understanding of the challenges Switzerland faced during the Second World War. Throughout the war the ideological defense of the country's tradition against defeatism or alien mindsets, the so-called "geistige Landesverteidigung", represented a vital effort. Another important and complex aspect not covered in this collection is Switzerland's role as

---

[14] The struggle between the various groups is featured by Alice Meyer, *Anpassung oder Widerstand. Die Schweiz zur Zeit des deutschen Nationalsozialismus*. Frauenfeld: Verlag Huber, 1965. Her central thesis is that Switzerland had been not only militarily, but also "ideologically-politically menaced" during the war. See also Heinz Bütler, *"Wach auf, Schweizervolk!" Die Schweiz zwischen Frontismus, Verrat und Selbstbehauptung, 1914–1940*. 2. Auflage. Gümligen, Bern: Zytglogge Verlag, 1980.

a "news center" and as a center of espionage, a role which tested to the utmost the nation's will to uphold the ideals of neutrality in the face of pragmatic necessity.[15]

The controversial issue of granting asylum to refugees, soldiers, and especially to persecuted Jewish people has only been alluded to in this set of essays since it has been widely addressed from the late 1950s onward, both within and without Switzerland.[16] Many accusatory investigations on this matter, however, pay insufficient attention to the international context within which the limitations of granting refuge occurred. The effective closing of doors by numerous nations, especially by Latin American countries and the United States, also suffering from unemployment and driven by a certain xenophobia, disabled Switzerland from serving as a country of transit for refugees.[17] As Thomas Mann publicly observed in 1943: ". . . small Switzerland deserves honorable mention because it has received many despite its lack of room and its precarious position; and it could have received many more if it could have served as a point of transit and if there had been the guarantee that the Jews would obtain another

---

[15] See the well-informed survey of Hans Rudolf Kurz, *Nachrichtenzentrum Schweiz. Die Schweiz im Nachrichtendienst des zweiten Weltkrieges.* Frauenfeld: Huber, 1972. The study shows that espionage and the gathering of information, while often intimately connected, are to be treated as two different facets, especially in times of war. See also Hans Rudolf Fuhrer, " Die Schweiz im Nachrichtendienst", in: *Schwedische und schweizerische Neutralität im Zweiten Weltkrieg.* Herausgegeben von Rudolf L. Bindschedler et al. (Basel: Helbing & Lichtenhahn, 1985): 405-426, with extensive bibliographical data; and Jacques Meurant, *La presse et l'opinion de la Suisse romande face à l'Europe en guerre, 1939-1941.* Neuchâtel: Editions de la Baconnière, 1976, a detailed study that transcends the narrow confines of the title.

[16] See Samuel Werenfels, "Die schweizerische Praxis in der Behandlung von Flücht-lingen, Internierten und entwichenen Kriegsgefangenen im Zweiten Weltkrieg" in: *Schwedische und schweizerische Neutralität*, Bindschedler et al., eds., 377-404; also Georg Kreis, "Die schweizerische Flüchtlingspolitik der Jahre 1933-1945", in *Schweizerische Zeitschrift für Geschichte* 47 (1997): 552-579, with extensive bibliographical data. The issue concerning refugees has also been featured by the Bergier Commission appointed by the Swiss government and has remained a contentious issue.

[17] See Roger Daniels, "American Refugee Policy in Historical Perspective", in: *The Muses Flee Hitler*, 61-77; also *Coming to America. A History of Immigration and Ethnicity in American Life* (New York: HarperCollins, 1990): 296-302; according to this author two events were symptomatic: The refusal by inaction of the American Congress to allow the requested entry of some 20,000 Jewish children and the similar refusal to permit the boat *St. Louis* with some one thousand refugees on board to land in Florida. For the years 1939 to 1945 only a total of 61,871 US visas, that is an average of merely some ten thousand visas per year, were granted to applicants from Germany; see US Bureau of the Census, *Historical Statistics of the United States, Colonial Times to 1970.* Bicentennial edition, Part 1 (Washington, DC 1975): C 89–101.

haven elsewhere."[18] Even the leaders of the Swiss Jewish community felt their capabilities to help strained to the utmost and suggested a slow-down, if not a halt, to admissions.[19]

As there are perhaps no untainted saints in the world,—those proclaimed as such can easily be unmasked as all too frail human beings—there are also no unblemished nations. Yet Switzerland deserves neither idealizing praise nor facile condemnation for its actions during the years of World War II, but instead recognition for what its people have done in their struggle for survival. The authors of the essays of this book show that the Swiss people, its leaders as well as its rank and file, fought valiantly, if often in different ways, on the military, economic, diplomatic, and ideological fronts and did what they could to mitigate the immense suffering surrounding their country. During the Second World War, genuine internal strength of the Swiss combined with the force of circumstance and with sheer luck. These three elements not only spared Switzerland the destruction of war, but also allowed the preservation of its independence and the fulfillment of its vital role as a 'protective power' for the belligerents.

The editor acknowledges the assistance of several people in making this work possible. George Gyssler initiated and helpfully critiqued the project and Donald P. Hilty excelled in patiently reviewing manuscripts and making suggestions with exquisite courtesy. Faith Whittlesey, former Ambassador of the United States to Switzerland and President of the American Swiss Foundation, and Architect Erdmann Schmocker, President of the Swiss American Historical Society, generously lent the full support of their respective organizations to the project. Gion Matthias Schelbert, President of Wellington Financial Corporation of Chicago, not only scanned materials, but also helped the editor understand the mysteries of the ever-changing world of electronic data processing. The authors of the various essays put up with numerous queries and eliminated mistakes that in the process of publishing so easily creep into impeccably crafted pieces. The staff of Picton Press, especially Marlene Groves, lent their expert and

---

[18] Quoted in Thomas Sprecher, *Thomas Mann in Zürich* (Zürich: Verlag Neue Zürcher Zeitung, 1992): 211. As to Switzerland's dilemma Heinz K. Meier observed in *Friendship under Stress. U. S.—Swiss Relations 1900-1950* (Bern: Herbert Lang, 1970): 299: "The one obstacle hampering all efforts to lend substantial help to the innumerable refugees in Europe, was, quite simply, though most disturbingly, the fact that no country desired to receive them. ... Switzerland did more in relation to the size of its population than any other country."

[19] Ludwig, *Flüchtlingspolitik,* 380, comment of E. von Steiger; see above footnote 1.

prompt assistance, and proved accommodating as always and Lewis Bunker Rohrbach, its President, was unhesitatingly generous in accepting the manuscript.

Permission to include some previously published materials in this work has been generously granted by the following publishers and is gratefully acknowledged: The Verlag der Neuen Zürcher Zeitung of Zürich, Switzerland (Maissen, "Unsung Dedication"); The Society for the Promotion of Science and Scholarship of Palo Alto, California (Bonjour, "Neutrality"); Herbert Lang Publisher of Bern, Switzerland (Meier, "Between Hammer and Anvil"); Allen & Unwin Publishers of London, England (Bonjour, "Neutrality Defined"); and HarperCollins, New York (Dulles, "Benevolent Neutrality").

Leo Schelbert   10 September 2000

PART ONE

DANGERS OF WAR

I: DEFENDING SWITZERLAND

The Impact of Armed Neutrality in World War II

Hans Senn

In the 1920s the general peace euphoria in Europe also spread to Switzerland, keeping the Swiss Army essentially unchanged at its status in 1918. Heavy weapons were totally lacking and the only new weapon was the light machine gun introduced in 1925.

The political situation, however, changed rapidly. After Hitler came to power in Germany in 1933, the racism and imperialism of the National Socialists began to threaten Switzerland's very existence as an independent state. The Swiss General Staff assumed that Hitler could not wage an offensive war for another ten years, but after his invasion of the demilitarized Rhineland in 1936 the Swiss began to reckon on a delay of only four to five years. Thus the Army leadership held that the next general war would break out during the first half of the 1940s.

Preparing for War

Fearing war, the Military Department of the Swiss government used the time of the late 1930s to rejuvenate the army. It equipped the infantry with mortar and infantry cannons and the artillery with its first series of 10.5-cm motorized cannons. Training periods for soldiers were extended in two steps and the composition of the army reorganized. A military order of 1938 transformed the previous six heavy divisions comprised of two brigades into nine light divisions, each divided into three regiments plus three mountain brigades, each composed of two regiments. The defense forces of the frontier regions formed nine border brigades, for whom construction of permanent fortifications were begun. In 1936 the Swiss people over-subscribed the government's defense loan of 235 million Swiss francs by 100 million Swiss francs. In 1937 the Social Democratic Party switched from its earlier pacifist position and began to support national defense and military preparedness.

In hindsight it seems clear that had the Swiss dismantled their army in the 1920s and had failed to rebuild and modernize it in the 1930s, Switzerland might well have met the fate of annexation to the German Reich, as was the case with Austria and with the Sudeten region of

Czechoslovakia. The readiness of most Swiss to defend the country successfully averted that threat.

The capacity of Swiss munitions firms had been greatly reduced during the 1920s and rebuilding needed time. The ammunition industry, furthermore, was under the shock of the Great Depression which began at the start of the 1930s. It was deemed desirable, therefore, to spread the work necessary for equipping the army over as many years as possible. This, however, conflicted with the need to rebuild Swiss armed strength by the time of the expected general war in Europe. Thus by the fall of 1939 only 250 million of the allocated 750 million Swiss francs for rebuilding the army had been spent. The army's arsenal contained some 800 mortars and as many infantry cannons as well as 12 reconnaissance tanks, 80 modern 10.5-cm motorized cannons, and 40 Messerschmitt E-109 fighter planes.

Even at that late date the army consisted mainly of soldiers on foot, and motorized units were still in their infancy. The main body of the artillery consisted of horse-drawn 7.5-cm batteries, while armored vehicles and anti-aircraft guns were lacking. Although the Swiss General Staff had closely scrutinized the German *Blitzkrieg* doctrine of the 1930s which called for mechanized combat forces, it did not discuss the possibility of obtaining its own tanks. The issue seems to have been taboo and the General Staff obviously feared the difficulties involved in the development and production of tanks as well as the concomitant military training required. It sought instead to contain the enemy's mechanized attack within the confines of the fortified zones. At the same time, however, there was a too-limited awareness of the great cost in time and money as well as of the technical problems inherent in building permanent fortifications. By the end of 1939 only about 400 tank barriers and 180 bunkers had been built.

Extending the length of military training could only be implemented in steps. The first longer four-months basic instruction period took place in the spring of 1940. The defense forces mastered the less sophisticated available weapons, but were inadequately prepared for active combat against tanks and aircraft. In addition the army's top leadership lacked experience and flexibility.

Despite this precarious situation on the eve of the war, the gaps in the army's training were largely closed during the war itself. However, in many areas this process took much time. Because of the previous emphasis on building fortifications, training standards could be rated as combat-ready only from 1941 on. During the war the Swiss military even reached the combat level of a standing army. General mobilization on May 11, 1940 activated 450,000 Swiss combat troops supported by 250,000 auxiliary troops.[1]

The build-up in the supply of arms proceeded at an astounding pace. The number of machine guns was doubled to reach 30,000 and was supplemented by 27,000 automatic rifles. The anti-aircraft troops received 3,000 guns. The supply of anti-tank weapons increased sixfold and was backed by some 2,000 flame-throwers. The number of mortars nearly tripled and that of 10.5-cm motorized canons rose to 360. Shortly after the outbreak of the war the army received 50 additional Messerschmitt fighter planes, a 125% increase.

The large number of men in uniform excepted, the defense-preparedness of the army at the end of 1940 was still at a relatively low level. Yet in planning the Western campaign, the German generals rejected after a brief consideration the possibility of by-passing the Maginot Line by moving through Switzerland. While the full extent of their discussions is not known, one can surmise them. The Swiss Jura mountains and lowland terrain in the northwest of the country were unsuited for rapid tank operations. The entire nation's resolve, furthermore, to defend Switzerland, as well as the determination of an although imperfectly equipped, but spirited Swiss army could block the many narrow passes of the region until the French forces across the border could adjust to the new threat. Despite the gaps in weaponry and in training, the combined assets of the mountainous terrain and the will to resist formed a sufficient deterrent. The route through Belgium, the Netherlands, and Luxembourg offered the German mechanized forces an incomparably better chance of success and the prospect of reaching such important strategic goals as Paris and the coast of the English Channel much faster.

The 1940 Threat of Invasion

In the fall of 1939 Poland had waited in vain for a French relief operation in the Ruhr region. Instead Poland itself was overrun and divided by German and Soviet forces. In contrast, the staunch Finnish resistance to the Soviet invasion in the Winter War of 1939-40 gave the Swiss an encouraging example. In April 1940 the German *Wehrmacht* attacked the poorly equipped small states of Denmark and Norway, and in May it lined up for the long-awaited Western campaign which after brief resistance led

---

[1]At its peak, over 850,000 men were mobilized in all branches of Swiss military service, exceeding 40% of the total male population of Switzerland of all ages. The comparable figure required in America today to match this would be over 55 million men - LB Rohrbach comment.

to the surrender of Luxembourg, Belgium, and the Netherlands. Great Britain withdrew its army from Dunkirk in full retreat, and the collapse of France was only a question of time. In mid-June the threat to the western frontier of Switzerland began to emerge (see Figure 1, page 45). Guderian's tank detachment pushed from the Langres plateau toward the Swiss border and the 7th German Army crossed the Rhine on both sides of Colmar, thereby exerting pressure on the 45th French Fortification Corps. Some 43,000 French and Polish troops retreated into Switzerland and were interned in accordance with international law. The efforts of the Axis powers, however, failed to cut off all Swiss links with France (see Figure 2, page 46) and the French Alpine Army under General Orly managed to hold its own. Italian troops were pinned down by artillery fire from the French outposts. Bitter resistance by the French mountain troops prevented the 12th German Army from taking Grenoble and Chambéry. On June 25, 1940 an armistice was concluded between France and the Axis powers, and German and Italian troops were once again available for further campaigns.

Expecting a German attack, the Swiss army had built up positions along the northeastern Limmat Front. Secret contingency agreements with General Gamelin held out the prospect of support by part of the French army (see Figure 3, page 47). In case of a German attack on Switzerland, the French troops would pivot over Basel and the Gempen plateau from the west and in a first phase thrust through the Aare valley to reach the Zofingen-Olten-Hauenstein line. Given a favorable outcome, they would then advance in a second phase to reach Brugg's moated castle where the Aare, Reuss, and Limmat rivers converge, there to relieve the Swiss 2nd Army Corps in the Jura.

Towards the end of the western campaign, the German advance in France through the Burgundy gate and from the Langres plateau to Pontarlier showed that the Limmat position would have to be weakened in order to reinforce the Jura from Basel to Geneva (see Figure 4, page 48). The Swiss army thus formed a weak front in all directions and therefore was highly vulnerable. No one had reckoned with such a rapid French collapse and no plans fit the unexpected situation. The Federal Council and the leadership of the army assumed that now Hitler no longer needed to conquer Switzerland militarily because he could vanquish it by political and economic means. The people were seized by a fatalistic mood and asked whether Switzerland would be Hitler's next victim.

In fact, however, Hitler made preparations for an attack on Switzerland because he was angered for three reasons: First, Germany's concerted efforts to bring the Swiss press into line and to impose a "neutrality of conscience" on the Swiss people had come to naught. Second, Swiss pilots had downed eleven German planes who had violated the airspace of neutral

Switzerland by returning over it from their bombing missions in France. The Swiss air force, in contrast, had suffered only three losses from these dogfights. In revenge, German Air Marshal Goering ordered a campaign of sabotage against Swiss airfields. Thanks to Swiss vigilance, however, all saboteurs were arrested before they could inflict any damage. Third, Hitler's goal of completely sealing off Switzerland early in the war also had failed.

In a furious mood, Hitler ordered preparations for an invasion of Switzerland on June 23, 1940. By invading rapidly with powerful forces he hoped to achieve these goals: acquisition of intact production and communication facilities, absorption of the working and military potential of the Swiss people, and the take-over of the gold reserves of the Swiss National Bank. Also enticing to him was the chance of smoking out an irritating ideological nest of democratic resistance.

Consequently, several *Wehrmacht* staffs developed plans of conquest. All of them involved the German forces attacking the Swiss army from the west, north, and east in order to cut off a retreat into the Alps, thus leading to an encirclement and isolation of the Swiss forces. The Germans proposed two basic models. The first model envisioned main attacks from the west and east along the pre-Alps into the Lucerne region, combined with advances from the north to link up with the other forces (see Figures 5–7, pages 49–51). The second model centered on attacks from the west, aiming at reaching the rear of the fortified Limmat position and engaging it through frontal advances from the northeast. (see Figures 8–9, pages 52–53). To reach these operational goals within a viable time frame required from 11 to 21 divisions (see Figure 10, page 54).

The German staff planning assumed that Italian forces would advance at the same time from the south up to the northern chain of the high Alps, encountering the German forces there and relieving them from operations in the mountains. Agreements concerning these plans had supposedly been made at a meeting between Hitler and Mussolini in Munich on June 18, 1940, but to date no proof has been found. As the collapse of the French armed forces was expected at that time, Mussolini feared that the German *Wehrmacht* might continue its victorious campaign in Switzerland. The prospect of having such a powerful northern neighbor in a dominant position in the central Alps poised for an attack on northern Italy horrified Mussolini. He decided therefore to cooperate, if necessary, and to divide the spoils while aiming to obtain the strongest possible natural border. By conquering the frontier regions he wanted to safeguard the pawns he might need for future negotiations.

The Italian plans of the summer 1940 are only partially known. On June 7 the chief of the Italian General Staff General Roatta named General Mario Vercellino as commander of the possible "Operation Ticino" (see

Figure 11, page 55). He made the conquest of the watershed from San Bernardino to the Gries Pass the goal of the operation. As resources he made available two mountain divisions, one Alpine division, a motorized division, and a tank division. These troops, when combined, would have meant a ratio of about 5:2 between Italian attackers and Swiss defenders. On June 10 Vercellino sketched his concept of attack, which was to be based on surprise. Using five division columns, he wanted first to conquer the crossings of the Splügen-San Bernardino passes as well as the St. Gotthard fortifications from the access routes of Chiavenna and Domo-dossola. He would then occupy the center of the Canton Ticino around Bellinzona and reach the Lukmanier Pass and Airolo via the Blenio and Leventina valleys.

In mid-July the operations department of the Italian army began to expand its plans, which previously had been limited to Switzerland's Canton Ticino. This action they justified by the claim that all border regions on the Italian-speaking side of Switzerland's watershed must be dominated by Italy. Unfortunately, of the complete plan of conquest only the featured attack on the Simplon pass still exists (see Figure 12, page 56). This plan consisted on the one hand of direct advances from the Alpe de Veglia to the top of the pass and the winding Berisal road, on the other hand it called for by-passing the Gondo gorge from the north and south with the intent of opening it from the rear. The planners of the Italian General Staff, furthermore, sketched two alternative plans by which a final solution of the Swiss problem could be achieved. A first proposal envisioned partitioning Switzerland among its neighboring powers along ethnic and linguistic lines (see Figure 13A, top of page 57). The second proposal envisioned modifying Switzerland's borders while maintaining a reduced neutral Confederation as a buffer state (see Figure 13B, bottom of page 57).

As the German-Italian campaign in the Balkans reached its end in May 1941, the Italian General Staff, ignorant of the German "Barbarossa" plan to invade the Soviet Union, still assumed that Hitler could use the army units freed from the Balkan theater of war for the liquidation of Switzerland. The Italian General Staff thus had the operations department draft new directives for a joint military campaign against Switzerland (see Figure 14, page 58). The Italian operational goal was the domination of the northern high Alps. In support of the planned German operations in the Swiss lowlands, the staff also considered the following proposed moves: into the Rhone valley to Aigle and from there into the Simmen valley; into the regions around Interlaken and Thun and also Sarnen and Lucerne; and into the Schwyz basin and the Linth plain. These moves envisioned a complete conquest of Switzerland.

The Italian operations department considered it necessary to deploy three armies with five divisions each in order to gain superiority over the Swiss forces. If one includes the planned use of an average of 15 divisions projected by the German planners, the total of the German and Italian invasion forces would amount to an average of 30 divisions. This very high figure, compared to the two and six divisions used against Denmark and Norway respectively, indicates how highly the Axis powers appraised the combat readiness of the Swiss troops. Such a substantial commitment for merely a secondary campaign seemed however inappropriate.

In early July Hitler demoted preparations for an attack on Switzerland to a lower priority; it was then that the country became the "porcupine" which the *Wehrmacht* would take care of after its expected triumph over England. Nonetheless, the 12th German Army under General List marched to the Swiss border on July 7, 1940 in order to prepare for the invasion which had already been ordered. Street and railroad lines which ran towards Switzerland were upgraded, reconnaissance was undertaken up to the southern foot of the Jura chain, and the necessary supplies were stockpiled. General List assumed that "Operation Switzerland" would be carried out in about three weeks, that is at the end of July. Yet he waited in vain for Hitler's order to attack. In keeping with his character, Hitler's indecision dragged out the project, yet he let the preparations continue until November 1940.

Why did he waiver? There were three possible military reasons. First, the low combat success of the Italian armed forces in the French Alps showed Hitler that they could not be counted on. This meant that after the conquest of the Swiss lowlands the *Wehrmacht* might have to enter a second extended battle with heavy German losses in the mountains. Second, a secondary campaign which might pin down extensive German forces for a prolonged period might endanger the far-reaching strategic plans to gain *Lebensraum* in the East and to annihilate Bolshevism. Third, given Switzerland's almost complete encirclement it seemed possible to pressure Switzerland into the Axis order of Europe by political and economic means rather than by invasion.

Despite great gaps in the defensive preparedness of Switzerland and an obvious wide dispersal of its armed forces throughout the country, Hitler called off the planned attack. The fighting spirit displayed by the Swiss fighter pilots made him fear that despite a growing Swiss fatalism a victory over Switzerland could be won only at an exorbitant price and would lead to time-consuming battles in remote valleys. Thus this victory was won by the Swiss themselves. Had the Federal Council and General Guisan given up, demobilized the army, and accepted the demands to conform to the agenda of the Axis, Switzerland undoubtedly would have been absorbed into the Third Reich.

The Réduit Concept

As noted above, one danger the German forces posed for the Swiss army was of the Swiss Army's being spread out too thinly along the country's frontiers. Because the Swiss could not know from where the invasion would be launched, it had to defend all its borders. This meant, however, that the army would be outnumbered against a concentrated attacking force and that the thinly positioned lines of defense could break easily. General Guisan devised an ingenious plan to solve this problem.

The mountain chain of the Swiss Alps had always been regarded as the last bastion of defense and the lowlands and Jura regions as more easily lost to an invader. Considering the emerging threat of a complete encirclement of Switzerland, Adolf Germann, a member of the Swiss Staff of Operations, and Colonel Hans Frick, commander of the Linth troops, proposed in June 1940 that the activated army *initially* be deployed in the Alpine region. They reasoned that concentrating the bulk of the Swiss army which had to expect attacks from all sides by modern armed forces would enable it to hold out far longer. The increased possibility of defensive success would put the federal government in a stronger position to reject any ultimatum that might accompany the threat of invasion.

The initiators of the concept of the *Réduit* or redoubt offered it in no way as a gesture of defeatism, but reasoned that Hitler's attack aiming at the control of the Alpine passes could be thwarted and that the very existence of the Réduit plan could deter an invasion. The concept, furthermore, was to serve less as a plan on how to wage a defensive war than as a signal to the Swiss people and to all the world that the nation was totally committed to resistance. This message was delivered for all to hear in a remarkable speech which General Guisan made before the bulk of the army's officers on the Rütli, a meadow where the Swiss Confederation is believed to have been initiated in 1291. After a phase of defeatism, the Swiss people thereby regained their trust in the ability of the military forces to safeguard the country. The aspect of deterrence implicit in the concept of the redoubt was noted also by foreign observers.

Three factors of the Swiss plan were designed to keep Hitler from invading Switzerland. First, the prospect of having to wage a prolonged battle in the mountains that would tie down German troops for a long time and would involve heavy losses could mar the Third Reich's military prestige. Second, the likelihood that the two main Alpine crossings, the Gotthard and Lötschberg-Simplon routes, would sustain lasting damage would mean the loss of the much-desired links between Germany and Italy.

Third, the likelihood that Swiss home guard units would destroy production facilities and stockpiles, rendering them useless, also held risk.

In addition, the *Réduit* could be attacked only during the months of June to September because the passes were not usable during winter. The conquest of the Balkans in the winter of 1940, furthermore, occupied center stage in Hitler's planning as preparation for the campaign against the Soviet Union. Thus Switzerland had become a *Wartegau*, that is a region in waiting, to be plucked like a ripe fruit after final victory.

Critics have proffered three reasons against the concept of the *Réduit*. They claim, first, that the Jura and the Swiss lowlands would have been abandoned unprotected to the German attackers. This objection overlooks, however, that the strategy was designed to prevent an attack in the first place, and also that troops at the frontiers were to hold their positions to the last man. According to the Operations Order No. 12 of July 17, 1940 the *Réduit* involved only half of the army on active duty. The other half was to take up positions behind the Limmat and Saane rivers as well as in the Jura to gain time (see Figure 15, page 59). It would retreat into the Alps only on the basis of Operations Order No. 13 of May 24, 1941 (see Figure 16, age 60). The light brigades were to remain in their positions using delaying tactics and were to engage in an extensive operation of destruction.

Critics claim, second, that the *Wehrmacht* could have contented itself with inflicting starvation on the Swiss army in the *Réduit*. It is to be remembered, however, that five months' worth of supplies had been stored in the central area. The attacking forces would not have been able to camp idly at the entry ways of the *Réduit* and suffer attacks from Swiss troops without losing prestige; also they would have been needed as soon as possible for operations elsewhere. Some argue, third, that Hitler could have bombed the Swiss cities until the government was willing to capitulate. This possibility, however, applied to any strategy the Swiss might have adopted. Furthermore, neither the British nor the Germans had allowed themselves to be demoralized by the air terror practiced in World War II. In short, the *Réduit* strategy did not mean bringing the army into security in a virtually inaccessible shelter. Rather it was a courageous and wise expedient, the goal of which was fully achieved in a situation almost beyond salvage.

The Phantom "Fortress Europe"

The German defeat at Stalingrad and the surrender of the German and Italian troops in Tunisia during the first half of 1943 signaled the onset of the downfall of the Axis military power. Experienced leaders of the *Wehrmacht* became convinced that the time of great offensives had passed and that a transitional strategic defense at the fringes of key European countries had to be established. In case, despite massive counterattacks, hostile breakthroughs in Germany's outer ring of defense could not be prevented, retreat into a second inner zone of defense would become inevitable. Such a zone would have to include the western, central, and eastern ranges of the Alps. Switzerland would play an important role in this endeavor since it was a country of transit and had the supply routes leading to the German troops which were to guard the outer ring of defense, thus being a pivotal region within the inner ring of defense.

Hitler, however, decided against the adoption of such a strategic retreat. He ordered that the *Wehrmacht* hold the lines it occupied and that it not relinquish a foot of ground. SS circles responsible for domestic security occupied themselves nevertheless with the demands involved in the creation of a "Fortress Europe." A memorandum which General Böhme completed in the fall of 1943 has survived. It assumed that the German leadership had decided to get rid of the last army hostile to Germany in central Europe before the Allies opened a second front. This move would eliminate the opportunity for the Allies to make Switzerland the epicenter of resistance, usable for their plans, whether as a landing strip by air or as a by-pass of stalemated fronts (see Figure 17, page 61). Böhme envisaged two particular tasks to be accomplished simultaneously and independently from each other by two separate German armies. In a first move, five infantry divisions and three tank divisions would invade from the north, occupy airstrips, and eliminate Swiss forces in the lowlands. The second move would occur by air and from the south. A German paratrooper infantry division would secure intact portions of the alpine passes and attack the Swiss *Réduit* at all points of access from the west, south, and east in order to discover its weak points and break through them with massive force. Fire from artillery and from the air directed at population centers, factories, and power stations would be avoided and transportation networks and industrial production be re-established as soon as possible. Böhme considered the deployment of German troops in the border regions to be indispensable. Even without including the necessary supplies, he estimated the need for 850 trains to transport the required 15 divisions which were to be taken from Germany's eastern front. Such extensive preparations would certainly have been discovered by the Swiss intelligence service in time and the remobilized troops would have been able to reach their deployment positions before the invasion began.

The Böhme memorandum only had real value if Hitler had reconsidered the idea of a "Fortress Europe." Böhme's plan had been initiated in the context of the 1943 "March alarm" of a threatened invasion of Switzerland during that month, but was not completed until the fall of that year. Hence the intended campaign in the mountains could not have occurred before the summer of 1944 and would have been paralleled by the opening of a second front by the Allies. In the fall of 1943, furthermore, the German leadership learned that the Swiss army would staunchly oppose an American march through Switzerland and would not join the Allied side. This seemed to make a preventative occupation of Switzerland superfluous.

Alarmed by rumors of the "Fortress Europe" concept in the summer of 1943, General Guisan ordered the drafting of plans to reinforce the southern front. He wanted to prevent a German use of that region as part of its European inner ring of defense. His Operations Order No. 16 implemented the concept of a frontal defense of Switzerland's borders, including the crucial Italian one (see Figure 18, page 62): and provided for five divisions and three brigades at the frontiers. Operations Order No. 17 similarly foresaw a highly graduated defense beginning at the country's borders (see Figure 19, page 63): however the successful defense of the northern chain of the High Alps remained of crucial importance. To achieve this purpose three Swiss army units would be deployed in each of the Bernese and Glarus Alps, the 9th Division was to defend the Gotthard massif, and one division would reinforce the brigades in each of the fortified St. Maurice and Sargans regions. In the areas of the enemy's approach at the country's frontiers, the 11th and 12th Mountain Brigades as well as the 9th Border Brigade would implement a highly graduated defense strategy.

It was above all the German SS that advocated a preventive campaign against Switzerland in the context of a possible "Fortress Europe". The leadership of the Swiss army could not know whether some day Hitler might still decide on a strategic retreat and attempt to conquer Switzerland as a necessary measure. Obtaining a Swiss pillar of "Fortress Europe" would have been a military imperative and for Germany would have far outweighed the benefits of Swiss neutrality.

Preserving Neutrality in the Fall of 1944

On August 23, 1944 reports arrived of the fall of Paris to the Allies and the rapid advance of American troops up the Rhone valley to Annecy. The German *Wehrmacht* seemed to make preparations for a defensive front west of the range of the Vosges. It thus became necessary to reactivate the Swiss troops in order to prevent tactical violations of the borders or operational by-pass campaigns through Swiss territory. During the first half of September Border Brigades 1 through 4 and Light Brigade 1 protected the western frontiers (see Figure 20, page 64). Four divisions and two light brigades stood ready to intervene at the southern foot of the Jura mountains. The troops called to active duty were divided at that time into two Army Corps and a reserve unit.

German reinforcements at the front in the Trouée de Belfort became apparent in mid-September and increased the danger of German tactical by-passes through the Bernese Jura. However, because no Allied reserves were observed in the Rhone valley, a use of the Swiss lowlands by the 7th US Army for an operational march-through became improbable. The Swiss defense had thus to be shifted further east. (See Figure 21, page 65). From September 20 on, the Swiss 2nd Army Corps guarded the bridges of Basel together with a regiment of elite troops, and two light brigades defended the Ajoie. To the rear of the 3rd and 4th Border Brigades, the 3rd Light Brigade took up a stand-by position in the Frick Valley, the 8th Division on the Gempen plateau, and the 4th Division in the Delémont basin. The 1st Army Corps took a waiting position in the Solothurn-Neuchâtel-Berne triangle and the 7th Division formed the reserve in the Olten area. In mid-October some active service units of the army were relieved (see Figure 22, page 66) and in their place the 4th Border Brigade of the 2nd Corps and the three newly reactivated 2nd, 5th, and 6th Divisions protected the border regions between Basel and the Ajoie. The 14th and 15th Divisions composed of mountain troops carried out maneuvers in the lowlands and could be used at any time as operational reserves.

On November 14, 1944 the 1st French Army opened its offensive through the Burgundy gate and reached the Rhine below Basel on November 19. Between November 21 and 24 two German divisions from the Dannemarie area advanced toward the heights of Porrentruy in order to interrupt the French supply line between Delle and Pfetterhouse. The battle at the Swiss border reached its climax on November 22 and turned in favor of the French. Warned in time, troops of the 2nd Division observed the action from the heights and interned 200 exhausted German soldiers.

With the Rhine fronts stabilizing at the end of November, the bridges of Basel gained in importance (see Figure 23, page 67). As in the past, their destruction was to be carried out at a moment's notice by a reinforced infantry regiment. The 14th Division controlled the Gempen plateau and closed the Ergolz valley while the 15th Division replaced the 6th as army reserves in the Aare valley. As the Allied forces began occupying southern Germany in the mid-March 1945 spring offensive, the 4th Division assumed the protection of the Basel bridges while most of the 7th Division secured the tip of the border at Schaffhausen (see Figure 24, page 68).

Had Switzerland not guarded its borders effectively at this time, it might have been drawn into the final phase of the war's turmoil. It also would have been placed into an extremely delicate position if the Americans had followed Stalin's advice and by-passed the German positions of defense via the Swiss lowlands in order to punish the "swine" (as Stalin called Switzerland) because of its coldness towards the Soviet

Union and its supposed collaboration with Hitler's Germany. Switzerland would not only have to turn down German support, but also to guard against German troops in order to live up to its position of neutrality. That would have led to war on two fronts until an accommodation could have been reached with the invading Americans.

To sum up: despite great gaps in armed readiness at the outset of the war and despite the late reaction of the leadership of the Swiss army to the changed situation caused by the collapse of France, the army fulfilled its task and successfully defended the country against invasion. The determination of the Swiss people at large as well as of its armed forces to turn back any invading troops and to make skillful use of the mountainous terrain for a forceful defense did not miss its mark. Admittedly, when in the summer and fall of 1940 the danger of invasion was most acute, Switzerland was left alone by Germany because Hitler feared that the divisions needed for a secondary campaign against the Swiss might not be available for his grand strategic design. The fact that German forces were pinned down in Russia as well as North Africa was also decisive, in contrast to the issue of war supplies from Switzerland to Germany which became important only after 1940. However, if the Swiss had not been prepared to defend their country with massive force, Hitler would hardly have missed the unguarded prey. Thus the Swiss nation was saved from war and destruction by the interplay of circumstance, by a forceful, determined, and heavily equipped armed defense, and by the conduct of business with all parties as required by the necessities of survival and the duties imposed on neutral nations by international law.

Armed Neutrality as a Moral Issue

In a report of May 1997 the American Undersecretary of State Stuart Eizenstat claimed that neutrality in World War II had been immoral. He argued that while the Allies made sacrifices in blood and wealth to combat the forces of evil, the neutral states greatly benefited from the collaboration with National Socialist Germany and prolonged the war by supplying it with strategic material. Did Switzerland indeed enrich itself by providing munitions to Germany and thus lengthen the conflict?

First, the fact must be considered that Swiss imports from countries controlled by the Axis powers exceeded exports to them by 500 million Swiss francs, thus Switzerland received more than it provided. Second, it was forced to export in order to get the necessary food and arms which the Allies could not or would not supply, yet were vital for Switzerland's survival. The substantial increase in the Swiss army's weaponry described above was possible only because of the import of raw materials and prefabricated items from Germany. Among these were ninety modern fighter planes as well as hundreds of armored plates needed for the loopholes of the numerous bunkers built by the Swiss during the war. Such imports occurred at the expense of German armaments and partially canceled out the munitions supplied by Switzerland to Germany. The surplus of strategic goods the Swiss supplied amounted to less than ½ of one percent of the total cost of equipping the German armed forces. Although these supplies involved key materials, the Swiss contribution was a mere pittance compared to other factors that prolonged World War II. These included the Allied demand for unconditional surrender in the summer of 1943, the missed Allied opportunity to occupy Italy before German troops moved in, the Allied bombing of German cities instead of the systematic destruction of the infrastructure producing armaments, and General Eisenhower's order in the fall of 1944 to stop the offensive against Germany on supply grounds instead of concentrating the supplies that were available at key points and thus exploiting the *Wehrmacht's* critical situation.

Switzerland invested four billion Swiss francs in improving its defense preparedness during the phase of mobilization and the operational funding for the army involved an additional four billion. The Swiss, therefore, supported their armed neutrality by some 53 billion dollars in today's value. In 1945 the Swiss national debt amounted to nine billion Swiss francs which the Swiss had to shoulder by paying interest on capital in the form of defense bonds as well as by assuming high taxes derived from defense needs. Aside from some war profiteers, therefore, the Swiss did not benefit. After 1940 war profits were effectively curtailed by taxing excess earnings above the average pre-war levels by fifty to seventy percent. The rapid economic upswing after the war derived not from profiteering during the war, but from the fact that Swiss industrial facilities had been spared, unlike those of other countries. Pent-up entrepreneurial activity, furthermore, that had been limited during the war by extended military service, stimulated rapid economic growth. The Swiss also contributed two hundred million Swiss francs to the rebuilding of the war-damaged countries, which amounted to 2% of Switzerland's national income at that time.

What would have happened if Switzerland had abandoned its neutrality in mid-1943, even though the Axis powers did not relax their stranglehold against it until the fall of 1944? First, if the country had stopped its munitions supply to Germany, deliveries of coal, iron, seed, and food to Switzerland would have stopped and would have led to widespread hunger and unemployment. Also the Wahlen plan, which effectively doubled the Swiss productive land use from 183,478 hectares (453,374 acres) in 1934 to 365,856 hectares (904,030 acres) in 1944, as well as the Swiss troops' rearmament, would not have been possible.

Second, had Switzerland openly joined the Allied side in World War II, Hitler still might have been able to defeat the Swiss militarily. The German assault planned for March 1943 and the "preventative" campaign advocated in circles of the National Socialist Party in part did not occur because the German leadership knew that Switzerland would observe strict neutrality even after a successful Allied landing in Western Europe. The German occupation of Hungary in the spring of 1944 and the Ardennes offensive at the beginning of 1945 showed that the *Wehrmacht* might have been able to muster even then sufficient forces for a successful attack on Switzerland despite the German shortage in resources. The consequences would have been grim. The Swiss elite noted for its fierce opposition to the Hitler regime, the nearly 100,000 refugees which included some 10,000 Jews harbored in the country, together with some 10,000 Swiss Jews, would have been liquidated or transported to concentration camps. German individuals and companies responsible for supplying equipment to the Third Reich would have received unlimited access to Swiss business and financial power. The country and its surviving armed forces would have been integrated into the German "Fortress Europe" and the Allies would have retaliated by bombing Swiss cities and industrial zones.

A German conquest would not only have been disastrous for Switzerland, but would also have disadvantaged the Allies. The services provided by the neutral country and the International Committee of the Red Cross would have ceased. These services included representing diplomatic interests among hostile powers, the caring for citizens and war prisoners of the Allies in enemy countries, mediating the surrender negotiations in northern Italy, and tolerating intelligence services and propaganda outlets on Swiss soil which were of special importance given their proximity to Germany, Italy, and France. Without these advantages concerning intelligence, the partisans in northern Italy and the French Vercors could not have been supported. Also the cost of liberating Europe would have increased and possibly prolonged the war. The Allied forces would not have been able to advance unimpeded along the Swiss border en route to the Rhine. They would have had to reckon with attacks on their right flank and, therefore, been forced to include the Swiss plateau in their operations, over-extending the available forces and thus postponing the Allied victory.

Switzerland acknowledges its debt to the liberators of Europe because the country would have otherwise fallen under the rule of the Axis powers. Swiss are also aware that despite their full ideological support of Allied values they could express that support only through relatively minor services. Yet premature abandonment of Swiss neutrality between the summer of 1943 and the fall of 1944 would have posed more problems than benefits for the Allies and would have meant a catastrophe of unimaginable scope for Switzerland.

Switzerland's joining the Allied side in the late fall of 1944, instead of mid-1943, might indeed have shortened the war and been less of a disaster for the country. It would have gained a place among the victors, it would have been treated with respect, and would have been invited to the founding conference of the United Nations in San Francisco. Yet opportunistic abandonment of perpetual neutrality, a role recognized for Switzerland since 1815, would have been tantamount to a breach of international law and would have meant also the loss of credibility. Remaining neutral and protecting it from the turmoil and destruction of war enabled Switzerland to take a decisive part in the rebuilding of Europe.

It seems that no alternative defense strategy during World War II that the Swiss government and Commander-in-chief General Guisan could have adopted would have guaranteed the survival of the Swiss nation. Although the authorities may have made mistakes concerning refugee and financial policies, they achieved their goal of successfully keeping the country out of war, and they were strongly supported by the vast majority of the Swiss people. Switzerland made its contribution to opposing National Socialist and Fascist dictatorships by maintaining itself as a lone island of freedom and democracy in the totalitarian storm tide and by successfully defying all attempts to force it into line with the designs of the Axis powers. Despite Great Britain's significant loss of people and great material sacrifice, this was freely acknowledged by Winston Churchill when he wrote to his foreign minister on December 3, 1944: "Of all the neutrals Switzerland has the greatest right to distinction. She has been the sole international force linking the hideously-sundered nations and ourselves. What does it matter whether she has been able to give us the commercial advantages we desire or has given too many to Germany, to keep herself alive? She has been a democratic state, standing for freedom in self-defense among her mountains, and in thought, in spite of race, largely on our side."

This article appeared first in German as Heft No. 18 of the Schriftenreihe der Gesellschaft für militärhistorische Studienreisen (GMS): Zürich, 1998, under the title *Unsere Armee im Zweiten Weltkrieg*. Translated into English by Lyn Shepard, American adaptation by L. Schelbert. Printed by permission.

II: THE THREAT OF THREE TOTALITARIANISMS

The Swiss Response

Jürg Stüssi-Lauterburg

The familiar tale of William Tell symbolizes not only Swiss marksmanship but also the fierce determination of the Swiss to maintain their independence and to repel anyone intending to invade their country. Not for nothing was Schiller's play *William Tell* performed in Switzerland during the darkest days of World War II, when the nation faced the threat of imminent invasion from National Socialist Germany to the north and Fascist Italy to the south.

From the perspective of the law of nations and the law of war, of course, by right Switzerland should not have faced this threat at all. Switzerland is, in the definition of international law, a neutral state which neither joins military alliances nor engages in war unless directly invaded. It is important, however, not to confuse the Swiss concept of armed neutrality with a posture that is indifferent to the conflicts surrounding the country, as though it made no difference to the Swiss people which side won either of the two World Wars, or that they were cheering the enemies of the United States and Great Britain. To the contrary: Switzerland has long been determined to preserve its independence and democracy and resolved centuries ago that a policy of neutrality in the wars of the European states surrounding it was the best way to do so. That neutrality, however, has not always been respected by others. It comes as no surprise that those states which were enemies of democracy were also those that have threatened Switzerland's neutrality and independence the most. Those who begin attacking their own people's freedom usually end up attacking the freedom of others as well.

Switzerland's neutrality is all the more at risk because the country occupies a position in the heart of Europe, a position vividly demonstrated especially during World War II when the two main European enemies of democracies were physically separated by the Swiss Alps. From 1917 to 1945, the most calamitous years of the twentieth century, Switzerland's existence as a democratic federal state granting equal rights to all its citizens without regard to race, ethnicity, or religion was threatened by three totalitarian powers: Soviet Russia, Fascist Italy and, most directly, by

National Socialist Germany. This article does not address all aspects of Swiss life or Swiss military strategy during the two World Wars, but intends to show how Swiss vigilance and military preparedness deterred invaders and helped to preserve Swiss independence. It will show, furthermore, that despite Switzerland's *political* neutrality the vast majority of its people *morally* supported the cause of democracy, and were reviled by the totalitarians for their democratic stance and their determination to preserve their independence.

Switzerland's form of democratic government is unique and has—in many parts of the country—existed for centuries. In 1848 the country reshaped its confederation and adopted a political system that incorporated some features of the American constitution, especially its bicameralism. In that reshaped form Switzerland has survived for some 150 years, some of which were pleasant, some difficult, some dreary, some terrible, some frightening. Its survival has depended on the institution of a "citizens' army", that is on universal military training, service in the reserves, and the keeping of arms and ammunition at home. It assures preparedness to defend the country whenever needed and to foster national unity. Bankers and bakers, lawyers, workers and farmers, academics and artisans serve in the militia side by side, thus mitigating divisions based on class, religion and, to some degree, also language. In the years before World War I the Swiss army was a model for republicans and even the democratic left. Jean Jaurès, the French socialist leader, viewed the Swiss militia system as a model and declared that "certainly the Swiss system comes nearest to the ideal of a democratic and people's army."[1]

The Threat of Soviet Totalitarianism

Voices like those of Jaurès, however, were silenced in 1914 when European armies of a very different character directed by political elites hurled Europe into one of the most violent of wars. In Germany, Austria-Hungary, and Russia the old orders were destroyed. In 1917 Czarist Russia had been transformed by two revolutions in the first Soviet Republic, the nucleus of the later Soviet Union. With the October Revolution of 1917 the ideology of Communism had found a polity to translate its anti-democratic ideals into practice. For European societies such as Switzerland, weakened by the need for permanent military readiness and by a much-reduced supply

---

[1] Quoted in Urs Brand, "Der französische Sozialistenführer Jean Jaurès und das schweizerische Milizsystem", in *Allgemeine Schweizerische Militärzeitschrift* 139 (October 1973): 513.

of food and fuel, the Communist revolutionary vision had genuine appeal among some segments of the population. Lenin, furthermore, hoped to fan the flames of revolution in the country where he had been given asylum. In two letters, dated October 14 and 18, 1918, he urged Ya. A. Berzin, then head of the Soviet mission in Bern, to spend money liberally to foment revolution in Switzerland. "And the Swiss leftists? Don't spare money!" Lenin advised; and he further counseled Berzin: "Two or three times a week you should get to see people like Guilbeaux, Hubacher, and the like from Geneva, Italians from Lugano, Germans from Zürich (not like Platten, but better—*workers* from among the Zürich leftists). Appoint agents from among them, and pay extremely generously for their trips and work."[2] Switzerland had been a country with which Russia had not been at war and which had provided asylum for the Bolshevik leader. Yet the Soviet authorities did not hesitate to seek to subvert the democratic order in any way possible.

The aftermath of World War I gave hope to those who believed with Lenin that revolution would immediately sweep throughout Europe. In Switzerland the pursuit of Lenin's ideals took the form of a revolutionary general strike starting on November 9, 1918, one year after the October Revolution. This thinly veiled attempt to overthrow the established democratic order, however, was met by a determined Federal Council, Switzerland's collective executive branch of government, with the help of the militia. No bloodshed ensued, but there remained an enduring skepticism in the Swiss left against the army and all things military, a tendency that in some ways survives to this day.

Although the documentary evidence of the Soviet intentions in Switzerland has come to light only in 1996, those intentions had been quite clear for some time, and led the Federal Council to expel the Soviet diplomatic mission in 1918. Although anti-Communism emerged at that time as an enduring theme in Swiss political life, for some 15 long years Switzerland's Social Democratic Party openly advocated the dictatorship of the proletariat.[3] In 1934 Switzerland cast the lone vote against the admission of the Soviet Union to the League of nations. Neither Stalin nor his followers ever forgot or forgave that vote.

The immediate threat of war had passed and this, combined with left-wing disenchantment with, or antipathy to, democratic institutions and the

---

[2] Richard Pipes, ed., *The Unknown Lenin* (New Haven: Yale University Press, 1996): 53, 59.

[3] Erich Gruner, *Die Parteien in der Schweiz*. Zweite Auflage (Bern: Francke, 1977): 141.

army, led in the inter-war years to a reduction in military spending. The position of both the democratic left, reacting as elsewhere in Europe to the horrors of World War I, and of the totalitarian left furnished reasons for those who wanted to hold military spending to a minimum. The never-ending haggling over a survival-level military budget contributed to the untimely death of Federal Councilor Karl Scheurer in 1929. For several years his successor Rudolf Minger did not fare any better. On December 23, 1932 a law was passed that decreed still further cuts in the already minimal military budget. This situation continued until the Social Democratic Party abandoned its pacifist stance and, in the face of Hitler's rise to full dominance in 1935, joined the political mainstream.[4]

The Threat of Fascist Totalitarianism

This late shift in attitude towards rearmament is all the more surprising because Benito Mussolini, the Italian *Duce*, a revolutionary turned Fascist and the originator of the term "totalitarian", had held Italy in his iron grip since 1922. Since the Swiss Canton Ticino is Italian-speaking, Mussolini dreamt of conquering it and thus completing what he saw as the unification of all Italian speakers under his rule, regardless of the wishes of the people concerned. He built numerous roads up to the Swiss Italian mountain passes to enable Italian artillery to reach vital positions in Swiss territory, especially in the Ticino, swiftly; these were to be followed by the Italian infantry once he had ordered an invasion of Swiss territory. The summer of 1929 saw the completion of what Switzerland saw as the most dangerous of those roads, the one leading up to the San Giacomo pass, thus directly menacing the St. Gotthard massif, the strategic heart of Switzerland.[5] Although quite real, at that time the threat was not taken very seriously in Switzerland on a military level because the Italian invaders would have to traverse very difficult terrain and also because the center of the population of Switzerland and of its economy was north of the Alps. Nevertheless, Italian fascism was, besides Bolshevism, a second and quite real totalitarian threat that Switzerland faced, although Mussolini desired only a part of its territory rather than the destruction of its democratic system.

---

[4] Even then the vote was relatively close, 382 supporting rearmament, 294 voting against. See Otto Lezzi, *Sozialdemokratie und Militärfrage in der Schweiz* (Frauenfeld: Huber, 1996): 171-177.

[5] *Badener Tagblatt* (September 16, 1929): 1.

The Threat of National Socialist Totalitarianism

After the Swiss vote of December 1932 to reduce military spending still further, Europe's political situation suddenly changed dramatically. On January 31, 1933 Adolf Hitler became *Reichskanzler* of Germany and his followers began systematically to dismantle the former democracy and to centralize all power in the hands of the party. Only a few months later the first concentration camp was established at Dachau to deal with the German opposition. Neighboring Switzerland and all of Europe now faced a third totalitarian threat and one of the most vicious tyrannies the world has ever seen.[6]

German is the language of some two-thirds of Switzerland's people, who share literature and culture with Germany in a more distant but still comparable way to that in which Americans share English literature and culture. The charismatic personality of Hitler, as yet still unsullied by the many and enormous crimes to come, and reaction to the general economic depression pulled some of the malcontents—broken men, extremists by temperament, and criminal elements—into the National Socialist orbit. There were in Swiss society representatives of the National Socialist totalitarian movement, flanked by Communists and Fascists.

In the Spanish Civil War some 700 Swiss fought in the International Brigades (although these were heavily dominated by Communists) against Francisco Franco and some 125 of them lost their lives.[7] What they were fighting for was certainly not the cause of democracy.[8] To fight in foreign wars, furthermore, was and still is a criminal offense under a Swiss law of 1927. These ideologically motivated fighters numbered only some 700 out of a Swiss population of 4,265,703 and a Swiss army of some 400,000 at full mobilization, hardly a significant number.[9] Somewhat later about 870 Swiss chose to fight in Pharaoh's army and served under the Nazi Swastika,

---

[6] In the elections of November 1932 for the *Reichstag* the National Socialists won 196 of 584 seats, the parliamentary base of Hitler's dictatorship.

[7] For a list of names see Helmut Zschokke, *Die Schweiz und der spanische Bürgerkrieg* (Zürich: Limmat Verlag, 1976): 110-11.

[8] The totalitarian outlook of the International Brigades in the context of Swiss volunteers is illustrated by Peter Huber, "Schweizer Spanienkämpfer in den Fängen des NKWD", in *Schweizerische Zeitschrift für Geschichte* 41 (1991): 335-353.

[9] 1941 census; see *Statistisches Jahrbuch der Schweiz 1970* (Basel: Birkhäuser, 1970): 20.

again a numerically small group.[10] Those who returned from this ignoble adventure were put on trial and received the proper punishment.

Communists, Fascists, and National Socialists continued, however, to operate as fringe groups in Swiss society. The sympathizers with the Hitler regime reached a parliamentary strength of one member in the Swiss National Council, while before 1945 the Communists had attained three seats.[11] In few countries of Europe were the fringe elements represented that poorly.

In mainstream politics the reaction to Hitler's rise to power was swift and decisive. On July 9, 1933, when such an act still took courage, Rudolf Minger, then head of the Swiss Department of Defense, chose the amphitheater of Windisch, a place with a Celtic rather than a Germanic name, to declare:

> Since the confederation came into being, there has never existed a true dictatorship in Switzerland. . . . [S]ince 1291 the people have held the principle of democracy in high regard, even though popular rights had been restricted over many centuries. Our people will never allow this democracy to be tampered with. Violent appetites for dictatorship, whichever side they come from, will always properly be dealt with. Never will our people accept a German-style *Gleich-schaltung* [forcing into line]. In Swiss fashion we will order our Swiss house. For this we do not need special shirts or flags; we are content with the white cross in the red field. Swiss, furthermore, will never allow themselves to be robbed of their right to criticize and speak their mind freely. If we did not have this right today, the young *Fronten* [Nazi sympathizers] would be in the most serious predicament. Also religious peace may not be tampered with. We will honor, furthermore, our federalism and count ourselves fortunate that our people is composed of different groups of languages and races. Herein lies the best guarantee that in times of war and in times of great international movements our nation will not be tempted into political adventurism.[12]

---

[10] This number relates to Swiss residing in Switzerland; it is larger if those living abroad, especially in Germany, are included; thus Vincenz Oertle, "Sollte ich aus Russland nicht zurückkehren ...", Thesis (Zürich 1998): 561; he ascertains 1,980 cases.

[11] After World War II the parliamentary strength of the Communists never exceeded 7 seats out of 200; see Gruner, *Parteien*, 186, for an overview of the parliamentary strength of the parties.

[12] Quotation transcribed from the original manuscript in the Bundesarchiv in Bern, J. I. 108, 329, "Rede von BR Minger an der Volksversammlung am 9. 7. 1933 in Windisch." A printed version in Hermann Wahlen, ed., *Rudolf Minger spricht* (Bern: Francke, 1967): 91-101.

Return to Military Preparedness

Minger asked for arms, fortifications, and training. Training was decreed, fortresses were built, and arms were bought. Switzerland's border regions significantly strengthened their defenses and anti-tank capabilities were much enhanced by the 47 millimeter infantry canon of 1935.[13] The air force acquired new planes, mainly some 100 of the type *Messerschmidt 109* with deliveries starting in December 1938; in addition Switzerland built under license some 300 *Morane-Saulnier M. S. 406s* (D-3800-3803).[14]

The figures for the military expenditures tell the story of a thrifty people thoroughly cognizant of new dangers and fully resolved to meet them.[15] Starting from a level of about 85-90 million francs in 1924 to 1933, military spending rose considerably to over 100 million francs in 1934, to over 200 million in 1938, to over 500 million in 1939, and to over a billion a year in 1940 to 1945. This represented about 1.4% of the net national product in 1934, 1.9% in 1937, 2.5% in 1938, 5.7% in 1939, and 11.6% in 1940, decreasing slightly to 9.2% by 1944. After representing 20 to 25% of the total governmental budget between 1923 and 1936, military expenditures reached 62% in 1940.[16]

This was serious money, derived to a large extent from extraordinary taxes decreed by the vote of a sovereign people, not known for throwing away valuable wealth, in a number of notable plebiscites.[17] Given the glaring lack of tanks, these military allocations did not guarantee a really strong defensive posture by 1939 or indeed even afterwards, but they did represent a credible effort derived from high commitment. Switzerland was not defenseless when Hitler sent his *Wehrmacht* against Poland. On June 22, 1939 Swiss President Philipp Etter proudly declared: "The Swiss will

---

[13] Kurt Sallaz and Peter Rilkin, *Panzer und Panzerabwehr* (Dietikon-Zürich: Stocker und Schmid, 1982): 197 and passim.

[14] *Cockpit* (July-September 1987):

[15] Figures based on Hans Rudolf Kurz, *Hundert Jahre Schweizer Armee* (Thun: Ott, 1978): 285-286. See also Albert Vogler, *Die schweizerischen Militärausgaben von 1850 - 1963 und ihre Auswirkungen auf die wirtschaftliche Entwicklung der Schweiz*. Dissertation Freiburg. Lungern: Druck Burch & Cie, 1965.

[16] Urs Schwarz, *Die schweizerische Kriegsfinanzierung 1939-1945 und ihre Ausstrahlungen in der Nachkriegszeit* (Winterthur: P. G. Keller, 1953): 81-82 and passim.

[17] See for instance Otto Schönmann, *Die ausserordentlichen Militär- und Kriegskredite im schweizerischen Bundeshaushalt*. Dissertation Basel (Basel: Druck Theodor Kestenholz, 1942): 109-110.

never part with his gun, symbol and protection of his freedom and independence."[18]

Holding Fast to Neutrality

For most Swiss, neutrality is an indisputable good, the value of which cannot be questioned. When World War II began, the Federal Council reaffirmed it on August 31 with these words:

> The international tension which has forced the Swiss Confederation to take military measures grants it anew the occasion to reaffirm its unshakable will, in no way to deviate from the principles of neutrality that have served for centuries as guidelines for its policies in that these principles correspond to the efforts of the Swiss people, its political legal status as well as its position towards other states and are, therefore, most dear to it.
>
> Implementing the instruction received from the National Assembly [Bundesversammlung], the Federal Council declares explicitly that the Swiss Confederation will maintain and protect, with all means at its disposal, the inviolability of its territory and its neutrality which has been viewed by the treaties of 1815 and the subsequent amendments to be in the true interest of the whole of European politics.
>
> The Confederation, as it has done already in the last wars, will make it a point of honor to promote humanitarian work which intends universally to soothe suffering arising from conflict.[19]

Swiss neutrality was explicitly recognized by powers entering the war. The British Foreign Office declared that Britain would "resolutely" respect Swiss neutrality "in full, so long as Switzerland for her part takes all possible measures to defend and maintain a strict neutrality."[20]

While neutrality applied to all belligerents, the military plans implemented by the army—its strength was typically 150,000, though during full mobilization some 450,000 men and women were under arms[21]—were clearly directed against an aggressive move by Hitler. For the

---

[18] Philipp Etter, *Reden an das Schweizervolk, gehalten im Jahre 1939* (Zürich, Atlantis Verlag, 1939): 64.

[19] Reprinted in Rudolf Kurz, ed., *Dokumente des Aktivdienstes* (Frauenfeld: Huber, 1965): 34-35.

[20] Edgar Bonjour, *Geschichte der schweizerischen Neutralität* 7 (Basel: Helbing & Lichtenhahn, 1974): 26. The whole chapter "Neutralitätserklärung" is relevant.

[21] "Bericht des Chefs des Generalstabes der Armee an den Oberbefehlshaber der Armee über den Aktivdienst 1939-1945;" copy in the Federal Military Library in Bern, pp. 46-53.

four very long years after 1940 the only onslaught against Switzerland could come from Germany, together with an auxiliary move from Italy. The Italian as well as German leadership had very clear plans about Switzerland. The nation was on the extermination list, being a people that simply could not in any conceivable way be fitted into a National Socialist and a Fascist Europe.

Preparing for Potential Invasions

The Swiss built the *Limmatstellung*, a strong defense line anchored in the fortress at Sargans, following from there to the Walensee, Lake Zürich, and on along the Limmat River to the pivotal point of Windisch, a place where earlier the Romans had built a camp for their legions fighting against the Barbarian invasions.[22] The Roman Emperor Tiberius nineteen hundred years earlier would easily have recognized what the Swiss were doing in 1939-40 to counter and deter the modern barbarians. From Windisch the line followed the Jura range to the plateau of Gempen where a link-up with the French was contemplated, should Hitler have struck there. Stretching the concept of neutrality to its furthest limit, General Henri Guisan, the Swiss Commander-in-Chief, actually arranged the necessary movements in concert with the French forces, but only in case of a German attack and at the explicit request of the Swiss.

When the Germans violated Swiss airspace, they were confronted with the Swiss air force. From May 10 to June 8, 1940 the Swiss shot down or forced a landing of 11 German war planes. An unknown number of others were shot at, but escaped.[23] The Swiss lost three planes, yet felt elated at what many perceived to be the first round of an impending struggle. Hermann Göring, the supreme commander of the German air force, was less happy and sent men to blow up planes at Switzerland's air fields. One man was denied entry because he did not have a visa, the rest were caught before they could inflict any damage. The would-be terrorists were tried and imprisoned. Seven Germans were released in 1950 and 1951, the two Swiss

---

[22] Walter Lüem and Andreas Steigmeier, *Die Limmatstellung im Zweiten Weltkrieg.* Baden: Baden Verlag, 1997; Hans Senn, *Basel und das Gempenplateau im Zweiten Weltkrieg* Frauenfeld: Huber, 1996. The works cited in both studies are significant.

[23] Werner Lindecker was one of the fighter pilots who, in 1998, turned 90. The Swiss Air Force Commander Fernand Carrel declared in his birthday greeting to Lindecker: "With your energy, your infectious enthusiasm as well as your courage in the air battles of June 1940 you have written one of the most notable chapters of our Air Force. You are and remain a memorable example for the coming generation of fighter pilots." Translated from *Luftwaffenzeitung*, No. 9 (February 1998): 51.

who had joined them in 1955.[24] Eventually General Guisan stopped the comprehensive interception of airplanes because it would not have been wise to deplete the planes of the Swiss air force without a chance to obtain replacements in the face of a potential German onslaught.

When France capitulated and had to conclude a humiliating armistice with Hitler on June 22, 1940, the Führer's armies were free to turn to unfinished business large and small. The Swiss were not far from the mind of the German leadership for after the *Anschluss* of Austria in 1938 and the conquest of Alsace- Lorraine in 1940, Switzerland included the last group of German-speaking people not controlled by the Reich, a true sting in Germany's side as the Swiss humor magazine *Nebelspalter* sarcastically pointed out, a Swiss publication like others banned in the Reich. On June 24, just two days after the armistice with France, a German army officer referred in his diary to his "first independent work." Otto Wilhelm von Menges had received the order to investigate "the possibilities of a surprise occupation of Switzerland by German troops operating from France and Germany, assuming that Italian troops attack Switzerland at the same time from the south."[25] Von Menges at that time was admittedly merely a captain on the German general staff and Great Britain had emerged as a far higher priority in the summer of 1940. The weather was still fine in the English Channel for a landing which, however, a band of committed defenders could defy.

Still, in August 1940 the Nazis worked out plans for an invasion of Switzerland, acting on the authority of the highest levels of the German army command. At the same time the Italians joined the planning under the authority of General Mario Vercellino, commander of the 6th Italian Army, although he was put on notice on August 22, 1940 that the Swiss case was not urgent.[26] The *Wehrmachtsführungsstab*, the general staff of the German armed forces, undertook an independent study of possible attacks on Switzerland because Hitler was furious that precision tools of Swiss origin had found their way to England and, also, because "it would have been

---

[24] See Ernst Wetter, *Duell der Flieger und der Diplomaten*. Frauenfeld: Huber, 1987.

[25] Quoted by Klaus Urner, *Die Schweiz muss noch geschluckt werden!* (Zürich: Verlag Neue Zürcher Zeitung, 1990): 150-151. Noteworthy is also the diary entry for June 24, 1940 by the Chief of the German General Staff, General Franz Halder: "It is again the same vexatious game as with the contact with the Russians in the campaign against Poland. The politician wants that Switzerland loses its direct contacts with France. This political desire shall be camouflaged by a military move. From this quite many undesirable consequences will result;" see Halder, *Kriegstagebuch* 1 (Stuttgart: W. Kohlhammer, 1962): 370.

[26] See Alberto Rovighi, *Un secolo di relazioni militari tra Italia e Svizzera 1861-1961* (Roma: Ufficio Storico, Stato Maggiore dell' Esercito, 1987): 557.

much more convenient to have at our disposal the railways through Switzerland not only for economic, but also for military transports."[27] The order for this study, which most likely had been submitted to Hitler, was given by Alfred Jodl who was later executed at Nüremberg in 1946. On August 26, 1940 Franz Halder, chief of the general staff of the German Army since 1938, ordered Army Group C to elaborate an operational plan for the conquest of Switzerland in cooperation with the Italians. In his order Halder asked for covert operations as well as a quick seizure of Bern, Switzerland's capital, and the industrialized regions around Solothurn, Lucerne, and Zürich. "The operations are to be conducted in such a way", Halder pointed out, "that would make it impossible for the armed forces of Switzerland to escape to the high mountains", the very thing the Swiss planned to do.[28]

Despite a partial demobilization as a measure of preserving resources, General Guisan spelled out Swiss policy in no uncertain terms in his order of the day, dated July 2, 1940 which concluded with these words: "We shall fight, even if it should prove impossible to win the contest of arms. We shall fight for every inch of ground, and we shall preserve this army's and this country's honor."[29] Ten days later Guisan sent a memorandum to Rudolf Minger, the head of the Swiss Military Department, which pointed out the importance of the direct means of communication across the Alps for Germany and Italy:

> Switzerland can only escape this threat of a direct German attack if the German High Command concludes that war against us would be long and costly, and that in a dangerous manner it would thereby create a focus of fighting in the heart of Europe and endanger the execution of its plans. From now on the goal and principle of our country's defense must be, therefore, to show our neighbors that this war would be long and costly. Should fighting ensue, we must sell our skin as dearly as possible.[30]

Creation of a National Redoubt

This was the reasoning that led to the concept of the National 'Reduit' [Redoubt], that is the transformation of the Swiss Alps into a fortress from

---

[27] Bernhard von Lossberg, *Im Wehrmachtsführungsstab* (Hamburg: H. H. Nölke, 1949): 103.

[28] See Lew Besymenski, *Sonderakte Barbarossa* (Reinbeck bei Hamburg: Rowohlt, 1973): 277-279.

[29] Kurz, ed., *Dokumente,* 80.

[30] Ibid., 83-85.

which the principal objective of an invader—use of the transit routes across them—could be thwarted, thus making the feasibility of an attack less likely.

General Guisan wanted to be clearly understood. On July 25, 1940, therefore, he ordered nearly five hundred commanding officers of the Swiss army aboard the steamship *Stadt Luzern*[31] to assemble on the Rütli meadow where according to tradition the Swiss Confederation had been founded in 1291. After a memorable speech the General issued an order to the whole army, the central passage of which stated: "At present there are more troops than ever beyond our borders, and they are excellent. What only weeks ago seemed unimaginable, today is in the realm of the possible: We may be attacked simultaneously from all sides. The army has to adjust to this new situation and to take a position which allows it to defend itself effectively on all fronts."[32]

The Axis powers were incensed. Who after all would attack Switzerland except they? So Caligula's cry "can there be an antidote against Caesar?" was heard again. On August 13, 1940 Federal Councilor Philip Etter, then in charge of the Swiss Foreign Office, had to endure the concerted protests of the Italian[33] and German envoys against Guisan's Rütli speech. Etter commented: "I had forced myself to accepting the protests in an absolutely quiet composure. I must confess, however, that it cost me something to remain quiet and friendly since the whole person, especially the [military] officer in me, rebelled against the task given me as representative of the Federal Council [i.e. the Executive branch of the Swiss government] to receive the—in my view objectively unjustified—protests from foreign powers. Durum officium [a hard task]!"[34]

The German secret intelligence digest *Laufende Informationen* reported on August 4, 1940 the continuing Swiss hopes for an English victory and added that the Jews in Switzerland were in fear of "liquidation".[35] On September 13 the publication again attributed to the

---

[31] Josef Gwerder, *Dampfschiff* 'Stadt Luzern', *Bordbuch* (Luzern: Keller, 1989): 40-44, 56-57.

[32] Kurz, ed., *Dokumente*, 90.

[33] Malcolm Muggeridge, ed., *Ciano's Diary 1939-1943* (London: Heinemann, 1947): 282: "Mackensen brings a plan for an identical protest to be made to Bern because of an insolent speech by a Swiss general. We agree on its general lines."

[34] Quoted in Martin Rosenberg, *Was war Anpassung, wo war Widerstand?* (Bern: Generalsekretariat der Konservativ-Christlichsozialen Volkspartei, 1966): 20-31. This work is a collection of historical essays first published in the daily *Vaterland*.

[35] Alfred Ernst, ed., *Neutrale Kleinstaaten im Zweiten Weltkrieg* (Münsingen: Tages-Nachrichten, 1973): 44.

Swiss increased sympathies for England and the belief that the German air offensive against Great Britain had failed, as it indeed had.

After the end of September when the weather in the English channel precluded any hope of successfully invading England, Hitler needed another victory. Switzerland once again presented a tempting target. Thus Benito Mussolini and Adolf Hitler met on the Brenner Pass on October 4, 1940. Afterwards Mussolini reflected on the discussions and wrote Hitler a letter on October 19. About Switzerland he commented: "I am sure that you will not be surprised to see Switzerland included in the remaining continental possessions of Great Britain. With its incomprehensible hostile allegiance Switzerland calls its own existence into question."[36]

In the fall of 1940 knives were indeed sharpened in Italy as well as in Germany. Planning for *Operation Tannenbaum*, that is the invasion of Switzerland, was approved on October 4 by Wilhelm Ritter von Leeb, the Commander of Army Group C. According to him it required 21 divisions for an attack. Leeb's plan, however, was criticized by the operational branch of the German general staff which reduced the estimate of forces needed to 11 divisions. On October 17 Franz Halder, Chief of the German Army's general staff, drafted independently the most dangerous plan of invasion: Five infantry divisions should attack in the Jura mountain range in the west of Switzerland with the goal of drawing the Swiss army out of its Alpine redoubt, only to be cut off and encircled by six motorized tank divisions.[37]

Perhaps it would have worked, perhaps not. In any event, the Swiss established themselves more and more strongly in the Alpine fortifications, gaining time by some concessionary measures as well as by the Axis' higher priorities elsewhere. Hitler decided in October that he wanted to close the Mediterranean at Gibraltar. Franco, the Spanish dictator, however, made such excessive demands that the talks came to naught. The problems posed by Vichy France, furthermore, as well as preparations for an assault on the Soviet Union diverted the Führer's mind from the issue of Switzerland. Yet even usually calm and level headed Swiss were all too

---

[36] "Col suo incomprensibile attegiamento ostile [a la Gran Bretagna] la Svizzera pona da sè il problema della sua esistenza;" quoted in Rovighi, *Un secolo di relazioni*, 558-561. See also the secret report of Colonel Hans August von Werdt, the Swiss Military Attaché in Berlin: "Italy demands foremost: All of Graubünden and further the territory to Lake Constance. Germany objected to this and wanted [all of] Switzerland to and inclusive of the Gotthard. The last demand of Italy has been the Canton Graubünden to Sargans." Copy of the report in file E 27/14336 of the Swiss Federal Archives. I thank Peter Kamber of Burgdorf, Switzerland, for having made me aware of this report.

[37] Ernst, ed., *Neutrale Kleinstaaten,* 50-51.

aware at that time that the German leader could change his mind at a moment's notice.

The Ideological Battle

In November 1940, 173 Swiss people in an infamous "Memorandum of the Two Hundred" demanded the dismissal of editors of leading newspapers and the purge of officials who denounced the Hitler regime.[38] It was to have no effect. On May 15, 1941 a well-known Swiss colonel, giving his impressions from a trip to Germany, observed that "it is as well possible for a good Swiss to think in a European way and to work for a new Europe as it is possible to declare allegiance to England or the United States."[39] As his *Denkschrift* became known, his views were hotly contested and its author was never able to live down the objections to its questionable contents.[40] The strong reaction in Swiss public opinion, however, did not endear the country to the dictators to the North and South.

Yet there was also a counter-movement afoot. At the same time that some Swiss called for accommodation to the Axis powers, a group of young military officers who feared that the Federal Council would capitulate to Hitler's demands formed a secret *Offiziersbund*, a league of officers.[41] Its 37 members pledged to continue resistance to the National Socialist regime at all costs. When the league, which clearly violated military discipline, was discovered, General Guisan put the officers under disciplinary arrest for a short time, yet allowed them to continue their military careers without impediment.

Both the 173 appeasers as well as the 37 officers calling for resistance at all costs were important, if in some sense marginal phenomena of a tense and frightful period. Most Swiss faced one of the hardest test in Swiss history with quiet determination. Arnold Lunn, the famous British mountaineer, observed in a letter written in London on March 27, 1942: "Even in 1940, the Swiss took the long view and knew that they would not die in vain, if they preferred death to surrender. Their children and their children's children would still be proud to be Swiss, and from the seed of their pride would flower the spirit of resistance which would one day liberate enslaved Europe from Nazi tyranny."[42]

---

[38] Gerhart Waeger, *Die Sündenböcke der Schweiz* (Olten: Walter Verlag, 1971): 257-259.

[39] Quoted in Willi Gautschi, *General Henri Guisan* (Zürich: Verlag Neue Zürcher Zeitung, 1989): 395.

[40] Full text in Bonjour, *Neutralität*, 8 (1975): 261.

[41] Gautschi, *Guisan*, 235.

[42] Arnold Lunn, *Mountain Jubilee* (London: Eyre & Spottiswoode, 1943): 277.

When Mussolini once again met Hitler at the Brenner Pass on June 2, 1941, the latter reserved much of his venom for the Swiss. In his irritation he even used the term "Schwaben", Swabians, a Swiss pejorative name for Germans.[43] The official record of that meeting recorded:

> The Führer called Switzerland the most vile and the most miserable people and state. He called the Swiss deadly enemies of the New Germany: It was telling that they declared that without a miracle the Schwaben were going to win the war. They were openly against the Reich because by separating from the fated community of the German people, they had hitherto hoped to make a better deal. This had been the case for a long time, but now, in light of the most recent developments, the Swiss realized that their calculation was wrong. Their attitude was driven by the renegade's hatred.
>
> The Duce, calling Switzerland an anachronism, asked what future it could well have. Smiling, the [German] Foreign Minister referred this question to a discussion between the Duce and the Führer. The Duce noted that in Switzerland only the French Swiss were in favor of France, the Italian Swiss however against Italy and the German Swiss against Germany. On the Jewish question the Führer said that all Jews had to leave Europe by the end of the war.[44]

While Hitler mused this way about Jews and the Swiss, the military planners of the Axis powers revived their plans against the country, Switzerland's strategic situation was grim indeed.[45] Yet although surrounded by the troops of the Axis and under severe economic pressure, Switzerland refused to cave in and to seek a permanent accommodation to the then-triumphant powers. Karl Barth, who had lost his university position in Germany due to his outspoken criticism of National Socialism, had stated

---

[43] "Schwobe", Swiss German for Swabians, became at times a Swiss slur word including all Germans. Shouted by Swiss across the river, the return compliment of Germans was "Kuhschweizer [cow Swiss]." Alfred Mahrer of Möhlin, Switzerland told the author that he also heard the following: "Hey Swiss, do you still have to eat? Tomorrow we will come over!—Na Schweizer, hast noch zu fressen [a word reserved for an animal's eating]? Morgen kommen wir rüber!"

[44] Quoted in Andreas Hillgruber, ed., *Staatsmänner und Diplomaten bei Hitler* (München: Deutscher Taschenbuch Verlag, 1969): 275-276. Franz Halder *Kriegstagebuch* 2 (1963): 450, noted: "Conversation Führer—Duce. Apparently general exchange of ideas, without binding agreement. (Switzerland vile)."

[45] Rovighi, *Un secolo di relazioni*, 562-563. An Italian intelligence assessment of May 17, 1941 refers to the Anglophile attitude of General Henri Guisan and the Officers League; see Antonello Biagini and Fernando Fratolillo, *Diario Storico del Commando Supremo* 4, tomo 2 (Roma: Ufficio Storico, Stato maggiore dell' Esercito, 1992): 27.

already in 1938 "that there is something worse than dying, there is something worse than killing, this something is the voluntary 'yes' to the shame of the Antichrist's rule." The Church, Barth further stated, "has . . . to admonish the democratic State to be at all cost, even of misery and destruction, a *strong* state: which means to demand that all dictatorships stop at its borders."[46]

A June 1941 map of Europe shows a Switzerland that was still independent, yet had no friends on the continent. France had fallen, the United States had not yet entered the war, and Great Britain stood alone, defending a precarious hold on Malta and Tobruk. There was no way that Great Britain could have come to the aid of Switzerland at that time, a fact to be pondered by those who now suggest that in 1941 Switzerland could or should have relinquished its neutrality and joined the Allied side.

The Long Wait

On June 22, 1941 Hitler unleashed his armies against the Soviet Union. Its great peoples heroically rallied to the oppressive Soviet regime because it was defending their homelands. Although Hitler was viewed then as he is viewed today by many as one of the greatest evildoers, Stalin in the view of many does not rank very far behind. Swiss felt relieved by the news of the German invasion of the Soviet Union and glad of being, at least for some time, removed from the immediate attention of the armies of the Axis powers. It was a sentiment not unlike that expressed by the *Chicago Tribune* in the issue of December 5, 1941.[47] Most Swiss, however, never thought of being liberated by Soviets, the destroyers of the Baltic republics, the aggressors of Finland, the partitioners of Poland, and the very power that in 1918 had tried to overthrow democracy in Switzerland. Yet this negative view of the Soviet Union did not prevent a person like Guido Pidermann from doing whatever possible in 1942 to help starving Soviet prisoners in Finland in cooperation with some Americans.[48]

By June 1941 the Swiss Army had settled in for its long wait. Physically this was possible because of Switzerland's mountainous terrain, morally because a strong belief of the Swiss people in democracy, freedom, and God, politically because of Great Britain's staunch defensive posture

---

[46] Karl Barth, *Eine Schweizer Stimme 1938-1945* (Zollikon-Zürich: Evangelischer Verlag, 1945): 64.

[47] Roy Douglas, *The World War 1939-1945: The Cartoonists' Vision* (London: Routledge, 1991): 86.

[48] Christine Gehrig-Straube, *Beziehungslose Zeiten* (Zürich: Hans Rohr, 1997): 209-231, esp. 211.

and the expectation of an American entry into the conflict. It is perhaps significant that the German intelligence service reported already on October 26, 1940 that the Swiss put their trust in the United States.[49]

During the war years Switzerland accepted a grand total of more than 5% of its resident population as refugees and, one has to agree, it should have accepted more, especially in regard to Jewish victims of the Hitler regime. Although much detail about their persecution especially after the invasion of the Soviet Union and the Wannsee Conference was not known in Switzerland, what had become known was unsettling enough. Since early in the war the division "Heer und Haus [Army and Home]" of the Swiss Army issued "Wehrbriefe", that is "Letters of Resistance", which addressed important issues of the day. Letter 26, dated May 25, 1943, dealt with the Jewish question. It was designed to combat anti-Semitic tendencies in the armed forces and to reaffirm that neither anti-Semitism nor any other religious prejudice had a place in the Swiss Army and among the Swiss people. It was an official document to be used as the basis for lectures and discussions and was well received.

The document strove to dispel concerns of the Swiss people about the scale on which Switzerland offered asylum to Jewish refugees. The letter made clear that it was not surprising "that 80 to 90 percent of refugees who enjoy asylum in Switzerland are Jews, in consequence of the persecutions of the Jews in our neighboring countries." It also stressed the significant financial support provided by the Swiss Jewish community for the persecuted. It reassured those concerned that the refugees consumed "an almost invisible crumb" of the nation's rationed food supply and that anti-Semitism provided an opening for alien propaganda. The letter concluded forcefully that "Anti-Semitism as it is propagated today involves convictions that are incompatible with our democratic thinking. If Switzerland admits anti-Semitism, it admits ideologies that are incompatible with its essence and existence."[50]

One may argue, of course, that this document only proves the need of fighting Swiss anti-Semitism in 1943, yet it certainly shows a serious and committed effort to oppose that dimension of the National Socialist ideology. The sight of armed Jews in Switzerland was yet another reason for Hitler's disdain for Switzerland, where Jews like other Swiss served in all ranks. In 1944 Herbert Constam of American Jewish origin, whose

---

[49] Ernst, ed., *Neutrale Kleinstaaten*, 44.

[50] *Wehrbrief 26*, issued by the Generaladjudantur of the Swiss Army, Division "Heer und Haus [Army and Home]", May 25, 1943; 9500 copies were printed and used to educate soldiers and civilians alike and to inure them to the poison of Anti-Semitism.

grandfather had fought in the American Civil War, became one of the four corps commanders of the Swiss Army, the equivalent of an American three star general.[51] Albert Mayer served as the first adjutant of General Henri Guisan and was a close confidant of the Swiss Commander-in-Chief.[52] Sympathy for the totalitarian regimes surrounding Switzerland as well as for Soviet Communism was minimal in the Swiss army since the soldiers served to combat the very threat those ideologies represented to Switzerland's independence.

Renewed Threats of Invasion

The deep aversion of the Swiss mainstream to totalitarianism was reciprocated in full. The last known German plan to invade the country was the so-called *Studie Böhme* of December 1943. As Allied pressure in Italy grew, German attempts to hold down its now unwilling erstwhile partner increased the importance of communications across the Alps. General Franz Böhme had been commanding general in Serbia in 1941, where he not only allowed the massacre at Kraljevo, but also boasted in the October 26 order of the day: "The enemy lost at least 80 dead, 1755 hostages were shot to expiate our own losses." He closed the document with the exhortation: "Onward to new deeds!"[53]

One contemplated such "new deed" was the conquest of Switzerland. In his 1943 plan Böhme called the Swiss Army "an extremely significant factor" and his methodical mind so typical for the German general staff detailed not only the strengths , but also the weakness of the Swiss. Thus he called for a swift withdrawal of any attacking German columns that became bogged down, aware that the Swiss would not pursue a withdrawing enemy.[54] An operation to outflank the enemy on the Rhine via the Swiss Jura mountains was in Böhme's view quite feasible. The Swiss Army could thus be pushed back to its Alpine redoubt and cordoned off there. As General Guisan had understood three years earlier, Böhme's objective was clear: "The prize is . . . possession of the important North-South communications. Only their unfettered possession—or at least the two

---

[51] Information provided by Benoit de Monmollin-Constam of Evilard, Switzerland who had Constam's autobiography privately printed.

[52] See Dominic Pederazzi, Jürg Stüssi-Lauterburg und Anne-Marie Volery, eds., *"En toute confiance." Correspondance du Général et de Madame Henri Guisan avec le Major Albert R. Mayer, 1940-1959.* Brugg: Effingerhof, 1995.

[53] Hannes Heer, Christian Reuther und Johannes Bache, *Vernichtungskrieg. Verbrechen der Wehrmacht 1941-1944* (Hamburg: Hamburger Edition, 1996): 52. Compare also Jozo Tomasevich, *The Chetniks* (Stanford: Stanford University Press, 1975): 97-98.

[54] Edmund Wehrli, *Schweiz ohne Armee—eine Friedensinsel?* (Zürich: Gesellschaft für militärhistorische Studienreisen [GMS], 1985): 25-26, with valuable bibliography.

western ones including the related electricity supply—signify a clear military victory over Switzerland."[55] Böhme summed up his plan with this comment:

> The prize to be realized by such an undertaking will be the elimination of the last anti-German army in central Europe, the taking of arms as booty, the possession of valuable industrial plants for the war industry, and the control of important railway lines. However, even after the subjugation of the Swiss army, German security forces will have to stay permanently to pacify the country. As to timing, in principle we might say that this must preclude an invasion of Allied forces in Europe. After a landing of Anglo-American forces, Germany will in no way be able to spare the necessary forces for an operation which is absolutely imperative against a well-defended mountainous country. Should Switzerland behave in a way unacceptable to Germany, the complete encirclement of the country already offers the possibility to press for policy changes by blocking all supplies.[56]

In the end Switzerland, which depended on Germany for coal imports, had the good fortune not to be "pacified" Böhme-style due to its strong military defense. As the war's end approached, army units were moved from the National Redoubt in the Alps to the frontiers in order to prevent incursions of Swiss territory by retreating German as well as advancing Allied troops, in conformity with the 1939 declaration concerning Switzerland's treaty-sanctioned obligations as a neutral state.[57]

The next serious threat of invasion originated with Josef Stalin, who despised Switzerland and suggested that the allies push back the German right flank over Swiss territory. Stalin seems not to have forgotten the expulsion of Soviet diplomats in 1918, Switzerland's lone vote against the

---

[55] Significantly Böhme stated further: "Given the tense German supply situation, it would be militarily not justifiable to undertake operations that would lead to a desert [die zu einer Einöde führen würden]. Thus the following situation is given: The Swiss defense of the country has an army at its disposal that alone for its numerical size is a most considerable factor. The vanquishing of the troops bitterly defending themselves in the redoubt of the High Alps will represent a task that is difficult to fulfill." See *Allgemeine Schweizerische Militärzeitschrift* 12 (December 1949): 850-851.

[56] Ibid., 859.

[57] The Hague Convention V, "Respecting the Rights and Duties of Neutral Powers and Persons in Case of War on Land", signed October 18, 1907, demands no less. The violation of this convention by Germany in attacking Norway, Denmark, Luxembourg, Belgium, the Netherlands, and the USSR was one of the war crimes of which the Nuremberg defendants were accused. See "Trial of the Major War Criminals before the International Military Tribunal, November 14, 1945–October 1, 1946" (Nüremberg 1947): 86, Charge IV.

Soviet Union's membership in the League of Nations in 1934, and the measures taken against Alexander Rado's wartime spy ring.[58] Nor was Stalin civil when in 1944 he rebuffed a Swiss request to resume diplomatic relations.

The end of World War II marked the end of the first and second, but not of the third totalitarian threat faced by Switzerland. Military preparations in the event of a third world war that might be unleashed by the Soviet Union were undertaken and, if need be, the *Limmatstellung* was to be activated against Soviet armies as it had been readied in World War II against the German threat. That Stalin intensely detested the Swiss is affirmed by none other than Winston Churchill: "I was astonished at U. J.'s [Stalin's] savageness against her", Churchill declared, "and much though I respect that great and good man, I was entirely uninfluenced by his attitude. He called them 'swine' and he does not use that sort of language without meaning it. I am sure we ought to stand by Switzerland." In the same passage Churchill also praised the role the Swiss played in World War II and claimed that "of all the neutrals Switzerland has the greatest right to distinction. She has been the sole international force linking the hideously-sundered nations and ourselves."[59]

The fact that the British held out against Germany, as well as the hope that eventually the United States would enter the war, undoubtedly strengthened the morale of the Swiss people during the dark days of World War II. It might well have been impossible to preserve Swiss independence and democracy if the Allied forces had not been able to vanquish the Axis powers. Thus most Swiss readily acknowledge the great debt they owe to Great Britain and the United States for their role in helping to preserve Switzerland's independence and, in Allen Dulles' phrase, its benevolent neutrality.

---

[58] Pierre-Theodore Braunschweig, *Geheimer Draht nach Berlin* (Zürich: Verlag Neue Zürcher Zeitung, 1989): 387, n. 247.

[59] Winston S. Churchill, *The Second World War*. Vol. 6: *Triumph and Tragedy* (London: Cassell, 1954): 616.

III: UNSUNG DEDICATION

Women in Switzerland's Mobilization

Thomas Maissen

"Heer und Haus" (its French equivalent being "Armée et Foyer") was a branch of the Swiss Army charged with defending the nation ideologically against the threat of defeatism and totalitarian propaganda. These names reveal the pillars on which the fatherland was to rest: On a husband as soldier, on a wife and family as the home that gives security and deserves protection. In the context of the ideological defense of the country traditional images of women were once again highly prized: The dynamic, short-haired, modish, urbane secretary of the twenties gave way to the earthy, healthy, kind, and devoted country woman in skirt and with pigtails. Especially in the Great Depression working women, above all unmarried ones, were often viewed as improper rivals of heads of families in distress. The proper tasks of women consisted mainly in the care of children, of home and hearth, in the numerous and, given the absence of today's technical means, time-consuming labors of washing, sowing, cleaning, and cooking as well as in the economical use of spare provisions.

After the mobilization of most men these women's tasks were inevitably augmented by many additional burdens. In the short run it meant that women helped out in the service sector and in industrial production, in the long run performed and organized those labors over again in the shop or on the farm that otherwise had been the domain of men. Conductors and letter carriers visibly proved to the public that it could be done without problems—and that at the same time it was only provisional. The women conductors of Zürich performed their duties for only two days a month and had to be accompanied by male colleagues. Labor unions did not want jobs to be lost by their members who had been called up for active duty. Employers did not see it differently. Labor contracts with women included the provision for a one to three days' notice of termination so that at demobilization male workers could again resume their employment. The lower esteem awarded the work done by women was also evident in the wages they received, which were generally a third to a half below that of men.

Interestingly, the widespread massive employment especially in farming did not lead to a statistically evident increase of women in the work place: only 30 percent were considered employed. In 1941 the number of 570,215 given for fully employed women even reached a low point, and only 9 percent of them were married. About 300,000 women worked in the service sector, half of them as maids or domestics, slightly over 200,000 in industry and some 90,000 in agriculture. In the years following, however, war production lead to a strong shift towards industry. These official data were deceptive as to the actual performance of women in that they failed to consider not only their widespread substitute or complementary work, but also their traditional engagement on the farm and in the shop which by then had grown to more than a full time occupation.

Precisely because of the customary tasks of being a mother and housewife, which implied additional demands given the absence of the husband, it was neither possible nor desirable that women should pursue full-time jobs. In contrast to the time of the First World War, the resulting financial problems were at least somewhat mitigated by the introduction at the war's onset of a system of wage and income supplements and by rationing. Nevertheless, the economic and personal situation for many women burdened by a variety of tasks was extremely taxing, especially if one considers the meager rations, the need to care for their own garden in the context of the so-called *Anbauschlacht* or agricultural battlefront, the close living conditions in comparison with today, and the large number of children, augmented by years of high births during the war as an expression of the will to survive which was fostered by official exhortation.

The activity of the civilian Women's Auxiliary Service was viewed as part of the country's military defense effort and, besides a woman's domestic and professional duties, was considered a task that was to remain uncompensated and limited. It could be fulfilled by working on farms, especially at harvest time: From 1941 to 1946 more than 170,000 women helped out on the average for a month in the agricultural domain. Others worked as Samaritans in hospitals, looked after refugees as they arrived or lived in homes, helped gather used paper or old metal, mended garments, and assisted widely in the care of soldiers by washing their clothes, by sending them care packages, by visiting their families, by cooking in military kitchens, and by providing books and games for recreation rooms. The kind and cordial "soldiers' mother" was the symbol of these activities who lightened the hard daily routine for many a man on active duty. An important function, furthermore, was the role of women in the civilian anti-aircraft defense where they formed, often with many years of experience in contrast to the frequently absent men, the very core of the firefighters at home.

The involvement of women in the anti-aircraft defense derived from the corresponding 1934 decision of the federal government which introduced the new principle that women could also be called upon to perform public service. In some way it was an early stage of the "Ordinance Concerning the Auxiliary Service", issued by the Federal Council on April 3, 1939, which declared: "In this sense also women may be accepted as volunteers in all kinds of the auxiliary service in which female assistants are feasible and in case their aptitude conforms to the demands of the given auxiliary service." Initially the organization of a Women's Auxiliary Service remained with the authority of the cantonal governments, which attended to the task unevenly. The coordination with existing institutions such as the Red Cross, or the automobile clubs ACS and TCS which possessed long lists of volunteer drivers, often met with defensive reflexes of cantonal military directors who adhered to the principle of states' rights.

The full-fledged Women's Auxiliary Service (FHD) emerged only after the outbreak of the war: On November 26, 1939, the modern Swiss army trained women for the first time as drivers for the Red Cross in a course given in Basel. The ideological sympathy with the Finnish struggle against the Soviet Union as well as the example of the Finnish female auxiliary organization "Lotta Svärd" had contributed to a favorable climate for the establishment of the FHD, for which General Guisan issued the pertinent guidelines on February 16, 1940. Analogous to the male auxiliary service categories, tasks were assigned in the realm of medical service, administration, publicity, communication, transport, equipment and clothing, care-taking for instance of refugees, the servicing of carrier pigeons and military dogs, as well as the "Intellectual Auxiliary Service", especially in the news service and in the observation of aircraft.

On April 10, 1940 a call was issued to all Swiss women to join the Women's Auxiliary Service which was to free soldiers for other tasks. Instead of a haphazard engagement of women in the army a systematic induction was planned as well as a two week training for those enlisting between the age of 18 to 40, to be conducted on the Axenfels above the Lake of Uri and in Castello di Rialto near Lugano. A contemporary report described the training as follows: "Gymnastics, sports and games, exercising (always with consideration for the specific female constitution): singing; and developing and firming up theory which for any further education is an indispensable basis of impeccable character traits: the spirit of joyful, faithful and exact fulfillment of duty, of disciplined thinking and acting." Also to be instilled were "Dependability, discipline and comradeship" To be rejected however, in the words of the FHD Chief Generaladjudant Rugero Dollfus, was "everything that could lead to a masculinization of women", that is to what was not "according to nature", especially the manipulation of weapons. Despite or because of such limitations, officers and soldiers as well as people at large seemed uncertain about the appropriateness of the Women's Auxiliary Service. By some, women in the military service were not fully accepted although, in Dollfus' words, " they fulfilled their duty in their domain more gladly, evenly, and conscientiously than the men."

At the end of 1941 some 15,000 Swiss women served in the military Women's Auxiliary Service (FHD) from one to four months, and by 1943 their number had risen to 23,000. However, despite intense publicity campaigns their ranks did not increase. Familial obligations held numerous potential candidates back as well as the threat of employers who, given the already precarious staffing in many branches of production, did not want to lose their female employees. After much urging the women, who until then were identified only by a gray FHD-apron and by an armband, were finally given permission in 1943 to wear a uniform for which, however, they had to pay themselves and which, therefore, was not obligatory. General Guisan himself had declared in his guidelines of 1940: "Uniformation is out of the question, only a federal armband will be distributed. A uniformed dress may be prescribed by the FHD at a person's own expense."

Conceived mostly by men, the military Women's Auxiliary Service shows that traditional assumptions had shaped the deployment of women during the war: The issue was for women to help out and to stand in, mostly in order to free men for other tasks. As large as the contribution of women in the military and especially also in the civilian sector may have been, women's work was judged as natural only in the privacy of the home and as merely temporary in the public sector. That also holds for the Women's Auxiliary Service, which in the eyes of many men had no further function after 1945. "When the war ended, women again retired, quietly, and as courageously as during the years of trial and endurance when they had shouldered the hard work of the men which had to be done behind the bunkers and barbed-wire entanglements." These words of Federal Councilor Philipp Etter expressed typically the widely held ideal that the home was a woman's place whose devotion to family earned the gratitude and love of her male relatives. This view ran counter to reality in that women had shown great independence in many public endeavors. At the same time the view also represented the self-understanding of many women who saw their main role as being a caring wife and mother. Yet due to the achievements during the war the demand for voting rights for women intensified, noticeably in middle class circles as well as in the military Women's Auxiliary Service, and was proof of an emerging change in consciousness. Although in 1945 the Swiss people accepted a constitutional provision concerning the protection of the family that derived from a conservative stance, efforts to introduce voting rights for women failed during the later 1940s in seven cantons. A corresponding postulate on the federal level was to disappear in the administrative drawers for twelve years. It was only in 1971 that women's suffrage was introduced by a referendum on the national level.

Adapted from the German by L. Schelbert. Excerpted from Katri Burri (Bildauswahl)/ Thomas Maissen (Texte): *Bilder aus der Schweiz, 1939-1945*. Zweite Auflage (Zürich: Verlag Neue Zürcher Zeitung, 1998): 107-109. Printed by permission.

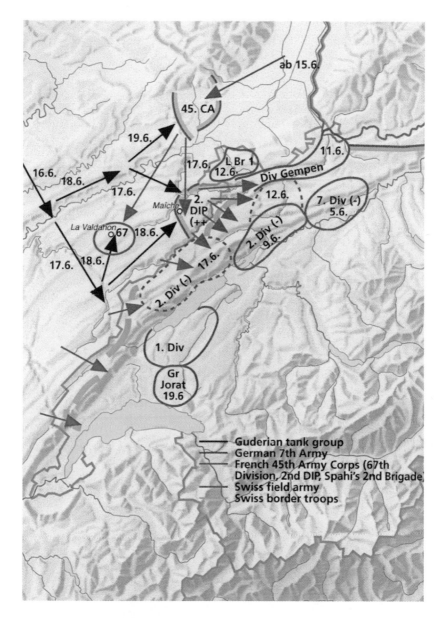

Figure 1: June 10-20, 1940: German Troops Facing Swiss Contingents on Switzerland's Western Border

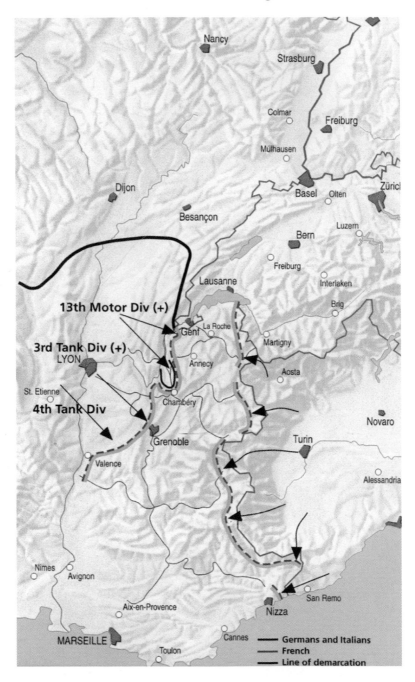

Figure 2: June 21-24, 1940: German and Italian Troops Facing the French Alpine Army in the Western Alps

Figure 3: April 18, 1940: General Besson's Plan of French Intervention in Support of Swiss Troops in Case of a German Attack

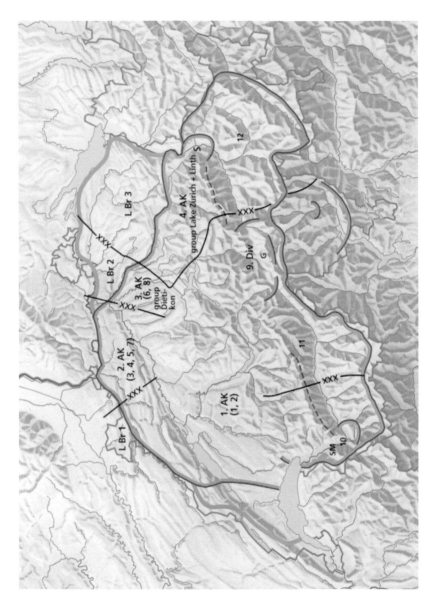

Figure 4: June 25, 1940: Regrouping of Swiss Troops According to Operational Plan 10

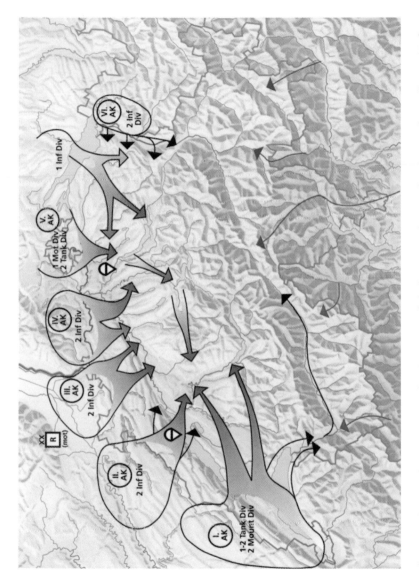

Figure 5: September 6, 1940: The German High Command's Draft "Tannenbaum" No. 12 for an Invasion of Switzerland

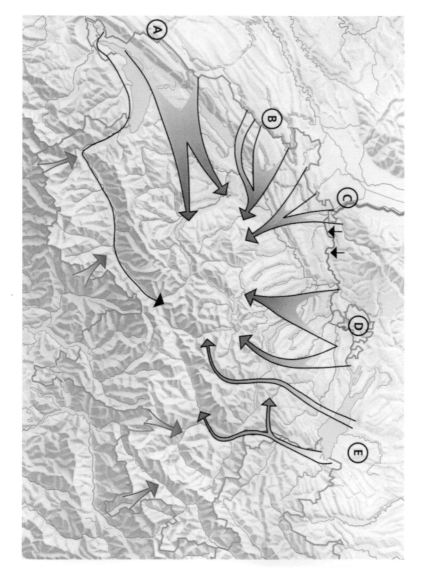

Figure 6: October 4, 1940: The German Army Group C's Draft for "Tannenbaum"

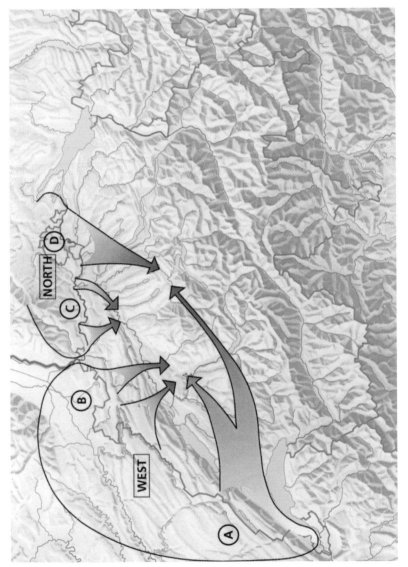

Figure 7: October 17, 1940: Draft for "Tannenbaum" prepared by German General Halder

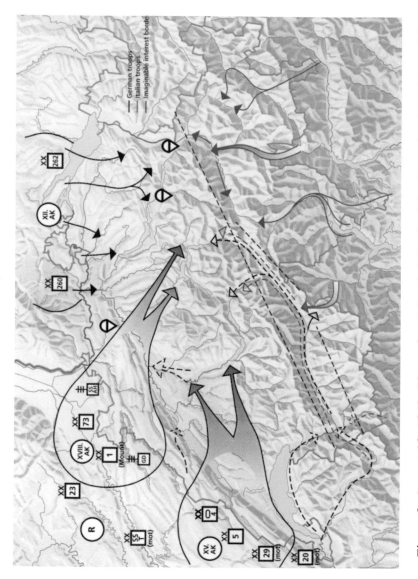

Figure 8: August 12, 1940: "Operation Schweiz," Draft of the Operational Division of the German Army High Command for an Invasion of Switzerland

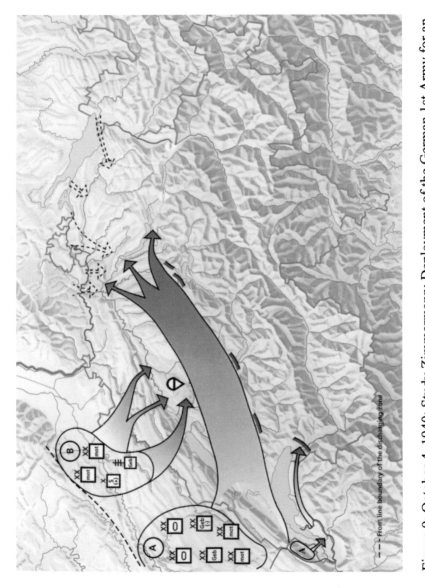

Figure 9: October 4, 1940: Study Zimmermann: Deployment of the German 1st Army for an Attack on Switzerland

Creator	Military Command	Army Corps	Tank Divisions	Motorized Divisions	Mountain Divisions	Infantry Divisions	Total Number of Divisions
Op Abt OKH	AOK 12	3	1	3⅔	1	5	10⅔
AOK 12	AOK 12	6	3-4	2	2	9	16-17
H Gr C	H Gr C 2 AOK	7	5	5	3	8	21
Halder	2 AOK	4	6 rapid			5	11
AOK 1	AOK 1	3	2	4 ½	2	3	11 ½

(Support forces stationed in Germany are not included)

Figure 10: Troops Needed for the Conquest of Switzerland as Calculated by German Planners

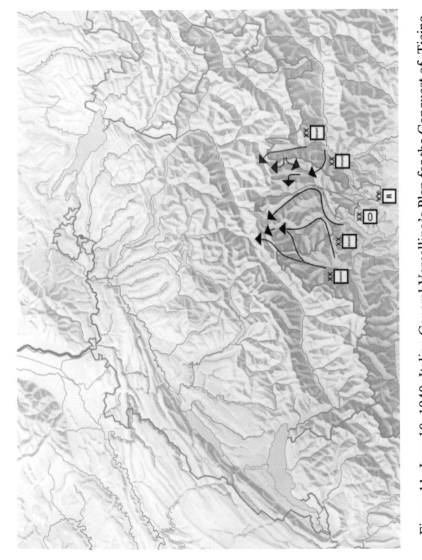

Figure 11: June 10, 1940: Italian General Vercellino's Plan for the Conquest of Ticino, Switzerland's Italian-Speaking Region

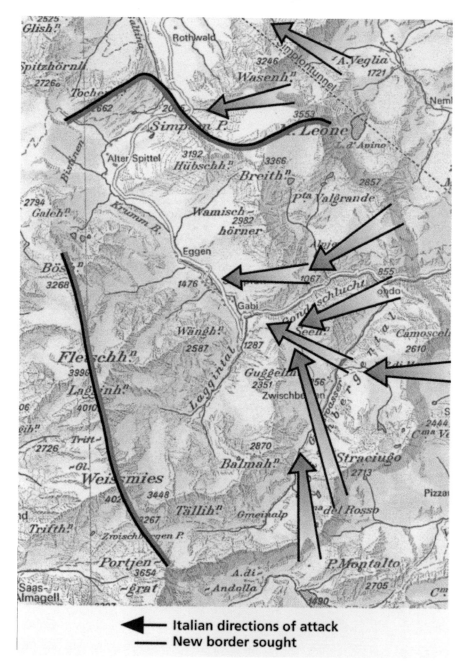

➤ **Italian directions of attack**
— **New border sought**

Figure 12: Mid-July 1940: Italian Operational Plan for the Conquest of the Simplon Pass

Italy's project to partition Switzerland, 15 July 1940

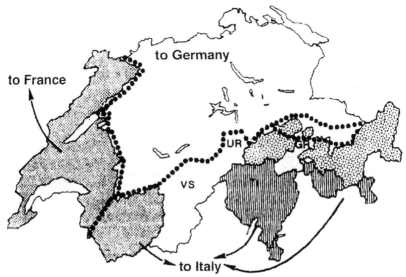

A: Radical solution (dismemberment)

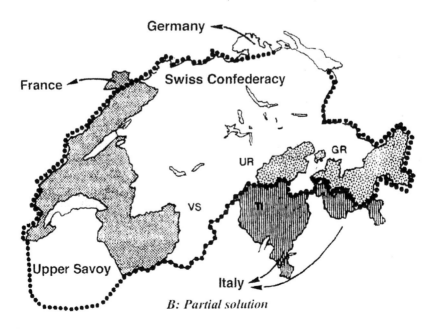

B: Partial solution

Figure 13: July 15, 1940: Italian Plans for Dividing Switzerland Between Italy, Germany, and France or for Repartitioning Switzerland

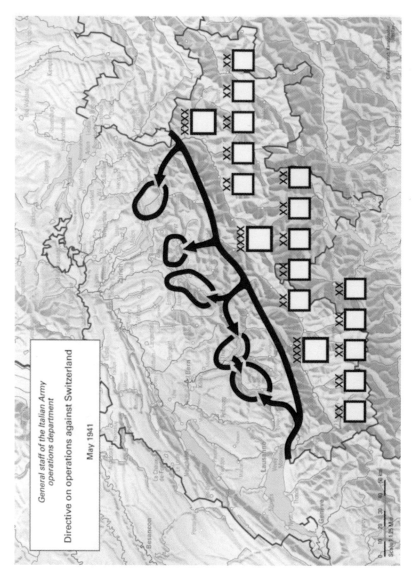

Figure 14: May 1941: Plan of Invasion of Switzerland by the Italian General Staff

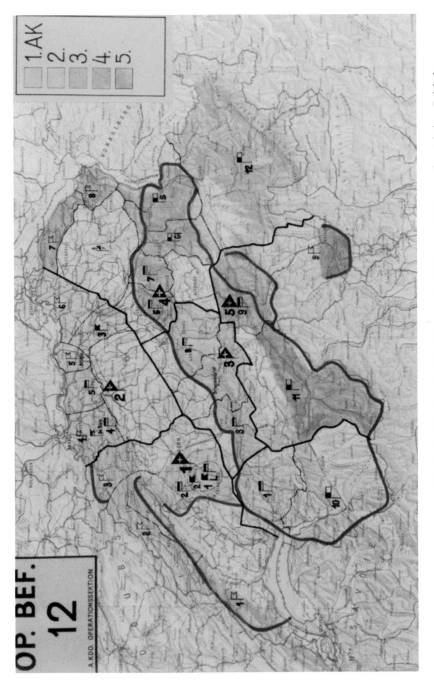

Figure 15: July 17, 1940: Initial Swiss Re-Deployment of Troops to Form the Alpine Réduit

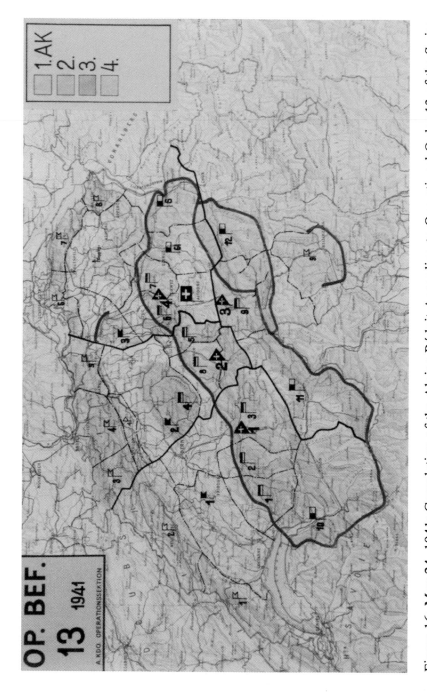

Figure 16: May 24, 1941: Completion of the Alpine Réduit According to Operational Order 13 of the Swiss General Staff

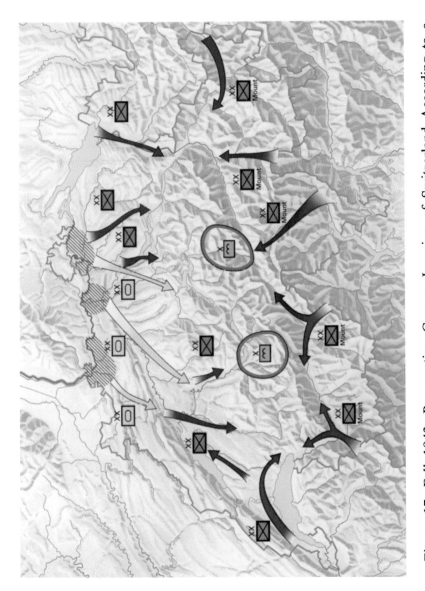

Figure 17: Fall 1943: Pre-emptive German Invasion of Switzerland According to a Memorandum of General Böhme

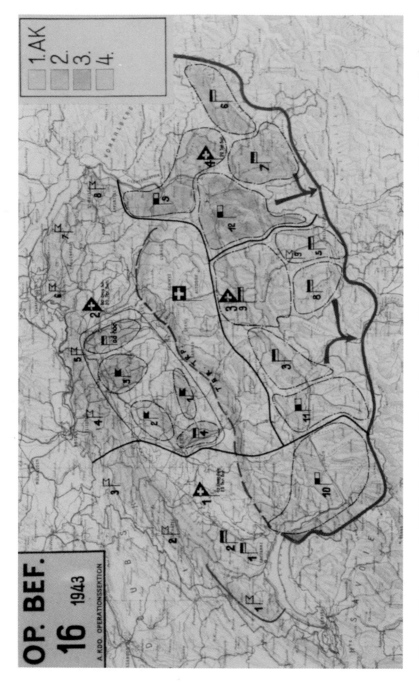

Figure 18: January 1, 1944: Southward Re-deployment of Swiss Troops to Defend Switzerland's Southern Border According to Operational Order 16

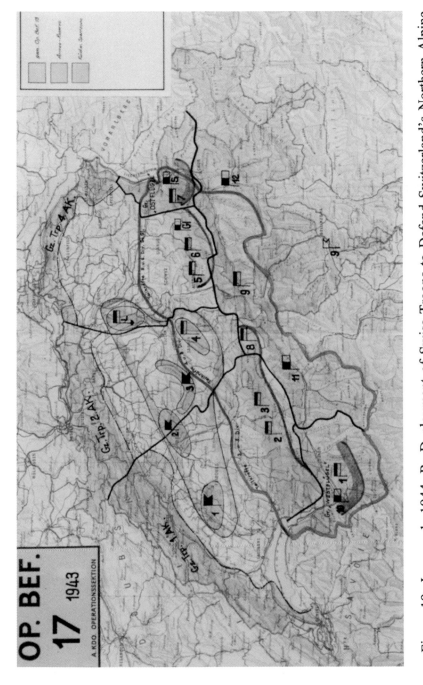

Figure 19: January 1, 1944: Re-Deployment of Swiss Troops to Defend Switzerland's Northern Alpine Mountain Range According to Operational Order 17

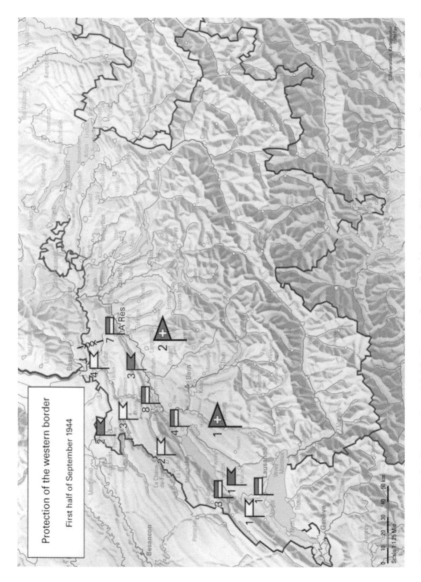

Figure 20: Early September 1944: Protection of Switzerland's Western Border to Prevent a German Attempt to Retreat Through Swiss Territory

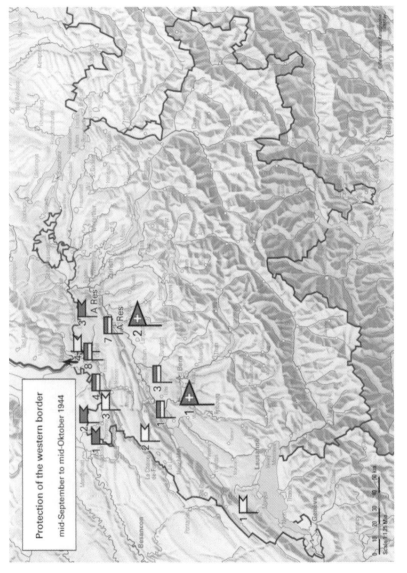

Figure 21: Mid-September to Mid-October 1944: Protection of Switzerland's Western Border to Prevent an Attempt of the Belligerents to March Through Swiss Territiory

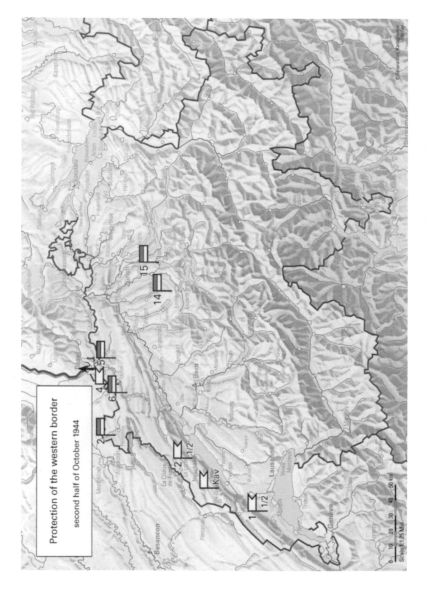

Figure 22: Second Half of October 1944: Protection of Switzerland's Western Border

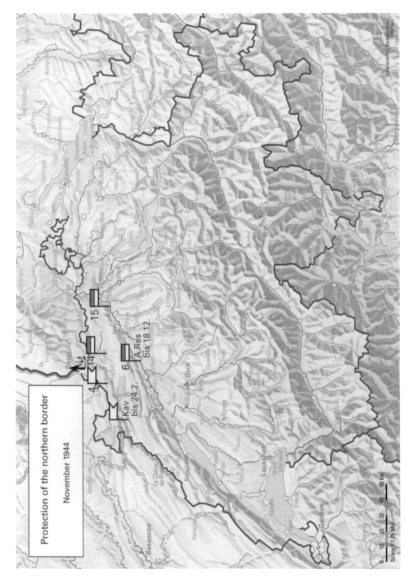

Figure 23: November 1944: Protection of Switzerland's Northern Border

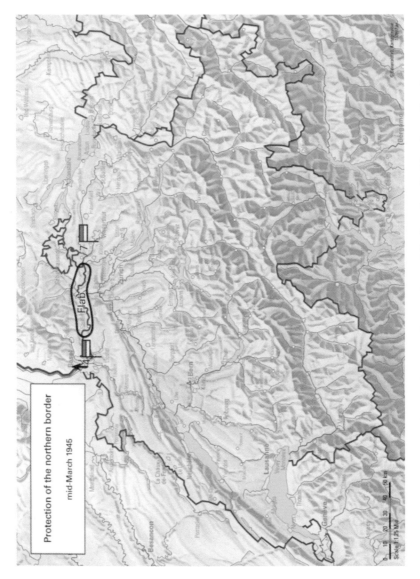

Figure 24: Mid-March 1945: Protection of Switzerland's Northern Border

IV: FATAL ERRORS

The Allied Bombing of the Sister Republic

James H. Hutson

At 11: 10 A.M., April 1, 1944, American military authorities in London received the following "strike message" from aircraft attacking a target in Europe: "392 Group bombed Last Resort with poor results at 10:50 hours."[1] This terse communication described the "gravest violation"[2] of Swiss neutrality during the Second World War—in fact, during the entire twentieth century: The bombing of the city of Schaffhausen by planes of the 2nd Division of the American 8th Army Air Force.

The Unfolding of an Event

The weather in Schaffhausen on Saturday morning, April 1, was good, but not perfect. A newspaper reported that the city enjoyed a "sunny, clear spring day."[3] Mayor Walther Bringolf called the weather "leicht bewölkt."[4] An eyewitness, who described the raid in a Zürich newspaper, wrote of the American bombers emerging from clouds.[5] The attacking American pilots reported to their superiors that Schaffhausen was "5/10"[6] covered with clouds, a description supported by photographs taken by American bombers as they flew over the city.[7]

---

[1] Eighth Air Force records, Center for Air Force History, Bolling Air Force Base, Washington, D.C. The records at Bolling Air Force Base are microfilm copies of the original records at The Air Force Historical Research Agency, Maxwell Air Force Base, Montgomery, Alabama. The microfilm reels consulted at Bolling Air Force Base were 520.331, 520.332, 526.331, 526.332, and BO 445. G.P. 392.

[2] *National Zeitung* (Basel): April 3, 1944.

[3] *Ibid.*

[4] Walther Bringolf, *Mein Leben. Weg und Umweg eines Schweizer Sozialdemokraten* (Bern, 1964): 340: "slightly overcast"; "Dennoch gelang es mir, ... einen Blick ... auf den leicht bewölkten Himmel zu werfen" (340-341).

[5] *Neue Zürcher Zeitung,* April 3, 1944.

[6] Report of Lead Bombardier (Joseph Whittaker): 392nd Bombardment Group, April 1, 1944, reel 526.332, Bolling AFB.

[7] See Ursel P. Harvel, *Liberators over Europe. 44th Bombardment Group* (San Angelo, Texas, 1949): unpaginated.

At 10:00 a.m. German radio, received throughout the city, reported the presence of enemy aircraft near the border between the Third Reich and northeastern Switzerland. Shortly after 10:15 a.m. the roar of engines was heard over certain parts of Schaffhausen. At 10:39 a.m. sirens began sounding in the city. Because of the continual violation of Swiss air space by Allied and Axis planes, air raid sirens had become a fixture in Swiss life by the spring of 1944. As a result of the "monotony of almost daily alarms", a Basel newspaper reported on April 3, "the population in large areas of the country paid hardly any attention to them."[8]

What the Basel newspaper meant was that the Swiss had ceased to respect the sirens as harbingers of possible harm. Complacency in Schaffhausen began from the top down, for the City Council, meeting on April 1 in a Saturday morning session, ignored the sirens and continued to work through its agenda.[9] It was also business as usual at Schaffhausen's weekly open-air market near the railroad station where operations proceeded in "full swing" as the sirens sounded.[10] Citizens continued to stroll along the streets. Some curious homeowners threw their windows open and scanned the skies to see what was happening above the city. A businessman described running into the street when he heard the sound of airplane engines. As the planes flew over, they dropped red flares, causing the businessman to linger in the street to see what would happen next. Suddenly, a violent explosion shook the neighborhood. Thrown through the air and temporarily knocked unconscious, the businessman came to his senses and saw the body of an acquaintance with its head and right shoulder blown off.[11] The decapitated corpse was gruesome testimony to the meaning of the flares: they were signals to the bombers to drop their payloads on Schaffhausen.

The bombing of Schaffhausen, carried out by American B-24 Liberators, lasted thirty to forty seconds. The target of the American planes was Schaffhausen's *Altstadt* [the city's old section], an area in the south central part of the city, along the Rhine River, that contained the Swiss National Railroad station, government buildings, museums, churches,

---

[8] *National Zeitung,* April 3, 1944.

[9] 'Mayor Bringolf reported that at the sound of the sirens he briefly adjourned the council meeting, went to the window, and scanned the skies. Seeing a smoke signal, Bringolf assumed that it indicated that Swiss fighters were attempting to intercept intruding aircraft. No sooner had the council resumed its deliberations than bombs began falling in the streets around the city hall. Bringolf, note 4, above, 340-1.

[10] *New York Times,* April 2, 1944.

[11] *Basler Nachrichten,* April 3, 1944.

quaint houses, and the Mühlenenquartier, "the old industrial area of the city." The railroad station took a direct hit, which killed sixteen people. A bomb that fell near the court house ripped up heavy paving stones and propelled them through the air, killing ten.[12] In a report to the Schaffhausen City Council, April 12, 1944, Mayor Walther Bringolf stated that the Americans had killed thirty-nine people, a figure later revised to forty; thirty-three remained in the hospital, some with potentially fatal wounds.[13] The dead were a cross-section of Schaffhausen's population—a city councilman, a cantonal judge, a chef, craftsmen, laborers, women, and children.

The mayor reported that scores of dwellings were destroyed, leaving 428 people homeless. Seventeen factories and businesses were wrecked, throwing two hundred people—some estimates ran as high as one thousand—out of work. The city's cultural patrimony suffered irreplaceable losses, for the American bombers destroyed a wing of the Allerheiligen Museum which contained the priceless paintings of the city's foremost artist, the sixteenth-century painter, Tobias Stimmer (1539-1584).[14] Providentially, Stimmer's portrait of the Zürich naturalist, Konrad Gessner (1516-1565), one of the first Swiss to study the Americas, miraculously survived the bombing, having been blown into the street and retrieved there relatively unharmed. Not so fortunate was Lucas Cranach's famous painting of Martin Luther, which was destroyed by the fire. The catastrophe at Allerheiligen alarmed museum directors across Switzerland, some of whom hastily removed their treasures from public galleries and put them in safekeeping.[15]

The Swiss Response

Officials and citizens of Schaffhausen were widely admired for their response to the bombing.[16] There was no panic; discipline, ingenuity, and public spiritedness prevailed. Having lost telephone service, the city administration dispatched town criers and citizens with handwritten signs to instruct their fellow citizens to report to emergency duty stations.

---

[12] Bringolf's report to the Schaffhausen City Council, April 12, is printed in the *Neue Ziircher Zeitung,* April 13, 1944.

[13] A total of 270 people suffered wounds of varying degrees of severity. Andreas Schiendorfer, *Schaffhauser Nachrichten,* March 31, 1944.

[14] Max Bendel, *Zerstörter Schaffhauser Kunstbesitz* (Zürich, 1944).

[15] As did officials at the Kunstmuseum in Basel. *National Zeitung,* April 5, 1944.

[16] For a vivid account of the impact of the bombing on one Swiss family and for the resilience of the citizens of Schaffhausen, see Peter Vogelsanger, *Mit Leib und Seele. Erlebnisse und Einsichten eines Pfarrers* (Zürich, 1977): 196-9.

Firefighting assistance was requested by telegraph and within an hour of the 10:50 a.m. attack an "unbroken line" of fire trucks from Zürich, Winterthur, St. Gallen and points-in-between were streaming into the burning city.[17] By 2:00 p.m. the largest fires were "isolated;" by 4:30 p.m. all fires were under control; and by 6:00 p.m. the visiting firefighters were preparing to return to their hometowns. To protect inhabitants and visitors from the danger of collapsing buildings and delayed action bombs, federal authorities closed Schaffhausen to most outside traffic until April 10, at which point life in the city began to regain some of its normal rhythm.

Assessing his city's response to the attack, Mayor Bringolf on April 12, 1944 recommended improvements in its civil defense operations: Air raid shelters needed to be more clearly designated and they needed to be stocked with more and better first aid supplies. Although the advice may have seemed gratuitous, Bringolf urged the citizens to pay more attention to air raid alarms in the future.[18] This became a common theme across Switzerland, as newspapers and public officials lectured the people of their locality about the "lessons" of Schaffhausen. Although the citizens of Schaffhausen were regarded as objects of compassion not reproach, a Zürich newspaper, *Die Tat,* estimated that few lives would have been lost in the city had proper civil defense procedures been followed. Writing in *Volk und Armee,* Schaffhausen's best-known soldier, Colonel Oscar Frey, calculated that one-third of the casualties in his hometown could have been avoided by a responsible reaction to the air raid warnings.[19] Especially distressing to Colonel Frey were the deaths of those people sucked through the open windows of the upper stories of houses by the turbulent air pressure created by the explosion of the American bombs. If it did nothing else, Schaffhausen transformed the detached attitude ("Zaungast Mentalität")[20] of the Swiss towards civil defense into anxious apprehension.

American newspapermen, who reached Schaffhausen on Saturday afternoon, April 1, while the fires were still blazing in the city, were amazed at the self-restraint of the local population. Thomas Hawkins of the Associated Press reported that the "Townspeople with whom I talked

---

[17] *Neue Zürcher Zeitung,* April 3, 1944.

[18] Pastor Vogelsanger relates an anecdote to demonstrate Schaffhausen's sudden respect for air raid sirens. A confirmation service over which he was officiating on April 2 was "interrupted by a new air raid alarm. While earlier one had paid little attention to these alarms, now we fled at the first sign to a large nearby shelter and there I continued with the ceremony. It was the most impressive confirmation service that I had ever experienced... ." *Ibid.,* 201.

[19] Frey's article was reprinted in *Der Bund* (Bern): April 12, 1944.

[20] *Neue Zürcher Zeitung*, April 3, 1944.

expressed grief at the casualties and regret at the loss of old buildings, but showed no anger saying simply they hoped it would not happen again."[21] A United Press dispatch, filed from Schaffhausen on April 1, marveled at the "stoic calm" of the suffering city. "There are no hard feelings toward the United States. Americans were being treated with the utmost politeness and friendliness by police, military authorities and the population."[22]

Swiss in other parts of the country were not so courteous. Inflamed by exaggerated accounts of the damage at Schaffhausen—*Der Bund* (Bern) reported that the city had been reduced to "an ocean of flames and a field of rubble"[23]—some Swiss lashed out at Americans. The *Washington Post,* April 3, 1944, reported that "in Bern anger flared after the first reports pictured Schaffhausen as almost completely destroyed. Youngsters shouted 'dirty Americans' at several members of the United States legation. One American was not permitted to rent an apartment he had tentatively accepted yesterday." The New York *Herald Tribune,* April 5, 1944, informed its readers that fistfights had broken out between Swiss and Americans and "to guard against incidents, Americans . . . received instructions to avoid bars and public places, to eat at restaurants only if necessary and to leave immediately after they were finished and to continue normally but apologetically their relations with Swiss friends, while avoiding possible bitter conversations with strangers." One Swiss newspaper, claiming to speak for the whole country, accused the American airmen who attacked Schaffhausen of being "war criminals."

The unhappiness of many Swiss extended beyond the devastation at Schaffhausen to the allied policies which, they believed, had sown the seeds of the disaster: The violation of Swiss neutrality by the unrelenting allied penetration of Swiss airspace. In the spring of 1944 the Swiss congratulated themselves on keeping their land boundaries inviolate, but were deeply frustrated by their inability to prevent the "incessant" overflights of their country by the belligerent powers, especially by the British and Americans.[24] Swiss diplomats deluged Washington and London with protests about the conduct of their air forces. They regularly received assurances that remedial measures would be taken, but the intrusions continued. Although the Swiss Air Force had not been totally passive in confronting the trespassers and although certain newspapers thought that a more vigorous air defense was possible, there appeared to be a general

---

[21] *Washington Star,* April 2, 1944.

[22] *New York Times,* April 2, 1944.

[23] *Der Bund*, April 3, 1944.

[24] *Journal de Genève,* April 4, 1944.

recognition in Switzerland that the air force could not halt the violation of the country's airspace by the powerful and increasingly sophisticated allied air armadas. The inefficacy of both diplomacy and force suggested to some Swiss that in an era of modern warfare neutrality might no longer be capable of achieving one of its objectives—the protection of the population—and raised the question of whether modern military technology had vitiated the effectiveness of the cherished neutrality policy which had helped to give the nation its identity. As the American minister to Switzerland, Leland Harrison, perceived, Schaffhausen aroused complex reactions in Switzerland, "resentment and indignation on material, moral and theoretical grounds."[25] *Der Bund,* April 3, 1944, also commented on the complexity of the Swiss reaction, noting that not only had the "personal feelings" of the Swiss been hurt, but that their "civil-democratic pride" had been wounded.

Although some Swiss professed to believe that the United States attacked Schaffhausen to staunch the flow of Swiss supplies to the German war machine, the factories hit in Schaffhausen, which produced consumer goods such as silverware, pottery, and leather, refuted this notion. Swiss newspapers were prompt to dismiss the suspicion that the raid was a "brutal reprisal" for the nation's assistance to the Third Reich. The attack was, most Swiss assumed, a "tragic mistake." The American bombers, most Swiss agreed, intended to attack Singen, a German city eleven miles northeast of Schaffhausen which was a rail trans-shipment point for goods bound for the Nazi armies in Italy and contained some significant heavy industry.[26]

That Schaffhausen was attacked instead of Singen the Swiss blamed on the American pilots' ignorance of geography. The Swiss believed that the Yankee fliers must not have known that the Swiss boundary ran north of the Rhine at Schaffhausen and must have assumed that anything north of the river was German and hence fair game. "The geographical and political ideas" of the American air force were "clearly inadequate", complained the *Journal de Genève.*[27] In a characteristic aside, *Der Bund* patronizingly remarked that "perhaps one ... should not expect an exact knowledge of the details of European geography from Americans".[28]

The assertions of American ignorance were, in some cases, a product of a strain of anti-Americanism that thrived in certain Swiss political and

---

[25] 'Harrison to Cordell Hull, April 2, 1944, Record Group 59, 411.54, National Archives.
[26] *Journal de Genève,* April 3, 4, 1944; *Gazette de Lausanne,* April 3, 1944; *National Zeitung,* April 3, 1944.
[27] April 4, 1944.
[28] April 5, 1944

intellectual circles in the 1930s, a view tinctured by an ideology that considered the United States as the citadel of vulgar, ill-informed monopoly capitalism.[29] Counteracting this "ugly American" image in Switzerland was a deeply rooted admiration (more abstract, perhaps, than personal) of the United States which was captured by the "sister republics" metaphor. Beginning in the 1770s and intensifying in the nineteenth century, the idea established itself that there was a special relationship between the United States and Switzerland because they were fellow republican nations in a hostile monarchical world. The bond between the two countries was thought to have been strengthened by the reciprocal borrowing of political institutions, the American Constitution of 1787 being a model for the first Swiss Federal Constitution of 1848 and the Swiss initiative and referendum being widely adopted by American state governments before World War I.[30]

The "great sister republic" metaphor was invoked by the Swiss Federal Council in 1939 as it sought to justify the country's participation in the New York World's Fair,[31] and its grip on the Swiss consciousness was one of the factors that predisposed many Swiss to the allied cause when World War II began and moved them to regard as "heroes" the American pilots who guided their crippled planes to the safety of Swiss airfields.[32] An anecdote, probably apocryphal, which appeared in *Time* magazine March 6, 1944, showed the presumption of mutual friendship that the sister republics theme encouraged. Purporting to be reporting a conversation between a Swiss anti-aircraft battery and "a trespassing formation of U.S. bombers", *Time* printed the following dialogue:

> Swiss ground commander: "You are over Switzerland."
> U.S. Air Commander: "We know."
> Swiss: "If you don't turn back we will shoot."
> U.S.: "We know."
> The conversation paused during a furious ack-ack [anti-aircraft artillery]
> barrage, then resumed.
> U.S.: "Your fire is 1,000 feet low."
> Swiss: "We know."

---

[29] See Heinz K. Meier, *Friendship under Stress. U.S.—Swiss Relations 1900-1950* (Bern, 1970): 146-147.

[30] For the development of the Sister Republics metaphor, see James H. Hutson, *The Sister Republics* 2nd ed., (Washington, 1992); French and German language editions were published by Stämpfli Verlag, Bern, 1992

[31] Meier, op. *cit.,* note 29, 263.

[32] *New York Times,* April 5, 1944.

The American Response

The attack on Schaffhausen made the front pages of the major American newspapers, which carried feature stories about the incident and pictures of the wounded city. The disaster destroyed American innocence, for the people of the United States had not yet been confronted with a lethal attack by their forces on a neutral nation. Earlier in the war Russia had struck Sweden, Germany struck Ireland, and Britain struck Switzerland; Geneva, Renens, Basel and Zürich were hit by the R. A. F. in 1940 with some loss of life. Americans, however, had been persuaded that their air force would not spill neutral blood because of what were represented to be its superior military skills and moral sensitivities. Unlike the British, whose nighttime area bombing many considered a form of indiscriminate violence, American commanders insisted on precision daylight bombing of military targets only, a strategy designed to minimize civilian casualties. The American Air Force had no intention, one of its top commanders asserted, "of throwing the strategic bomber at the man in the street."[33]

But when the man in the Schaffhausen street was killed, many ordinary citizens were outraged. They found their voice in one Raymond B. Young, Jr., who wrote the *Washington* Post on April 7, 1944 that "however great the anger or sorrow caused in the heart of the Swiss people, directly affected, it will never surpass the anger found here at the news: the 'maddest' people of all will be Americans." Describing the massive outpouring of sympathy for the Swiss, the *Neue Zürcher Zeitung* reported that Americans condemned the "unforgivable sin" of their airmen and offered their condolences and apologies to ordinary Swiss citizens in the United States through "visits, letters, telegrams and telephone calls." Americans, the Zürich newspaper reported, held the Swiss in the highest esteem as "true democrats and compassionate helpers" and claimed that "Switzerland was the last land that they wished to see harmed by the United States.[34]

American newspapers, reflecting Swiss assumptions, informed their readers that the target of the raid on Schaffhausen was Singen.[35] The proximity of Schaffhausen to Singen did not, however, excuse what the *Washington Post* in an editorial of April 3 denounced as an "unpardonable" attack. In an editorial of April 5 the *Washington Star* demanded an investigation of the Schaffhausen raid, since "it is difficult to understand how, in daylight, our bombers could have mistakenly attacked a peaceful

---

[33] Michael Sherry, *The Rise of American Air Power. The Creation of Armageddon* (New Haven, 1987): 144.

[34] *Neue Zürcher Zeitung,* April 8, 1944.

[35] *New York Times,* April 2, 1944.

city across the Rhine and eleven miles from the intended German target."
The most influential voice in American journalism, that of Walter
Lippmann, was aroused by the Schaffhausen incident. In a column of April
4, 1944,[36] Lippmann expressed the nation's regret over the attack and
criticized officials of the Board of Economic Warfare for attempting to
compel the Swiss to modify their commercial policies by what Lippmann
regarded as ill-conceived economic sanctions. Lippmann's tribute to
Switzerland deserves to be quoted at some length:

> Neutrality does not arouse much sympathy in nations who are
> desperately at war. But the neutrality of Switzerland is a very special
> thing, indeed unique. Only Switzerland in all of Europe has made no
> concessions. Surrounded by the Fascist world, its neutrality has been
> much more than a policy of staying out of war. The Swiss have
> maintained intact their democratic liberties because they hold them dear
> and because their hearts are stout. That is a great contribution to
> mankind. Through the darkest days of the war, when Hitler seemed
> about to sweep all Europe before him, the moral resistance of the Swiss
> has reassured us that once a nation has known liberty, it will never
> willingly surrender it.
>
> Their example should never be forgotten and if there is anything
> this government can do to express not only its regret for the
> Schaffhausen bombing but its appreciation of the part Switzerland has
> played, it should do it. It should take the risks of giving the Swiss the
> benefit of the doubt as between the judgment of some official here and
> their honest representations. We shall be amply repaid if we come out
> of this war with the confidence and friendship of the Swiss nation.
>
> Let us not forget the indispensable part which Switzerland has
> to play in the healing of the nations. By long historical tradition
> Switzerland is the seat, so to speak the capital, of mankind's works of
> charity and of mercy. We shall need Switzerland when the war is over.
> It will stand there, firm and free, in a sea of misery and hatred. We shall
> need the Swiss because they alone perhaps will be able to go
> everywhere, feared by none and trusted by all.
>
> Realizing all that, we shall be wise if, jolted by this terrible
> mishap, we go beyond the obvious regrets and indemnities to larger
> actions which express our moral solidarity with this admirable people.

Swiss newspapers supplied their readers with generous summaries of
the "condolences of the American press."[37] Sympathetic editorials in the
New York Times and the *Washington Post* were reported in full, as was

---

[36] *New York Herald Tribune*, April 4, 1944.
[37] *Basler Nachrichten*, April 3, 1944.

Lippmann's salute to Switzerland, which appeared on the front page of the *Neue Zürcher Zeitung*.[38] Commenting on the role of the press in the crisis, Minister Harrison observed: "The attitude of the American press was very helpful in convincing the Swiss of the factual state of American opinion in the matter and contributed materially to assuaging anger and resentment and restoration of calmness here. I am pleased to report that the Swiss press evinced no hesitation in presenting fully the American reaction."[39]

The American political and military establishment shared the ordinary citizen's anguish and guilt over Schaffhausen and was profuse in its apologies to the Swiss. Secretary of State Cordell Hull issued a statement on April 3[40] in which he expressed "my own and all Americans' deep regret over the tragic bombing", adding that Secretary of War Henry Stimson "has expressed to me the deep regret he and the American Air Force feel over this tragedy." "Every precaution", Hull advised the Swiss, "will be taken to prevent in so far as is humanly possible the repetition of this unfortunate event." Assistant Secretary of State Breckinridge Long and Director of the Office of European Affairs James Dunn delivered Hull's message to the Swiss ambassador, Charles Bruggmann, on the afternoon of April 3 and the next day Stimson wrote Bruggmann a personal letter, expressing his "deep feeling of horror" at the attack on Schaffhausen.[41] In Europe Minister Harrison called on the Swiss foreign minister, Marcel Pilet-Golaz, on the afternoon of April 1 to express his regrets and sympathy. American consuls in various Swiss cities called on local authorities to express their condolences. On the afternoon of April 3, General Carl Spaatz, commander of the United States Strategic Air Forces in Europe, and the American ambassador to the Court of St. James, John G. Winant, called on the Swiss chargé d'affaires in London to convey regrets and explain "how sincerely sorry our airmen were that this had happened."[42] The next day Spaatz's superior, General Henry H. "Hap" Arnold, wrote his counterpart, General Rihner, commander of the Swiss air force, to "express personally . . . my extreme regret over the sad occurrence at Schaffhausen on April 1. I know that you understand that the bombing of this peaceful and friendly town could only have taken place as the result of error."[43]

---

[38] April 5, 1944.

[39] Harrison to Cordell Hull, April 20, 1944, Record Group 59, 411.54, National Archives.

[40] Record Group 165, National Archives.

[41] Ibid.

[42] *Foreign Relations of the United States*, 1944, IV, 793.

[43] Memorandum, April 5, 1944, Spaatz Papers, Box 17, Manuscript Division, Library of Congress.

The chief of staff of the American army, General George C. Marshall, personally interested himself in Schaffhausen and urged Secretary of State Hull to pay compensation without quibbling: "Seek Switzerland's bill", Marshall advised Hull, "and pay it promptly."[44] Minister Harrison was, accordingly, instructed on April 5 to procure from the Swiss a full account of the damage done at Schaffhausen so that "appropriate reparations" could be paid. In the meantime Harrison was authorized to disburse $1,000,000 to the Swiss as a downpayment on the Schaffhausen account. In October 1944 the United States paid another $3,000,000, although everyone recognized that the final bill would be far higher.

The bombing of Schaffhausen could not have come at a worse time for the American Air Force. The Air Force was a "brand new" arm of the American military which "had come to maturity almost overnight, just as the great war got started."[45] It was resented by traditionalists who accused it of overselling its capacities. Skeptics about air power were not averse to seeing the pretensions of their brash young brethren deflated and were prepared to seize upon any failure to make a case for reducing the Air Force's role in the war. The fiasco at the famous battle of Cassino, Italy, in mid-March 1944 played into the hands of the Air Force's critics. Bombers saturated Cassino with high explosives, inducing the commander of the operation to proclaim "exuberantly . . . that the town had been wiped out.[46] Far from being obliterated, German defenders emerged from their bunkers at Cassino and decisively repelled an allied ground offensive. To make matters worse, the Air Force was compelled to admit that because of "mistakes in target identification",[47] it had bombed and killed allied troops invading Cassino.

The debacle at Cassino and the Air Force's failure to sweep the skies of the Luftwaffe, as it had set out to do in the first months of 1944, produced in the United States what a commentator in the *Washington* Star on April 9, 1944, called a "tendency in some quarters to begin doubting its [the Air Force's] amazing potency." Enthusiasts, the commentator explained, had trumpeted the Air Force's potential "in terms of hyperbole, as if it could win the war by itself. . . . Accordingly, now that it has been found to be less than omnipotent, there is danger that its shortcomings will be equally exaggerated in a sort of reverse hyperbole." Faced with incipient

---

[44] General Thomas T. Handy, memorandum, April 5, 1944, Record Group 165, National Archives.

[45] *Washington Star,* April 9, 1944.

[46] General Ira Eaker was the boaster. *Washington Star,* April 1, 1944.

[47] *New York Times,* April 7, 1944.

disillusion with its capabilities, the Air Force feared that critics would cite Schaffhausen as fresh evidence of systematic incompetence.

The Air Force's strategy in dealing with Schaffhausen was to hunker down (an appropriate Vietnam War term): say as little as possible about the incident, and hope that it would quickly recede from the public's consciousness. Reporters were permitted to interview participants in the raid, but "censors stopped all direct quotations from the fliers and their commanding officers pertaining to the actual bombing, evidently on instructions from higher up."[48] A small crack was opened on the raid by fliers who said they were driven off course by unexpectedly high winds. The official Air Force communiqué, issued early in the morning of April 2, was extremely brief. As carried over American wire services, it stated that "Liberators penetrated deep into southwest Germany to blast industrial and communications targets", but that "due to difficulties of navigation in bad weather some bombs fell on Swiss territory by mistake."[49]

Reuters, the British news agency, paraphrased the statement about the weather, subtly but significantly altering it, to read "in consequence of poor visibility" bombs erroneously fell on Switzerland. Carried in several Swiss newspapers,[50] the Reuters dispatch irritated the Swiss, because, as the *Basel Nachrichten* declared on April 3, "all reports agreed that the bombardment of Schaffhausen occurred under clear skies." The American military attaché in Switzerland, General Barnwell R. Legge, urged the Air Force to disavow the claim (which it never made) that "poor visibility" was responsible for the disaster at Schaffhausen,[51] but the Air Force declined, having no interest in keeping the story alive. By revealing that high winds and unspecified weather and navigational problems were instrumental in the bombing of Schaffhausen, and by not contradicting public speculation that Singen was the actual target of the B-24s, the Air Force evidently assumed that it had a plausible explanation for the disaster of April 1. It did not seem so farfetched that planes could be blown ten miles off course. That the wind-buffeted bombers had hit a neutral city was painful, of course, but far less damaging to the Air Force's credibility than a nightmarish story of a raid gone haywire because of the failure of newly introduced high technology, resulting in squadrons of American bombers getting lost, frantically crisscrossing southern Germany in a futile search for targets, only to bomb the wrong targets in three different countries and to identify incorrectly the

[48] *Ibid.,* April 3, 1944.
[49] *Washington Post,* April 2, 1944.
[50] *National Zeitung,* April 4, 1944; *Basler Nachrichten,* April 3, 1944.
[51] To War Department, April 4, 1944, Record Group 165, National Archives.

targets wrongly bombed. A misadventure of precisely this magnitude befell the 8th Air Force on April 1 and resulted in the disaster at Schaffhausen.

The target of the American B-24s on April I was not Singen. Their primary target was some two hundred kilometers north of the Singen-Schaffhausen area, specifically, the I. G. Farben plant at Ludwigshafen, Germany, described by the Air Force as the "largest and most important manufacturer of wartime chemical products in Europe" and luridly stigmatized by the American press as "the poison gas manufacturing center" of Germany. The secondary target for the American fliers was the "center of the city" of Ludwigshafen. The "last resort target" was "any military objective positively identified as being in Germany."[52]

Ludwigshafen was a favorite target of the 8th Air Force. The Farben works were bombed on December 30, 1943, and again on January 7, 1944, but little damage was inflicted.[53] In September 1944 the giant chemical complex was attacked ten times. A raid against Ludwigshafen was scheduled for March 31 but was canceled because of "turbulent weather" that grounded all missions over western Europe, that of April 1 excepted, until April 7. Bad weather was as formidable an enemy of the 8th Air Force as the Luftwaffe itself. The Air Force Weather Service calculated that in an average year the weather over Germany was clear enough for visual bombing only 20 percent of the time; only thirteen days, the weathermen estimated, were suitable for visual bombing between January and March.[54] If only a handful of raids were possible, an air offensive against Germany would be futile, for her factories could be repaired or dispersed during the intervals between attacks. What the American command needed was a technology that would permit it to prosecute the air war unceasingly, in good weather and bad. What it found was radar.

Recognizing the potential of radar for warfare, the British in 1941 began developing H2S, a self-contained system using a beam of transmitted energy to produce a map-like picture on the indicator of a cathode ray tube. The British mounted H2S on "pathfinders", specifically modified aircraft that led squadrons to targets obscured by clouds. Following the British lead, the United States Air Force developed its own radar bombing technology,

---

[52] Tactical Report of Mission of April 1, 1944, written on April 25, 1944; reel 526.331, Bolling Air Force Base.

[53] Report of Operations, January 7, 1944, reel 520.331, Ibid.

[54] Hugh Odishaw, "Radar Bombing in the Eighth Air Force", pp. 11-12, Spaatz Papers, Box 80, Manuscript Division, Library of Congress. Odishaw's essay is a thorough post-war assessment of the effectiveness of the use of radar by the 8th Air Force. The author was a staff member of the Radiation Laboratory at MIT.

which it called H2X. Installed in American pathfinders, the H2X systems was first deployed in combat on November 3, 1943.[55]

At the time of the attack on Schaffhausen, radar bombing was still an experimental technology, subject to the usual glitches and malfunctions. Assessing H2X on March 22, 1944, General Spaatz conceded that it was "interim equipment about which much remains to be learned." Since "we cannot run before we learn to walk", Spaatz was prepared to bear with H2X during its period of "growing pains."[56] The major virtue of the new technology was that by taking the weather out of play, it allowed the 8th Air Force to attack Germany unremittingly. Spaatz claimed that because of H2X "fighters and bombers operate in weather which was never conceived to be suitable for combat operations and, as a result, we have been able to maintain approximately five times the pressure on the enemy than would have been possible if we were restricted to visual bombing.".[57] Without H2X American planes would not have attempted to fly in the foul weather of April 1. That Ludwigshafen was target on that day was no accident, because one of the strengths of H2X was its ability to discriminate between land and water, and extending, as it did, three miles along the east bank of the Rhine, the Farben works, it was assumed, could be located and attacked in the worst of conditions.

The Air Force planned to commit 467 bombers and 489 fighter escorts (mostly P-47s, but some P-51s) against Ludwigshafen.[58] The Third Division of the 8th Air Force supplied 259 B-17s; the Second Division 208 B-24s. Leaving their bases in England early on the morning of April 1, the B-17s encountered such bad weather just inside France that they aborted their mission and returned home.[59] Plans called for the three combat wings of the Second Division to assemble near Orfordness, England, and begin crossing the Channel at 8:40 a.m. The 20th Combat Wing, consisting of the 448th, 446th and the 93rd bombardment groups, led the division; following at a three-minute interval was the 14th Combat Wing which on this day consisted of two rather than the customary three bombardment groups. The two were the 392nd group, based at Wendling, England, and the 44th, based at Norwich. These were the units that bombed Schaffhausen. At the rear of

---

[55] *Ibid.,* 39.

[56] *Ibid.,* 61-2.

[57] Spaatz to Arnold, March 14, 1945, Spaatz Papers, Box 21, Manuscript Division, Library of Congress.

[58] Figures about the number of planes that were airworthy on April 1 vary slightly in different Air Force accounts.

[59] "Narrative of Operations", 8th Air Force, April 1, 1944, reel 520.332, Bolling Air Force Base.

the division was the 2nd Combat Wing, consisting of the 453rd, 389th and 44th bombardment groups. Two H2X pathfinder planes flew at the head of each combat wing. Assigned to lead the planes to Ludwigshafen, they were the eyes of the division.

A Double Jeopardy: Bad Weather and Failing Radar

The 20th Combat Wing, with the two other wings following, left the English coast at 8:47 a.m. Trouble began shortly after the French coast was reached, for there the wing's 446th Bombardment Group "became scattered due to a dense cloud layer and haze and abandoned the mission."[60] The other B-24s proceeded eastward into the same weather that had repelled the Third Division's B-17s. Solid clouds prevailed above 19,000 feet and an impenetrable "undercast" obscured the ground; throughout the whole route, one navigator reported, "the haze was extremely thick making it difficult to identify anything on the ground."[61] Threading their way through the layers of clouds and haze, the B-24 crews must have had the sensation of flying in a tunnel. Under these conditions their radars must perform flawlessly! No sooner, however, had the division made landfall in France than the H2X equipment in both pathfinder planes leading the 20th Combat Wing and hence the entire division malfunctioned. As a result, the pathfinders and the entire division following them veered off course. As an officer of the 392nd Bombardment Group later complained, "the PFF (pathfinder) ship led us completely astray, being continually south of course."[62]

The proper course, "the briefed course" in Air Force terminology, required the Second Division to cross the French coast northeast of Dunkirk and then to fly southeast; when it reached the Mosel River north of Trier the division was instructed to turn due east until it was over Bad Kreuznach, near the bend of the Rhine River at Bingen; there the division was ordered to take a 45° turn to the southeast to make its bombing run on Ludwigshafen. Because of the errant pathfinders, when the Second Division had flown far enough east to begin its bombing run, it was one hundred miles south of where it should have been.[63] There was, consequently, a "great deal of uncertainty as to position."

---

[60] Tactical Report of April 1, 1944, mission, April 25, 1944, reel 526.331, *Ibid.*

[61] Report of Lead Navigator (Christian Koch): 392nd Bombardment Group, April 3, 1944, reel 526.332, *Ibid.*

[62] 392nd Bombardment Group, report, reel BO 445, GP 391-92, *Ibid.*

[63] 8th Air Force, Report of Operations, April 1, 1944, written June 24, 1944, reel 520.33 1, *Ibid.*

In fact, the division was lost, as crewmen admitted to each other over their radios.[64] The B-24s now engaged in a period of hectic zigzagging across the skies, "essing back and forth sharply trying to get into position."[65] By this time the H2X equipment in the 14th and 2nd combat wings had also failed.[66] Every piece of radar in the division was now out of order! Amidst the confusion, seventeen of the twenty-six B-24s of the 20th Combat Wing's 93rd Bombardment Group misinterpreted the actions of another squadron and accidentally bombed Strasbourg, France, although the inhabitants of the city were fortunate enough to have most of the bombs fall five miles west of town.[67]

The 2nd Combat Wing now took the division lead and executed a sharp turn to the southeast, since the target run on the briefed course required such a maneuver. The problem was that since this turn was begun one hundred miles south of the briefed course, it carried the B-24s even further away from Ludwigshafen, in the direction of the Swiss border. In due course it was recognized that "a considerable navigational error had been made" and a 180° turn to the north was executed.[68] For the next thirty minutes a mixed formation of 2nd and 20th combat wing planes flew north. The H2X equipment in the pathfinders was working again and they located a target that they identified as Ludwigshafen. The B-24s bombed the city, although some of the units believed that they had attacked Reutlingen, a city southeast of Stuttgart, while others thought they might have bombed Stuttgart itself. The target actually hit, with "poor results" as photo reconnaissance later showed, was Pforzheim, a town forty-five miles southeast of Ludwigshafen.[69]

Pforzheim was bombed at 11:04 A.M. Since the attack on Ludwigshafen was scheduled to begin at 9:57 a.m., the planes of the 2nd and 20th combat wings spent more than an hour searching for a target which most of the time was more than one hundred miles to their north. Unable to find the B-24s over the briefed target area, the P-47 and P-51

---

[64] Report of Lead Navigator (C. E. Shuler): 44th Bombardment Group, April 2, 1944, reel 526.3321 *Ibid.*

[65] *Ibid.*

[66] Report of Operations Officer (Heber Thompson): 448th Bombardment Group, April 2, 1944, reel 526.332, *Ibid.*

[67] Report, June 24, 1944, note 63, above.

[68] *Ibid.*

[69] Report of Lead Navigator (Arthur Kline): 448th Bombardment Group, April 2, 1944, reel 526.332, Bolling Air Force Base; Report of Formation Commander (Carl Fleming): 445th Bombardment Group, April 2, 1944, Ibid.; Tactical Report of April 1, 1944 mission, April 25, 1944, reel 526.331; Spaatz to Arnold, April 1, 1944, Arnold Papers, Box 190, Manuscript Division, Library of Congress.

fighters never made a planned rendezvous with them[70] and were unable to protect them from German interceptors. Not that it mattered, because the weather was too bad for the *Luftwaffe* to take off and challenge the American bombers.

The 14th Combat Wing reacted to the disorientation differently than did the 2nd and 20th wings. Instead of following these wings on their turn to the southeast and then on their abrupt reversal to the north, the 14th Combat Wing took an east by southeast course that carried it even further from Ludwigshafen than its comrades. As the wing proceeded eastward, its H2X equipment came back to life with tragic results. First, the pathfinder aircraft, leading the 392nd Group and the 44th Group, directed "several runs on unidentified targets that were for the most part fields."[71] Then, the pathfinders identified a target, which faded from their screens, as Bad Kreuznach,[72] the point on the 'briefed route' northwest of Ludwigshafen at which the bombing run on the city was to begin. Having flown eastward beyond what it supposed was Bad Kreuznach, the wing reversed course and turned back toward the west. Soon thereafter, at 10: 19 A. M, the 392nd's pathfinder picked up a target. Claiming that he had "the target in scope", the pathfinder operator led a bombing run on what the 392nd believed to be Ludwigshafen.[73] The H2X equipment failed just as the attack began and a visual bombing run was ordered. A visual run was possible because for the first time during the entire mission "a few large breaks in the undercast" opened up above the target,[74] affording visibility that one of the 392nd's navigators described as "five to seven tenths" obstructed.[75] The visual run was orchestrated by the bombardier aboard the lead pathfinder and, like every other aspect of this hapless mission, it miscarried. As described by an officer in the 392nd, "the PFF bombardier took over and he got a pre-release falling short of the target he was aiming at."[76] Since the twenty-two other B-24s of the 392nd dropped their bombs on signal flares released by

---

[70] Report of Operations, June 24, 1944, note 63, above.

[71] Report of Lead Bombardier (John King): 44th Bombardment Group, reel 526.332, Bolling AFB.

[72] Report of Operations, June 24, 1944; Tactical Report, April 25, 1944; see notes 60 and 63 above.

[73] Report of Lead Bombardier (Joseph Whittaker): 392nd Bombardment Group, April 1, 1944, reel 526.332, Bolling AFB; General Thomas Handy to General Barnwell Legge, April 6, 1944, Record Group 165, National Archives. Other participants in the raid recognized that they were attacking a "target of opportunity", not Ludwigshafen.

[74] Report of Command Pilot (James McFadden): 392nd Bombardment Group, April 3, 1944, reel 526.332, Bolling AFB.

[75] Report of Lead Navigator, 392nd Bombardment Group, note 61, above.

[76] Ibid.

the pathfinder plane, their payloads also fell short of the target and landed "three miles south and east of the city of Schaffouson, Switzerland in woods area."[77]

A Reconstruction of the Bombing Mission

The Swiss confirmed that one squadron of B-24s had bombed a wooded area outside of Schaffhausen. In his report to the City Council on April 12, Mayor Bringolf mentioned that one wave of American bombers had bombed along the left bank of the Rhine, hitting Kohlfirst, identified on contemporary maps as a "park and forest." One spectator reported seeing numerous columns of smoke arising" from Kohlfirst; another asserted that a forest fire had broken out there.[78] Kohlfirst was obviously the wooded area southeast of Schaffhausen that the 392nd Bombardment Group reported hitting as a result of the accidental pre-release of its bombs.

The actions of the 44th Bombardment Group are more difficult to reconcile with descriptions of Swiss ground observers. The 44th, which had flown behind the 392nd during the entire mission, somehow realized, as it reversed its course and headed west, that it was over Lake Constance, south of the German city of Friedrichshafen, which the 14th Combat Wing had bombed on March 16. Since the 44th had been assigned to fly at a higher altitude than the 392nd, some of its crew members were able to catch a glimpse of the Alps, "just visible" to their south.[79] The navigator and bombardier of the 44th's second section concluded, accordingly, as they flew west that they must be over Switzerland.

Three of the second section's planes had become detached during the chaotic conditions afflicting the mission and had joined the 44th's first section with the result that, as the 44th approached Schaffhausen, fifteen B-24s flew in its first section, nine in its second section. What happened next is not entirely clear, but the mission reports of the 44th's Lead Navigator, lst Lt. C. E. Shuler, and its Lead Bombardier, lst Lt. John F. King seem to indicate that the fifteen B-24s of the Group's first section, seeing red signal flares released by the 392nd, assumed that it had bombed Schaffhausen and followed suit, taking as its aiming point "the buildings south of the town by the large bend in the river."[80]

According to Lt. King, the navigator and bombardier leading the nine B-24s of the second section "both knew their position, so did not release

---

[77] Report of Lead Bombardier, 392nd Bombardment Group, note 73, above.

[78] *Neue Zürcher Zeitung,* April 3, 1944; Harrison to Cordell Hull, April 20, 1944, Record Group 59, 411.54, National Archives.

[79] Report of Lead Bombardier, 44th Bombardment Group, note 64, above.

[80] Report of the Lead Bombardier, 44th Bombardment Group, note 71, above.

their bombs when the first section's bombs started to fall."[81] The second section proceeded on a northwesterly course and once it was certain that it was over Germany bombed, as a "target of opportunity", the small town of Grafenhausen, although what military objective in the town justified such an attack is not clear. Fortunately for Grafenhausen, the release mechanism in the section leader's plane malfunctioned and, as a result, the section's bombs "were seen to fall over the aiming point."[82]

A major mystery of the bombing of Schaffhausen is why the second section of the 44th Bombardment Group did not radio its comrades in the first section that the group was over Switzerland and should not bomb. Why, in fact, was the 392nd not alerted as well? The records offer no explanation for a silence so portentous for Schaffhausen.

If the preceding reconstruction of the actions of the 14th Combat Wing over Schaffhausen is correct, the following happened: the 392nd Bombardment Group, leading the wing, bombed the forest at Kohlfirst; the 15 B-24s of the first section of the 44th Bombardment Group then bombed Schaffhausen; the third and final unit, the nine B-24s of the second section of the 44th Bombardment Group, recognizing that Schaffhausen was in Switzerland, flew over the city and bombed Grafenhausen, Germany. This recreation of the raid is at odds, however, with the unanimous testimony of Swiss ground observers, who asserted that the third, not the second, section of B-24s bombed Schaffhausen.

American records and Swiss observers agree that three waves of B-24s were involved in the attack on Schaffhausen and vicinity. On April 2 General Legge, the American military attaché, sent Washington a summary of the official Swiss version of the bombing: "3 waves of US AAF planes coming from direction Frauenfeld crossed Schaffhausen altitude 5,000-

---

[81] *Ibid.* Charles McBride, who flew in the 448th Bombardment Group on April 1, published a book in 1989 that presents an account of the attack on Schaffhausen that is consistent with Lt. King's description. According to McBride, Lt. A. N. Williams, identified as the lead navigator of the second section of the 44th Bombardment Group, knew he was over Switzerland and ordered the section to withhold its bombs. McBride's account is based on some documentary research and on reminiscences of surviving crewmen forty-five years after the event. How much credence is to be given to his description of Lt. Williams' actions is not certain since elsewhere in his book there are substantial errors, i.e., "on 22 February 1945 Schaffhausen was struck again" with considerable loss of life. It is odd that there is no report filed by Lt. Williams in the official Air Force records nor is his name mentioned in the official investigations of the bombing of Schaffhausen. See Charles McBride, *Mission Failure and Survival* (Manhattan, Kansas, 1989): 79, 126.
[82] Ibid.

7,000 meters at 10:50. Leading wave circled, dropped smoke signal . . .
Second wave did not bomb. Third wave same as first."[83]

At a news conference on April 1, Schaffhausen Mayor Bringolf
asserted that it was "the unanimous opinion" of observers that "three waves
of 30, 20 and 24 bombers" had approached the city and that only the third
wave had done the actual bombing.[84] A correspondent of the *Neue Zürcher
Zeitung,* who had climbed the tower of the Catholic Church in Neuhausen
to obtain an unobstructed view of the raid, confirmed Bringolf's statement,
asserting that after the first group of B-24s "emerged from a cloud" and
bombed south of the Rhine "about two minutes later a second squadron
flew over without dropping any bombs", followed by a third squadron that
attacked the city.[85]

Swiss and American accounts can be reconciled only by assuming that
Lieutenants Shuler and King, the 44th's lead navigator and bombardier, had
found themselves during the day's confusion leading the entire Group from
a position in front of the second section. If Shuler and King were, in fact,
the navigator and bombardier described in King's mission report who "both
knew their position", they would have led the smaller second section over
Schaffhausen without dropping bombs, while the larger first section,
following, would have committed the fatal error. Thus, the third wave of
American B-24s would have conducted the bombing, as Swiss observers
said that they did. If Shuler and King were, in fact, leading the entire Group
at the head of the second section (but how, then, could King have seen the
bombs of the first section, which would have been flying behind him?):
their failure to inform the Group that it was over a neutral city is
inexplicable and would seem to be nothing short of criminally negligent.
The evidence available, however, is not clear enough to convict Shuler and
King of anything; all that it tells us is that fifteen B-24s of the 44th
Bombardment Group dropped their payloads on Schaffhausen on the
morning of April 1, 1944.

To suggest that Schaffhausen had escaped lightly on April 1, that it
had been lucky, would have been regarded in Switzerland as an obscene
frivolity, but consider what would have happened had the 14th Combat
Wing attacked the city at full strength. Had a third bombardment group
been flying with the wing on April 1, as was customary, an additional
twenty-four B-24s would have made the bombing run against Schaffhausen.
Even as it was, the city did not absorb the full weight of the American
attack. The 392nd Bombardment Group dropped 868 hundred-pound

---

[83] Legge to War Department, April 2, 1944, Record Group 165, National Archives.
[84] *Basler Nachrichten,* April 3, 1944.
[85] *Neue Zürcher Zeitung,* April 3, 1944.

incendiary bombs and 264 hundred-pound explosive bombs in the forest at Kohlfirst. The section of the 44th Bombardment Group that passed the city by, hit Grafenhausen with 358 hundred-pound incendiaries and 180 hundred-pound explosives. The fifteen planes that actually bombed Schaffhausen dropped less than half of their payload on the city; they released 598 hundred-pound incendiaries and 180 hundred-pound explosives.[86] If Mayor Bringolf's figures are correct, if Schaffhausen was struck by 331 bombs as he reported on April 12,[87] more than half of the fifteen B-24s' bombs must have fallen in the Engewald, a forest in the hills west of the city where a Major Notz of the Swiss Army told the *Journal de Genève* that a large number of incendiary bombs had fallen.[88] Had the 14th Combat Wing accurately dropped all of its ordnance directly on Schaffhausen, the city would have been hit, not by 331 bombs, but by 1,824 hundred-pound incendiaries and 552 hundred-pound high explosives. Lucky Schaffhausen to have been spared such an inferno!

Design or Error?

The 8th Air Force promptly and aggressively investigated the bombing of Schaffhausen, causing an officer of the 392nd Bombardment Group to complain that "a great deal of explaining had to be done."[89] Because the facts about Schaffhausen, if revealed, would have been a public relations disaster, the Air Force controlled the results of the investigation as tightly as possible. On April 6, 1944 General Legge at Bern was furnished with what amounted to a summary of a summary of the investigation which did not even reveal the target of the mission.[90] Bad weather and navigational problems were blamed for the raid and, although Swiss newspapers jeered at this explanation when the Air Force offered it on April 2, it was substantially true. Legge was authorized to share these crumbs of the investigation with Swiss military officials in Bern with the understanding, which the Swiss faithfully observed, that they be given "no publicity or explanation which would probably lead to press criticism and be unconvincing to laymen."[91]

---

[86] Figures on the number of bombs dropped are derived from the mission reports of King and Whittaker; see notes 71 and 73, above.

[87] A recent writer has asserted that Schaffhausen was hit by 366 bombs and nine duds. Andreas Schiendorfer, *Schaffhauser Nachrichten,* March 31, 1994.

[88] *Journal de Genève,* April 3, 1944.

[89] Report, 392 Bombardment Group, April 1944, reel BO 495; GP 391-2, Bolling Air Force Base.

[90] War Department to Legge, April 6, 1944, Record Group 165, National Archives.

[91] Legge to War Department, April 22, 1944, *Ibid.*

　　　The same "investigation" was submitted to the Swiss ambassador in Washington, Charles Bruggmann, on April 25, 1944, again with the understanding that "the matter should be treated as confidential and not given publicity either here or in Switzerland."[92] When Ambassador Bruggman asked for more information a week later, officials at the State Department told him, truthfully, that they themselves did not know the target of the raid against Schaffhausen, which was being treated by the Air Force "in the category of military secrets."[93] In the absence of further information, most Swiss have assumed that the target of the American bombers on April 1 was Singen.[94] In some quarters, however, the view still persists that the attack on Schaffhausen was not an accident, but a punitive expedition, mounted by the Americans "to teach the Swiss a lesson for supporting Germany with weapons deliveries and for laundering dirty money."[95] After fifty years it is at last possible to drive a stake through the heart of this dark suspicion.

---

[92] Henry Stimson to Cordell Hull, April 18, 1944, *Ibid.*

[93] Memorandum of conversation between Bruggmann and Paul Culbertson, May 2, 1944, *Ibid.*

[94] *Neue Zürcher Zeitung,* March 31/April 1, 1984.

[95] Franco Battel, "Zum 50. Jahrestag der Bombardierung Schaffhausens am 1. April 1944", *Schaffhauser Mappe* (1994): 12. Noting that speculation still exists that the attack against Schaffhausen was a reprisal for Swiss economic support of the German war effort, Paul Stahlberger asserts in the *Neue Zürcher Zeitung,* March 26-7, 1994, that in his opinion there was the "highest probability" that the attack was a tragic error and that the target of the American pilots was "presumably Ludwigshafen." Two Swiss military writers, who appear to have had access to some American sources, state in commemorative articles that the target of the American fliers was Ludwigshafen. See Hans von Rotz, "Es war ein fataler Irrtum", *Schaffhauser Nachrichten,* March 31, 1994, and Kurz, "Vor 50 Jahren wurde Schaffhausen bombardiert", *Schweizer Soldat* (April 1994): 16-7. In a letter to the editor, *Neue Zürcher Zeitung,* April 15, Toni Schob cites Charles McBride's *Mission Failure and Survival* (Manhattan, Kansas, 1989) as proof that the attack on April 1, 1944, was an error. An American bombardier who participated in the attack, McBride verified in his memoir that the American target was Ludwigshafen. The same conclusion was reached by the diplomatic historian Jonathan Helmreich. See his "The Diplomacy of Apology. United States Bombings of Switzerland During World War II", *Air University Review,* 28 (May-June, 1977): 20-37. All of these accounts suffer from limited use of American archival sources; hence, they contain errors and are incomplete. Massive documentation about the bombing of Schaffhausen exists in American military and diplomatic archives, most of it not declassified until the mid-1970s; it irrefutably proves that the 14th Combat Wing of the 8th Air Force was under orders to bomb Ludwigshafen when it attacked Schaffhausen on April 1, 1944. Franco Battel is certainly wrong when he states that "it is doubtful, whether sources really exist, that would be able to unequivocally clarify the question" of whether the raid on Schaffhausen was an error or a reprisal. Battel is quoted from "Die Bombardierung", *Neue Zürcher Zeitung,* March 26-7, 1994.

Swiss officials were satisfied by one piece of information that the American military was willing to share with them in the aftermath of Schaffhausen. On April 20, 1944 General Legge informed General Rihner, commander of the Swiss air force, that American planes were under orders not to attack targets within fifty miles of the Swiss border unless they were positively identified. Legge reported to the War Department that Rihner was "extremely pleased" with this information.[96] What the Swiss officer did not know, however, was that Legge was simply affirming an American policy that had been in effect since 1943 and which governed the B-24s that struck Schaffhausen. The policy offered no additional security to Switzerland, whose territory was, in fact, bombed by the American Air Force thirty-seven more times before the war ended.[97]

Some of these thirty-seven incidents can scarcely be dignified by the term attack. As Legge reported to the War Department on April 30, 1945, "many of them were apparently considered of such slight significance at the time by Swiss military authorities that the M/A [military attaché] was not even informed of their occurrence."[98] Typical of these episodes was damage inflicted on a "steep slope" near the remote hamlet of Sulsana in Grisons on November 16, 1944 by a crippled American B-24 which jettisoned eight bombs before making an emergency landing in Ticino. One of the bombs exploded on the hill, causing what was later computed at $375 damage to a cultivated field and a surrounding forest.[99]

Other strikes were not so innocuous, however, and as the ground war moved closer to Switzerland after June 1944, American authorities cautioned the Swiss that American fliers, despite their best intentions, might

---

[96] "Legge to War Department, April 20, 1944, Record Group 165, National Archives.

[97] In making claims for compensation, the Swiss government considered the attack on Schaffhausen to have comprised three separate attacks: Schaffhausen, Flurlingen-Feuerthalen and Schlatt. By Swiss reckoning, therefore, the United States had bombed—and the Americans accepted the responsibility for—forty attacks on Switzerland from April 1, 1944, until the end of the war. In addition, the Swiss claimed that American planes had attacked Samaden in Grisons on October 1, 1943, an attack which the United States acknowledged in the summer of 1944 and for which it paid compensation of $56,515 (Hull to Bruggmann, July 4, 1944, Record Group 59, 411.54, National Archives.) Thus, the United States accepted responsibility for forty-one attacks on Switzerland during World War II. The Swiss government asserted that American bombers conducted eight additional attacks against its territory, for which the United States denied responsibility. Recapitulation of Bombing Claims, Headquarters, U.S. Forces European Theater, Office Theater Chief of Claims, Feb. 12, 1947, Ibid.

[98] "Legge to Military Intelligence Service, April 30, 1945, Record Group 165, *Ibid.*

[99] "Swiss Aide-memoire, July 16, 1946, Record Group 59, 411.54, *Ibid.*

stray over the Swiss border and launch unauthorized attacks. Responding on July 26, 1944 to a Swiss complaint about a bombing in Thurgau, the State Department asserted that, as the allies closed in on Germany, "it is manifestly impossible to hope that occasional violations will not occur."[100] No two Americans were more solicitous of Swiss sensitivities than Secretary of State Cordell Hull and Army Chief of Staff George C. Marshall, but both of these leaders accepted that there was no way to insulate the Swiss completely from inadvertent American attacks. Writing to Secretary of War Stimson on September 15, 1944, Hull admitted that "incidents of this nature are bound to occur, and even possibly to increase, as fighting develops in close proximity to the Swiss border."[101] Three days earlier, evaluating a Swiss proposal to assign observers to American ground forces, Marshall observed that "repeated violations of Swiss frontiers and neutrality and the likelihood of similar future incidents might indicate desirability of approving requests." Swiss observers could "provide basis for mutual understanding, appreciation by Swiss of difficulty in determining the border in all cases and understand confusion in targets, and would likewise remove in large measure basis of Swiss protests over continued violations."[102]

Although the Swiss were not prepared to concede officially that attacks on their territory were inevitable and thus absolve the Allies of responsibility for them, they appreciated that the eastward thrust of the American and British armies placed their border areas in jeopardy and took steps to minimize the danger. On September 9, 1944, for example, Swiss diplomats called at the War Department to express fears that Basel might be attacked because the land there was "very similar to surrounding French terrain" and because there were three marshaling yards in the area, one in France, another in Germany, and the third in Switzerland, all of which looked alike from the air.[103] The Americans were also notified that Swiss trains were electrified, while German and Italian locomotives used coal and hence could be distinguished by the steam they emitted. Large Swiss crosses were painted on buildings, power plants, military installations and in open fields along the Swiss-German and Swiss-Italian borders in hopes that they would catch the eyes of American pilots and alert them to their

---

[100] Memorandum, July 26, 1944, Record Group 165, *Ibid.*
[101] Record Group 59, 411.54, *Ibid.*
[102] Marshall to SHAEF Main, Sept. 12, 1944, Record Group 331, SHAEF 373.5, *Ibid.* 103War
[103] War Department, memorandum, Sept. 10, 1944, Record Group, 59, 411.54, *Ibid.*

positions. The crosses produced mixed results. In February 1945 American pilots reported that, as they were strafing a train, "a Swiss frontier boundary marker was seen one half mile to the south" and they broke off their attack. On the other hand, planes of the 1st Tactical Air Force bombed Thayngen on Christmas Day, 1944, under the impression that they were attacking the "Singen railroad bridge in Germany;" one Swiss citizen was killed, four wounded and "important damage" was inflicted on buildings with large Swiss crosses painted on their roofs.[104]

A Neutral Nation's Impotence

Although attacks on Switzerland in the fall of 1944 were infrequent and relatively harmless, American overflights of Swiss territory continued to annoy Swiss officials and aroused the State Department as well as the embassy at Bern to intercede with the War Department in an effort to improve the situation. Hull reminded Stimson that American self-interests were served by mollifying Switzerland because that country's neutrality permitted it "to perform certain invaluable services on behalf of American prisoners of war."[105] General Legge made a similar point, when he wrote General Dwight D. Eisenhower's headquarters on November 9, 1944, that the "repeated violations of the frontier are bringing about a feeling of bitterness on the part of the Swiss" upon whose good will the "interest of some 1000 Air Force internees" depended.[106]

The American command was unmoved by these pleas as long as nothing horrific—no new Schaffhausen—occurred to prick its conscience. There were also, in its view, extenuating circumstances for some of the episodes that provoked Swiss complaints. The Air Force, which was admirably forthcoming about admitting culpability for attacks on Switzerland, was unable to confirm that its planes had participated in a series of attacks in the Basel area in early September 1944 and suggested that the offending aircraft might have been downed American fighters, rehabilitated and flown by the Nazis, as part of "deliberate efforts by the Germans to injure Allied relations with Switzerland."[107] The Air Force agreed that it had attacked the bridge across the Rhine at Diessenhofen on

---

[104] Neutral and occupied countries folder, Switzerland, Box 139, Spaatz Papers, Manuscript Division, Library of Congress; Bruggmann to Hull, December 29, 1944; Divine to Culbertson, January 26, 1945, Record Group 165, National Archives.

[105] Hull to Stimson, September 15, 1944, Record Group 49, 411.54, *Ibid.*

[106] Legge to W. B. Smith, November 9, 1944, Record Group 331, SHAEF 373.5, *Ibid.*

[107] General J. E. Hull, memorandum, October 10, 1944, Record Group 165, *Ibid.*

November 9, 1944, as the Swiss charged, but contended that American planes had hit only the German side of the bridge—a legitimate military objective—and that the damage that had resulted in Swiss territory because of "flying debris" was regrettable but unavoidable.[108] Nor did an incident at Chiasso on January 11, 1945, enlist much Air Force sympathy. The Swiss complained that American fighters had attacked a railyard at Chiasso and killed a locomotive engineer. An investigation revealed that the engineer had, in fact, been killed by American planes that had been strafing an Italian train, heading north from Como. As the train neared the Chiasso railyard, it stopped in a tunnel. Spotting a steam engine, north of the tunnel in the Chiasso railyard, an American pilot, having been instructed that all Swiss trains were electrified, fired upon it under the assumption that it was the fugitive Italian locomotive. The train turned out to be Swiss, a fact that might have been established had the Swiss cross on the roof of the Chiasso rail station not been covered with eighteen inches of freshly fallen snow.[109]

More flagrant examples of Air Force malfeasance would have to emerge before the American high command would take further action. These occurred on February 22, 1945, during operation CLARION. CLARION was conceived as an offensive against heretofore neglected targets in smaller German towns—"relatively virgin areas"—in the words of an American planner.[110] CLARION spilled over into Switzerland with ugly results. According to an Air Force investigation, planes from the 8th and 15th air forces, flown by inexperienced crews, encountered bad weather over Germany, became "confused" and strayed over northeastern Switzerland. Confronted with "diminishing fuel supply and bombs still aboard", they dropped their payloads, "believing they could not fall on Swiss soil."[111] In fact, twelve different locations in Switzerland were struck, resulting in at least twenty deaths, a considerable number of injuries and substantial property damage; particularly hard hit were Stein-am-Rhein and Neuhausen in Canton Schaffhausen.

One of President closest advisers, Lauchlin Currie, was caught, to his surprise and embarrassment, in Operation CLARION. A New Deal economist, Currie had been appointed by Roosevelt at the end of 1944 to

---

[108] Stettinius to Bruggmann, December 22, 1944, Record Group 59, 411.54, *Ibid.*

[109] Col. F. E. Cheatle, Report, January 15, 1945, Record Group 165, *Ibid.*

[110] For Operation CLARION, see Ronald Schaffer, "American Military Ethics in World War II: The Bombing of German Civilians", in *Journal of American History* 67 (June 1980): 327-30.

[111] Switzerland folder, note 104, above.

lead an Anglo-American delegation to Switzerland to negotiate a shrinking of Swiss economic relations with Germany—a reduction of Swiss exports to the Reich, restrictions on transit traffic between Germany and Italy and limitations on the supply of hydro-electric power to both Axis nations. Currie's modest title of administrative assistant to the president belied his importance. Representing Roosevelt in negotiations with Chiang-Kai-shek in 1942, Currie carried a personal letter from the President, informing the Chinese leader that he, Currie, had "my complete confidence [and] access to me at all times."[112] Swiss feared that Currie would assume a dictatorial posture in the negotiations—the "Currie served to Bern will be hot and concentrated", one Swiss newspaper quipped[113]—but the American emissary proved to be mild and conciliatory.

The Anglo-American delegation presented its credentials in Bern on February 12. At the ceremonies the leader of the British delegation, Dingle Foot, expressed his relief at having escaped the din of the constant air raid sirens in London, to which a Swiss minister, Walter Stucki, "somewhat jokingly" replied with a request that Foot ask Currie "to arrange for the bombers to leave us in peace at least for the duration of the negotiations", his point being, a Swiss newspaper explained to its readers, that there were more air raid alarms in neutral Bern than in the beleaguered British capital.[114]

On February 22, as Operation CLARION unfolded, Currie and a group of his colleagues made an official visit to Schaffhausen, stopping at Zürich on the way. Present in the American delegation was Allen Dulles, whose activities in Bern as the United States' O.S.S. representative were an open secret. Curiously enough, shortly before Dulles became Central Intelligence Agency (CIA) director in the postwar period, Currie was denounced as a Communist and fled the United States for South America where Dulles' agents kept him under surveillance. The activities of the American Air Force on February 22 literally came close to wrecking Currie's goodwill visit, for according to a Geneva newspaper, the American party was "almost hit by their own compatriots' bombs" on their way to Schaffhausen.[115] Escorted by Mayor Bringolf, Currie and his associates visited the mass

---

[112] Earl Latham, *The Communist Conspiracy in Washington* (Cambridge, 1966): 242.

[113] *Neues Winterthurer Tagblatt,* quoted in Harrison to Hull, January 31, 1945, Record Group 59, EW 740.00112, National Archives.

[114] *Der Bund,* February 24, 1945.

[115] *Journal de Genève,* quoted in Harrison to Hull, February 24, 1945, Record Group 59, EW 740.00112, National Archives.

grave of the victims of the April 1 bombing and paid their respects by laying a wreath. They then toured the damaged portions of the city and visited the still charred Allerheiligen Museum, where Bringolf, in a shrewd act of psychological gamesmanship, arranged a reception. In officially greeting his guests, Bringolf asked them to use their influence to prevent bombings of the kind that were occurring in the vicinity of Schaffhausen even as they spoke.[116] A chastened Currie promised, in his response, to intercede with President Roosevelt as soon as possible to stop the attacks.

Currie cabled Roosevelt when he returned to Bern, asking the President to take action to spare the Swiss further agony. It is difficult to assess the impact of this cable, but it is probably no accident that on February 24, 1945 Acting Secretary of State Joseph Grew issued a press release, announcing that he was "profoundly shocked and distressed" at the "series of bombings and strafing of Swiss towns on February 22", that on February 26, General Marshall, always sensitive to Switzerland's plight, ordered General Eisenhower to do something "towards preventing a recurrence of these incidents", and that two days later Eisenhower "issued orders to the Tactical Air Forces prohibiting attacks under visual conditions on any objective within 10 miles of the Swiss frontier and under instrument conditions within 50 miles."[117]

The attacks of February 22 produced in Swiss newspapers another round of denunciations of the geographical ignorance of American pilots and of complaints that the Swiss were weary of promises that were constantly undercut by the actions of the American military. "Words are cheap, " snapped *Der Bund,* "actions count and convince."[118] The frustration of the Swiss with their inability to prevent the violation of their neutrality surfaced in sharp questions about the inactivity of the country's armed forces. "Where is the Swiss air defense?" became an embarrassing question. That the United States was in danger of depleting its fund of goodwill in Switzerland was illustrated by the *Basel National Zeitung* which declared with resignation that "All sympathy for the large sister republic notwithstanding, we find it difficult that the liberation of Europe is accompanied with suffering and death brought so indiscriminately by American flyers over the border into Switzerland."[119]

---

[116] *Der Bund,* February 23, 1945.
[117] Grew's press release is in Record Group 59, EW 740.00116, National Archives; Marshall's and Eisenhower's orders are in Record Group 331, SHAEF 373.5, *Ibid.*
[118] February 24, 1945.
[119] February 23, 1945.

Fatal Errors Renewed

In laying prohibitions on the tactical air forces on February 28, General Eisenhower assured General Marshall that the attacks on Switzerland were "a matter of extreme concern to this Headquarters and the Air Force", but warned that it might be impossible to stop the violation of Swiss air space by administrative fiat. "Under existing conditions", cautioned Eisenhower, "there can be no positive guarantee that such incidents will not occur. . ."[120] Eisenhower's apprehensions were prophetic because within a week of his statement, on March 4, 1945, American B-24 bombers struck two of Switzerland's major cities, Basel and Zürich. These raids were the proverbial last straw, for they aroused the American high command to take quick and decisive action to end, once and for all, the air attacks on Switzerland.

The bombing of Basel and Zürich was a less lethal reprise of the raid on Schaffhausen: some of the same Air Force units participated; they were disoriented by bad weather; plagued by the unreliability of high-tech equipment; and bombed only when the clouds beneath them suddenly broke. Making the resemblance between the raids still more uncanny, one American unit recognized at the last moment that it was over the wrong target and refrained from dropping its bombs. One significant difference between the attacks was that by March 1945 American commanders were holding pilots to a higher level of performance and were less willing than their predecessors to accept equipment failures as excuses for navigational errors. The leader of the American formation that attacked Zürich was, in fact, court-martialed but acquitted of negligence.

The March 4 mission was planned as an assault against German jet aircraft production facilities and airfields. All three of the 8th Air Force's divisions, a total of 990 B-24s, were scheduled to participate. One additional combat wing, the 96th, consisting of the 458th, 466th and 467th bombardment groups, had been added to the Second Division's other wings—the 2nd, 14th, and 20th—that had flown against Ludwigshafen on April 1, 1944. Unlike the April 1 raid, on March 4, 1945, the 14th Combat Wing had its full complement of bombardment groups, the 491st having been added to the 44th and 392nd.[121]

---

[120] Eisenhower to Marshall, February 28, 1945, Record Group 33 1, SHAEF, 373.5, National Archives.

[121] Planning for Mission of March 4, 1945, report of March 12, 1945; Bombing Results, 2nd Division, operation no. 863, reel 520.332. Bolling AFB.

The weather over the English coast, the usual assembly point for American bombers headed to Europe, was so bad on March 4 that the Second Division was ordered to fly to the continent and assemble northeast of Paris.[122] From there it was to proceed to a point south of Strasbourg, then go directly east to Freiburg, fly southeast again in the direction of Lake Constance, then turn north, northeast and overfly Stuttgart. From Stuttgart the division was ordered to continue in a north, northeasterly direction. Along the course the 20th Combat Wing was assigned to attack an airfield at Schwäbisch Hall. The 2nd and 96th combat wings were to proceed to the Würzburg area to attack airfields at Kitzingen and Giebelstadt; the 14th was then directed to turn to the northwest to attack a tank depot at Aschaffenburg near Frankfurt.[123]

The weather on the continent was, if anything, worse than over the English coast: solid clouds up to 24,000 feet and dense, persistent haze and undercast, described by pilots as 10/10, meaning the downward vision was 100 percent obscured. As on April 1, 1944, the Second Division had the sensation of flying in a tunnel, with no visibility above or below. As the division flew east from Paris, the entire 2nd Combat Wing, some sixty B-24s, abandoned the mission,[124] as the 446th Bombardment Group had done on April 1, 1944, because the planes could not see each other well enough to fly in formation. The division's other wings continued eastward, flying into increasingly miserable conditions. According to a report filed on March 5, "clouds made adherence to any formation extremely difficult. At times group leaders lost sight of the groups ahead and squadrons lost sight of their group leaders . . . all available information indicated that primary targets could not be reached and that targets of opportunity should be selected as soon as possible."[125]

Since the Second Division was near Stuttgart, it elected to attack that city using "H2X methods." Clouds over the city were so dense that the division's planes dodged each other as they maneuvered for their bombing runs. A collision between planes of the 20th and 96th combat wings was barely averted. In taking evasive action the 466th Bombardment Group became separated from the remainder of the 96th Combat Wing and headed south in the direction of Freiburg which it decided to attack as a target of opportunity. As the group approached the target, the H2X in the leader's

---

[122] Planning for Mission of March 4, *Ibid.*
[123] Track chart, March 4, 1945, *Ibid.*
[124] Bombing of Neutral Territory, March 4, 1945, report of March 5, 1945, *Ibid.*
[125] Two incidents of bombing Swiss territory, March 4, 1945, *Ibid.*

plane failed. The group leader, a Colonel Jacobowitz, then ordered visual bombing, since a break in the clouds suddenly occurred, as it had at Schaffhausen. The more Jacobowitz looked at the target area the less certain he was about its identity, so he ordered his section to close its bomb doors and head back to England.[126]

The leader of the second section of the 466th, which consisted of nine planes—eight B-24s from the 466th and a stray from the 392nd—was confident that the city below him was Freiburg. According to a subsequent investigation, "the H2X navigator was the man who positively identified the target as Freiburg",[127] although as a precaution the section leader checked the "target identification over with all the people in the aircraft"[128] and they all agreed that Freiburg was below them. General Spaatz's staff later concluded that the bombing of Basel—for it was Basel not Freiburg that the second section bombed—"resulted from the using of instruments that failed during the flight and gave false readings."[129]

The bombs of the second section fell on the Swiss railway freight station near downtown Basel. Seven people were injured and thirty houses were damaged. Swiss authorities estimated that approximately sixty-five hundred-pound high explosive bombs struck the freight station (there were actually seventy-six) as well as one thousand small, stick-type incendiaries, some of which drifted into the Swiss railway passenger station and started fires there. American authorities concluded that "many fortunate circumstances" attended the attack on Basel, the principal one being that the bombs fell on a deserted freight station rather than on the nearby passenger station "filled with the usual Sunday crowd" of travelers."[130] At least as fortunate for Basel was that, as at Schaffhausen, one squadron of American bombers refrained from releasing its payload. Colonel Jacobowitz's squadron contained fifteen B-24s, carrying at least 126 five-hundred-pound demolition bombs—thirty-two tons of high explosives—which, if dropped, might have created a bloodbath at Basel.

Only six B-24s attacked Zürich: a hybrid group of three planes from the 392nd Bombardment Group, two from the 491st group and one from the

---

[126] *Ibid.*

[127] *Ibid.*

[128] Swiss folder, note 104, above.

[129] *Ibid.*

[130] For detailed American accounts of the bombing of Basel, see John A. Lehrs (American Vice Counsel) to Cordell Hull, March 7, 1945, Record Group 59, 411.54, National Archives, and Col. F. E. Cheatle, report, March 16, 1945, Record Group 165, *Ibid.*

445th.[131] In command of the group was a plane from the 392nd. The B-24s from the 392nd and the 491st participated with other units of the 14th Combat Wing in the attempt on Stuttgart. The 44th was leading the 14th Combat Wing, the 392nd being in second position (the reverse of the order on April 1, 1944). While maneuvering over Stuttgart, the six-plane squadron became separated from the 44th and, in fact, "from all other formations due to weather and did not have visual contact with any other units."[132] Turning to the south, the squadron also intended to attack Freiburg as a target of opportunity. The H2X equipment in the lead aircraft was "getting very poor returns" and giving the navigator "downward visibility only."[133] Worried about his position, the leader tried to obtain readings from another H2X plane but its equipment was broken.[134] The lead navigator suddenly saw a break in the clouds and led the section on a bombing run on what was assumed to be Freiburg. Hit instead were the northern suburbs of Zürich "between Schwamendingen and Strickhof."

The area was heavily forested and sparsely populated but five people were, nevertheless, killed and twelve injured. The American fliers later reported that clouds covered the southern part of Zürich, including the lake, and that haze at ground level obscured their vision.[135] Commenting on the bombing of Zürich, the American air attaché in Bern, Colonel F. E. Chittle, remarked that "considering the proximity to an important and closely settled area in which these heavy bombs had fallen, it can be considered a very fortunate circumstance that so much of this potential force was dissipated harmlessly in woods and open fields."[136]

American officials reported that the Swiss affected by these latest attacks displayed the same stoicism as had the citizens of Schaffhausen. According to the American consul at Basel, the population "preserved throughout an admirable discipline. The people with whom I have had occasion to talk about this regrettable incident were reticent in any criticism of the Allies which they may have felt, advancing instead suggestions that such accidental bombings appear to be unavoidable in modern warfare."[137] The Swiss media strove to find fresh language to articulate its familiar complaints. The geographical ignorance of the American military was once

---

[131] Two incidents of bombing of Swiss territory, March 4, 1945, note 125, above.
[132] *Ibid.*
[133] Bombing of Neutral Territory, March 4, note 124, above.
[134] *Ibid.*
[135] *Ibid.*
[136] Report, March 10, 1945, Record Group 165, National Archives.
[137] Lehrs to Hull, March 7, 1945, note 130, above.

again denounced[138] as was the hollowness of American diplomatic professions. The frustration over Switzerland's inability to defend its neutrality and to achieve its aims diplomatically became even more palpable. "We are simply not in possession of the requisite means of power to give the necessary weight to our protests", lamented a Zürich newspaper.[139] Warning that it was dangerous "to show the white flag" to "air pirates", the *Basler Nachrichten* had no suggestions about how the country could achieve its objectives.[140] A new element in the press was an imaginative variation on the conspiracy theory that the United States was deliberately bombing Swiss cities to punish the country for helping the Nazis. Some Swiss now thought it possible that the Soviet Union, which was in the midst of a public relations campaign against their country, might have orchestrated the raids which, it was thought, could have been concocted at the Big Three meeting at Yalta.[141]

The March 4 raids incensed Currie whose credibility they impaired. Currie's assurances after the bombings of February 22 that he would prevent their recurrence by personally intervening with President Roosevelt received the widest publicity in Switzerland. "We hope", a Geneva newspaper taunted Currie on March 5, that "he is not waiting to return to the United States to do this."[142] Whether Currie was spurred to action by such reproaches is not clear, but on March 5 the irrepressible envoy sent cables to both Generals Eisenhower and Marshall calling their attention to the attacks on Basel and Zürich. "I can not urge too strongly", Currie entreated the generals, "that the Allied Air Forces be impressed that every possible precaution be taken to avoid these accidents . . . violations of neutrality and loss of Swiss lives create most painful impression. You might also want to consider the advisability of making public statement which I am sure would help situation here."[143]

The American High Command Takes Charge

Currie's pleas were unnecessary because the attacks of March 4 exhausted the patience of the American high command and produced

---

[138] See , for example, *Die Tat,* March 6, 1945.

[139] *Ibid.,* March 8, 1945.

[140] March 5/6, 1945.

[141] Harrison to Hull, March 7, 1945, Record Group 59, EW 740.00112, National Archives.

[142] *Journal de Genève,* March 5, 1945.

[143] Currie to Eisenhower, March 5, 1945, Record Group 331, SHAEF 373.5, National Archives.

immediate, decisive action. Spaatz's superior, General Arnold, denounced the bombings as a "blunder" caused by "aggressive, but sometimes careless leaders."[144] General Marshall was "personally concerned about the recurrent, accidental bombings of Swiss territory"[145] and issued the following order to General Eisenhower on March 5: "Spaatz to report to Switzerland to clear up Bombing Mishaps."[146] The next day Spaatz received an urgent, top secret cable from Marshall's headquarters, amplifying his orders: "the successive bombings of Swiss territory now demand more than expressions of regret. It is desired that you personally leave immediately for Geneva or such other place as may be necessary and present to the appropriate Swiss officials first hand information as to the causes of these incidents, the corrective action undertaken, and a formal apology. . . . No publicity and maximum secrecy."[147] If this order had the ring of a rebuke, it was intended to be one.

Spaatz was immersed in planning what the American generals hoped would be the decisive thrust against Germany and could not have relished taking enforced leave to travel to Switzerland, but he complied with his orders with alacrity. Accompanied by his chief of staff, General E. P. Curtis, Spaatz flew to Lyons on March 7 and traveled by automobile to Bern, arriving there at 7:00 p.m. the same evening. At nine o'clock the next morning Spaatz and his party presented themselves at the Federal Palace and were received by a Swiss delegation that included Minister of War Karl Kobelt, Foreign Minister Petit-Pierre, General Henri Guisan, Air Force Commander Rihner and others.[148] On behalf of the War Department and the United States Strategic Air Forces, Spaatz "expressed to the Minister of War our official and my personal regrets for these incidents and particularly for the Swiss lives which had been lost as a result." In a working group with his Swiss military counterparts, Spaatz explained the specific steps he had taken on March 6 to eliminate the bombing of Swiss territory. He had, he revealed, drawn two lines around Switzerland. Within the first line, roughly fifty miles north of the Rhine, extending from Strasbourg to Innsbruck, no

---

[144] "Arnold to Spaatz, March 28, 1945, Spaatz Papers, Box 21, Manuscript Division, Library of Congress.

[145] Grew to Harrison, March 5, 1945, Record Group 59, EW 740. 0011, National Archives.

[146] Record Group 331, SHAEF 373.5, Ibid.

[147] War Department to Spaatz, March 6, 1945, Spaatz Papers, Box 23, Manuscript Division, Library of Congress.

[148] Spaatz's description of the meeting, March 10, 1945, is preserved in his papers, Box 23, *Ibid.*

attacks could henceforth be made without specific permission from Spaatz himself. Within a second line, drawn one hundred miles north of the first, clearance to bomb "by other than absolutely visual means" must be obtained from Spaatz's headquarters. Spaatz also disclosed General Eisenhower's order of February 28 to the tactical air forces, forbidding them to attack any target within ten miles of the Swiss border and to attack "only after positive identification in a zone extending 10 miles to 50 miles."

According to Spaatz, General Guisan and Air Force Commander Rihner seemed to be "more than satisfied with the steps which had been taken and assured me that information with regard to the prohibited zone would be kept strictly confidential." Spaatz responded by cautioning the Swiss that if the Germans learned of the sanctuary around the Swiss border and began to exploit it, he might be compelled to order new attacks. The Swiss military leaders raised other issues with Spaatz. They indicated "very strongly their desire to obtain 10 P-51s from the Air Force."[149] Evidently, they did not intend to use them to shoot down American bombers, for Spaatz supported their request on the grounds that granting it would generate goodwill for the United States. The War Department declined to accommodate the Swiss, however, because the supply of P-51s was inadequate for pressing American needs.[150] The Swiss also reminded Spaatz that they were repairing and maintaining downed American planes and could pay for the P-51s by deducting their purchase price from the maintenance bill which they would present the United States at some future date. Finally, the Swiss stated that they would paint even larger crosses at their borders as signals to errant aircraft. Spaatz informed Marshall's headquarters that the "attitude of all of the Swiss authorities was very understanding and even cordial. They seemed to be genuinely impressed with our visit." "To impress public opinion with the efforts being made by the Americans to avoid further difficulties", the Swiss asked for and received Spaatz's permission to issue a communiqué, discussing in general terms the results of his mission.[151] This they did at a press conference on the evening of March 8, as Spaatz was returning to France.[152] War Minister Kobelt presided at the press conference and thanked Spaatz for coming to Switzerland "in spite of his heavy duties." Kobelt reported that Spaatz had

---

[149] Spaatz to Arnold, March 11, 1945, is preserved in his papers, Box *23, Ibid.*

[150] General Barney Giles to Spaatz, March 23, 1945, *Ibid.*

[151] Spaatz's description, March 10, 1945, note 148, above.

[152] An English language translation of the official Swiss communiqué, dated March 10, 1945, is in Spaatz's papers, Box *23, Ibid.*

expressed his regrets over the recent bombings and had assured the Swiss that he "would immediately make new arrangements to assure the security of our country and had ordered even more effective steps to be taken", although what those steps were Kobelt did not disclose. The minister assured his countrymen that "henceforth the situation will improve", which it did. After Spaatz's visit there were no more bombings of Switzerland.[153]

Currie did not participate in the meeting of March 8. He was, in fact, preparing to return to the United States, because he had concluded his negotiations on March 5, having obtained the agreement of Switzerland to reduce its economic ties with Germany. That Spaatz appeared in Bern three days after the conclusion of Currie's negotiation proves that the general's mission was not designed to assist Currie by offering military concessions to procure economic objectives. The motive for Spaatz's mission was the need for the American military to salvage its professional pride, for the persistent bombings of Switzerland were a standing reproach to the competence of the American Air Force which exposed itself to the world as an organization apparently unable to implement its own policies vis-à-vis neutrals.

The missions of Spaatz and Currie augured well for the future of Swiss-American relations. Spaatz's visit was received with "deep appreciation" by the Swiss government and seems to have had "the most beneficial effect on public opinion."[154] The Swiss press also welcomed the general's initiative. Spaatz, the *Gazette de Lausanne* asserted on March 10, had "demonstrated in a preemptory manner that the American military attributes the greatest importance to the bombing question." Currie's negotiations were also considered by the Swiss to have turned out well. Swiss neutrality had emerged "unscathed", the *Neue Zürcher Zeitung* remarked approvingly,[155] and many Swiss now looked forward to a western reorientation of the nation's economics and politics. Currie was praised for practicing a kind of shirt-sleeves diplomacy in which he sought out the views of ordinary Swiss people and learned, so it was hoped, that they were not pro-Fascist, as some had represented them to be.

---

[153] On October 5, 1945, the American government acknowledged causing trifling damages some months earlier in Brusio, Grisons. The raids of March 4 were the last significant attacks on Switzerland.

[154] Harrison to State Department, March 8, 1945, Record Group 59, 411.54, National Archives.

[155] March 9, 1945.

Currie did not disappoint Swiss expectations, for he reported to Marshall and Eisenhower that he found the Swiss to be "overwhelmingly pro-Ally."[156] Was Currie merely hearing the transient enthusiasm of people impressed by the impending Anglo-American military victory—an everyone loves a winner euphoria—or was he recording an attitude toward the United States that had deeper roots? Consider in this regard Minister Kobelt's remarks to General Spaatz at the opening of the March 8 meeting, when he told the general that "we are proud to be considered the oldest democracy of the world together with the United States."[157] Or consider the declaration of a highly placed Swiss Red Cross official to Minister Harrison on November 10, 1944, which was said to represent the "opinion of a great many Swiss citizens": "Switzerland has a close affinity with his own [President Roosevelt's] country from the viewpoint of the constitution and of the fundamental principles of her home organization."[158] Although these remarks might be dismissed as flattery calculated to establish a rapport with representatives of an emerging superpower—as the cynical dusting off the words of a long forgotten hymn—the readiness of Swiss officials to invoke them suggests that the traditional concept of the sister republics still had sufficient influence in Switzerland to sustain a bias toward the United States strong enough, as Currie discovered, to survive the fiery ordeal of American aerial bombardment.

The end of the war in Europe in June 1945 did not close the curtain on the American bombing of Switzerland, for a final accounting of the damages had to be made and, more challenging, the American Congress had to be persuaded to pay the bill when it was presented. After the war the United States sent investigators to Switzerland to authenticate Swiss claims and by the spring of 1947 most claims had been resolved to the satisfaction of all parties. The State Department, therefore, requested Congress to authorize an interim indemnity payment of ten million dollars, a payment that was to be distributed to the bombing victims as well as to those whose property had been damaged by the crashing of disabled American planes (forty-six incidents amounting to one-sixtieth of the bombardment indemnity).[159] The State Department's bill passed the Senate and was sent to the House of Representatives, where it was favorably reported to the

[156] Cables, March 5, 1945, Record Group 331, SHAEF 373.5, National Archives.
[157] Spaatz papers, Box 23, Manuscript Division, Library of Congress.
[158] Louis Micheli to Harrison, November 10, 1944, Leland Harrison Papers, *Ibid.*
[159] Swiss Bombing Claims, draft statement, State Department Legal Adviser's Office, July 1949, Record Group 59, 411.54, National Archives.

floor by the Foreign Relations Committee. The full House failed to act, however, with the result that the Swiss Compensation Bill languished in Congress for the next two years.

In July 1947 the State Department urged Congress to pass the bill, "since certain sections of the Swiss press and individuals in Parliament are always eager to enlarge upon any slight dissent between that country and the United States."[160] In September 1947 the Swiss government (which, having paid some local claims, had become a creditor of the United States) requested Washington to make "a substantial advance payment"[161] and in October the Schaffhausen City Council went on record as being dissatisfied with Congress's stalling. The next summer, as the compensation bill continued to be immobilized in the House of Representatives, Swiss commentary became sharper. Mayor Bringolf wrote an article in a Schaffhausen newspaper in which he complained that "with the best of understanding for the frequent cumbersomeness of parliamentary machinery in a democracy, we find ourselves forced to voice our amazement and disappointment over the incomprehensible dragging out by the American parliament of an affair of such importance to us."[162] The editor of Zürich's *Die Tat* was even more exercised, charging that "these delaying tactics on the part of the American Representatives can hardly be qualified as anything but a deliberately unfriendly act towards Switzerland."[163] What was particularly galling to Switzerland was that through the Marshall Plan the American Congress was lavishing billions of dollars on neighboring European nations even as it was refusing "to settle what the Swiss consider to be a just debt of a few millions."[164]

In May 1949 the House of Representatives finally came to grips with the "Swiss Bombing Claims" bill and was treated to some remarkably unedifying floor debate. Congressman Stephen Young, Democrat of Ohio, assailed the Swiss as "callous and hard; cunning and cold blooded, and always looking out for their own interests and seeking an unfair advantage." "They plotted World War I in Switzerland", Congressman Young complained, and "the Swiss became rich out of World War I. World War II was plotted there, and the Swiss became wealthy from World War II while we

---

[160] "Memorandum, Office of the Director of European Affairs, July 9, 1947, *Ibid.*
[161] Harrison to State Department, September 9, 1947, *Ibid.*
[162] John Carter Vincent to State Department, June 23, 1948, *Ibid.*
[163] *Ibid.*
[164] Vincent to State Department, July 10, 1948, *Ibid.*

were expending our blood and treasure."[165] Responding to these "disobliging remarks", the editor of the *Journal de Genève* on May 13, 1949, professed to be "astonished" that they could be directed "at a nation which has always felt the most friendly sympathy for the great American republic." The anti-Swiss rhetoric made little impression on the House, however. It passed the bill and sent it on to the Senate and, after the interest on the claims was reduced from 5 percent to 3½ percent, the bill became law on June 28, authorizing a payment to Switzerland of up to $16,000,000. On October 21, 1949, more than five and one half years after the bombing of Schaffhausen, Switzerland accepted Swiss Francs 62,176,433 in discharge of her claims. In so far as money could compensate Switzerland for the damage inflicted upon her, a settlement had at last been achieved.

The bombing of Switzerland by the United States during World War II was a tragedy. At least seventy Swiss citizens were killed and considerably more were hurt and maimed. The bombings were also a tragedy for the American crews who participated in them, crews that were sent aloft in impossible weather with unreliable equipment to attack unreachable targets. The grief of American fliers when they learned after the fact that they had bombed Schaffhausen was deep and genuine. Some airmen, the *New York Times* reported, were "too distressed to talk" while others could only murmur that they were "terribly sorry that this could have happened."[166] American anguish was particularly sharp because of the widespread goodwill towards Switzerland at all levels of American society, including at the highest ranks of the military. The Swiss grossly underestimated the breadth of American esteem because they mistook the strident voices of a few shortsighted bureaucrats and parochial politicians for the opinion of the American public at large.

The attitude of the Swiss toward the United States during and after World War II appears to follow a similar pattern. From the 1930s onward a vocal minority of Swiss criticized the United States, often from an ideological stance that held it to embody the worst features of modern capitalism. But the majority of Swiss were well disposed toward the United States and these sentiments survived the provocations of the American Air Force during the war and the hectoring of a few American politicians after it. It may seem naive and sentimental to ascribe Swiss goodwill to a shared institutional heritage that is captured by the sister republics metaphor, but

---

[165] *Congressional Record,* House of Representatives, May 9, 1949, volume 95, part 5, Ist session, 81st Congress, 5914.

[166] *Neue Ziircher Zeitung,* April 3, 1944.

skeptics about the power of metaphors and symbols are obliged to produce an alternative explanation for the persistence of Swiss-American friendship through the dark days of 1944 and 1945, a persistence that fifty years after the fact appears to be an extraordinary testimony to the power of common democratic ideals.

This study first appeared in the *Swiss-American Historical Society Review* 31 (February 1995): 3-49. Reprinted by permission.

PART TWO

CHALLENGES OF NEUTRALITY

V: SEVERELY TESTED

Swiss Neutrality During Two World Wars

Edgar Bonjour

Swiss neutrality was not established by a single voluntary act. This axiom of Swiss foreign policy evolved only slowly out of the structure of the old Confederation, the religious schism, and the policy of alliances. Only gradually did it come to realize its own character in the twilight of international entanglements. The painful experiences of several centuries, hard-won insights into the vital necessities of the Confederation, and a renunciation of all further territorial growth were necessary to train Switzerland to the political abstinence of neutrality. For a long time neutrality remained an elastic formula in which the most manifold possibilities of a reserved foreign policy found an expression. Not until 1815 did it take on its final form and gain international recognition. In the course of the nineteenth century, Swiss neutrality was questioned both in fact and in theory. But as such crises were successfully overcome, Switzerland's faith in the inviolability of her neutrality was confirmed. It blended with the republican and democratic ideals to form a myth of almost religious sanctity. It seemed as if the country were protected by high ramparts behind which her citizens could live in political introversion.

Armed Neutrality During the First World War

The outbreak of World War I brought a rude awakening from these illusions. On August 4, 1914, at the behest of the Federal Assembly, the Federal Council announced to the signatory powers of the Neutrality Act of 1815, as well as to all other governments, Switzerland's firm determination "faithful to her century-old tradition, not to depart in any way from the principles of neutrality which are so dear to the Swiss people and which exist in accordance with their aspirations, their constitution, and their attitude toward other States." The Confederation would employ all means at her disposal to safeguard her neutrality and her territorial inviolability. This attitude, dictated by historical developments and the actual situation, was so obvious that it surprised no one either at home or abroad. The neighboring States assured Switzerland of their most scrupulous respect for her neutrality. Even before this declaration, when an armed conflict seemed

111

imminent, the Federal Council had ordered the mobilization of the entire Swiss Army and had taken initial military and economic precautions. It was the Council's belief that, with Switzerland being so plainly ready to defend herself, an enemy attack could be averted.

The foremost task seemed to be the immediate occupation of Switzerland's borders. Within a few days, the mobilization of the entire army of 250,000 men was completed. The main body was assembled in the northwestern corner of the country, thus protecting the border against both France and Germany. A merciful fate spared the Confederate army the necessity of having to prove that it would have been equal to an attempted enemy invasion. On average, the deployed troops did 600 days of border duty; this was the longest period of service in centuries. Their patience and spirit were severely tested by the prolonged stand-by, not knowing what to expect, brought about by a situation that was neither peace nor war. Belligerent activity can spur on the will to defend one's country, whereas inactivity, often perceived as a denial of heroism, has a destructive effect in the long run. As this war proved again, demoralization tends to appear particularly among troops which are not under fire. But the Swiss Army overcame this crisis.

In contrast to earlier European wars, this one brought no grave military violations of neutrality. Most incidents were only cases of flying over projecting parts of the territory; at times foreign patrols wandered onto Swiss soil.

Besides the obvious military danger, Switzerland was in economic peril as well. Would not the small, landlocked State in the heart of a belligerent Europe soon be starved to death? Switzerland's agricultural production did not suffice to feed the population, and her industry was largely dependent on the good will of her neighbors for the further maintenance of her foreign food sources.

When the Powers at war began to blockade each other totally, the continued supply of food and raw materials became the prime and most critical concern of the Swiss government. From the outset, Switzerland was painfully aware that she could not rely on the international agreements concerning trade with neutral parties. In their battle for existence, the belligerents did not uphold the principles of international law and did not concern themselves with Switzerland's protestations. Their sole concern was the economic strangulation of the enemy, his death by starvation. Therefore, they did not tolerate the neutrals' re-export of imported merchandise to the countries of their enemies. In order to safeguard supplies for herself Switzerland was forced to submit to a control of all imports, especially of imported foods and raw materials from overseas. This was a severe infringement of Swiss sovereignty.

If the belligerent nations did not allow Switzerland to starve, it was not solely for humanitarian reasons, but also for utilitarian ones. It seemed advisable to respect Swiss neutrality from a military point of view, in order to shorten battle lines and to intern sick prisoners of war. Both parties also took advantage of the neutral country for the supply of war materials as well as goods for civilian use. The high degree of industrialization in Switzerland made it possible to fill most orders of the belligerents. If the other nations wanted to keep open this source of supplies, Switzerland needed to be supplied not only with raw materials, but with food as well.

The German invasion of Belgium had a startling effect on large parts of the Swiss population. Especially in French Switzerland, prevailing attitudes were greatly affected. The central European States were regarded more and more as representatives of sheer power and of the absolutist, anti-democratic principle which stood in total opposition to the national liberal ideals. Germany was perceived as the greatest threat to law and democracy in Europe. Immigration from Germany had been taking on menacing proportions. In the intellectual sector, German influence was indeed quite strong, and the German dominance in the economic sector caused widespread uneasiness. For years, German-speaking Switzerland had followed with admiration the German rise in technology, economy, and international prestige. German-speaking Switzerland felt united by a bond of blood and culture, with southern Germany in particular. Firmly entrenched in their Alemannic peculiarities, which are also expressed in their dialect, the German-speaking Swiss believed themselves able to think and feel along with the Germans without having to sacrifice any of their own characteristics or give up their cultural ideal. Many, indeed, condemned the invasion of Belgium, and the Federal Assembly expressed its regret at this violation of Belgian neutrality. But this did not prevent the German Swiss from continuing to believe in Germany.

However, these attitudes of German- and French-speaking Switzerland toward the belligerents were not universal. With a population as racially mixed as the Swiss, it was impossible to define the two camps clearly, either geographically or ethnically. The battle of opinions was further poisoned by an unchecked influx of foreign lies and propaganda. A struggle for the soul of the neutral nation began, resembling an ugly continuation of the war, fought out with pen and ink, on Swiss soil. As had been the case in all previous European wars, now too the followers of the various parties clashed violently in Switzerland. But never had the battle of opinions taken on such passionate extents. Intellectual leaders then spoke up in order to motivate their compatriots to reflection and to help bridge the gap. The speech by Carl Spitteler[1] in particular has become famous. With inner independence, without arrogance, but with humanity and dignity, he outlined the Swiss ideal of neutrality and expressed his sympathy for all belligerent parties.

While both Federal authorities and private citizens made every effort to avoid demonstrations of siding with one of the belligerents, there was, at a very visible position in the Army Command, an incident detrimental to neutrality. Two colonels had regularly supplied the German and Austrian military attachés with the Bulletin of the Army Staff, which contained news of the military operations of the belligerents. This action of the colonels had little objective import, but it caused an uproar of public opinion. The offenders having been punished, the oppressive atmosphere seemed once again cleared. But in 1917 the public learned that the most influential member of the national government, Arthur Hoffmann, had violated the country's neutrality. He had indicated to the Russian revolutionary government that Germany would be interested in a peace agreement with Russia, with mutually satisfactory honorable terms. Motivated by a serious concern about the increasingly critical economic situation in Switzerland, Hoffmann had attempted to shorten the war. Although a neutral State may take measures to bring about peace, it must contact each of the Powers at war; it may not intervene unilaterally in the war policy of one of these Powers. The *Entente* had begun to suspect that the exposed Swiss Magistrate had been asked by the Federal Government to work toward a special peace treaty for Russia. Hoffmann's resignation as well as the swift and clean disposal of this incident prevented a threatening intervention. A further threat to Switzerland was caused by the national strike *(Landesstreik)* in November 1918, at the end of the war. Fearing foreign intervention, the Federal Council mobilized the troops, expelled the Soviet legation, and refused to give in to the strike committee's demands. The strike subsequently collapsed, but some of the demands were soon satisfied by democratic majority decisions.

In spite of such social upheaval, Switzerland did not for a moment interrupt her humanitarian activities, which thus far had been so successful. However much the country may have been divided in her sympathies with the belligerents, she stood united in her desire to help. When a Swiss thinks back to this activity, he does so not with complacent satisfaction about a good deed well done, but with a feeling of profound gratitude for a merciful

---

[1] Carl Spitteler, "Unser Schweizer Standpunkt", in *Gesammelte Werke,* Vol. 8 (Zürich, 1947): 579-5.

Fate that spared his country, surrounded by a flaming ring of nations at war, from armed conflict. He has always regarded his humanitarian activities as a sacred duty. He might have had the quiet hope that with this expression of an active neutrality, he could help to pay off a small portion of the general guilt.

Immediately after the outbreak of the war, several nations entrusted Switzerland with the protection of their citizens in enemy countries. Since this task grew continuously, the Swiss Political Department had to establish a special service for the protection of foreign interests. The Confederation was put to an even greater task with the repatriation of foreign civilians, the exchange of invalid or severely wounded persons, and the internment of invalid prisoners of war. Between 1916 and the end of the war, Switzerland gave shelter to approximately 68,000 internees. The International Red Cross in Geneva accomplished tremendous feats. The city of Geneva, true to its philanthropic tradition, developed widespread activities in international aid. The Committee of the Red Cross employed a veritable army of volunteer workers. Among other things, it set up a clearing-house for military personnel missing in action and prisoners of war. Lists were kept of the dead or imprisoned, inquiries were made concerning missing persons, and families were informed as soon as possible about their whereabouts and their state of health. But the generous charity of the Swiss people was by no means exhausted in these institutions. They regarded it as their privilege to alleviate pain and pursued this task with great dedication. Innumerable charitable organizations were created, each pursuing its own particular goals, helping all those in need, even far into the postwar era.

The Treaty of Versailles, which was celebrated in several Swiss towns by ringing of the church bells, contained several regulations of direct concern to the Confederation: the shipping on the Rhine, the international agreement on the Gotthard railroad, and the neutrality of Northern Savoy. In Article 435, the Treaty Powers recognized an agreement between France and Switzerland, abolishing all regulations pertinent to a neutral zone in Savoy; and the Confederation renounced all rights to a military occupation of Upper Savoy. The new generation in Switzerland regarded this point, to which their forefathers had clung so tenaciously, as a remnant of the past of no political or military value. Motivated by a similar interpretation of her neutrality, Switzerland also denied the request of Austrian Vorarlberg to join the Confederation.

From Absolute to Differential Neutrality

When, toward the end of the war, the ancient idea of a League to unite all peoples on an equal basis began to take shape, it was met with great enthusiasm in Switzerland. It was assumed that, among other factors, Swiss neutrality had played a role in the choice of Geneva as the seat of the League of Nations and the International Labor Office. However, disappointment was great when the text of the League of Nations Covenant was publicized: Large population groups in Switzerland, in criticism of the Covenant, contended that the vanquished were treated too harshly, and that there was no real guarantee of peace. In spite of such serious reservations, the Swiss were willing to participate actively in the establishment of a lasting world peace. But before Switzerland could consider joining the League of Nations, the question of her permanent neutrality had to be settled. No one wished to give up this national maxim, this vital principle which the Confederation had upheld for four centuries. After Switzerland had renounced her right to neutralize Northern Savoy, the other nations recognized Swiss neutrality as an international obligation for the preservation of peace, as laid down in Article 435 of the Treaty of Versailles. Yet Switzerland still requested an official declaration which would detail the rights and the essence of Swiss neutrality within the context of the League of Nations. This was accomplished in 1920, in the London Declaration of the Council of the League of Nations. This Declaration stated that Switzerland, due to her centuries-old tradition, was in a unique situation. It therefore recognized the permanent neutrality of Switzerland and the guaranteed inviolability of her territory, as they had been incorporated into international law by the treaties of 1815, to be justified in the interest of universal peace and as such in accordance with the principles of the League of Nations. The Confederation would not have to participate in military operations; nor would she have to tolerate the passage of foreign troops through her territory, or military preparatory actions on her soil. But she was obligated to participate in the economic sanctions imposed by the League of Nations against a nation that violated the League's principles.

Only on the basis of this special position did the Federal Council see fit to recommend to the people that Switzerland join the international union of nations. The Council had originally intended to join the League of Nations with the proviso that the United States of America (USA) join as well, but it then dropped this clause. Those opposed to joining did not wish to leave the ground of fundamental law, i.e. of indivisible neutrality, and wanted to avoid what might, at any rate, become a moral dependence. They thought it especially embarrassing that the Federal Council had had Swiss neutrality confirmed, as if this maxim did not exist in its own right and volition. The proponents of membership, however, declared that sacrificing Swiss neutrality on the altar of the League of Nations was not at issue.

Rather, the international covenant granted the greatest possible liberty to each member. Neutrality did not mean an egotistic aloofness, but active assistance in the establishment of a new ideal of humanity. Caught up in the postwar atmosphere, with its idealism of the brotherhood of people, they did not believe that the great Powers' former policy of preserving the balance of power would ever be resumed, and that Switzerland would thus find herself regretting the relinquishment of her absolute neutrality. On May 16, 1920 the people voted in favor of joining the League of Nations by 414,830 to 322,937 votes. The majority margin of the Cantons was even slimmer: 11½ to 10½ votes.

Era of Differential Neutrality

Whatever subsequent opinions about Switzerland's accession to the League of Nations may be, one thing is certain: After the great political dangers of the war years, being a member of the international peace organization gave the small Swiss State a welcome feeling of security which it would not have experienced in self-imposed isolation. Switzerland succeeded in contributing to the international policy of solidarity while safeguarding her own interests. This accomplishment is primarily due to the structure of the Swiss Federal State, which is a miniature League of Nations and thus had certain vital qualities in common with the League.

From the outset, Switzerland sought to specify her special neutral position in the Assembly of the League of Nations. In principle, she refused to take any responsibility for actions of the Council of the League of Nations in which she did not participate. Based on her tradition, she furthermore refused to honor any of the territorial guarantees which the League of Nations stipulated in favor of the victorious Powers. Switzerland did find herself in a rather precarious situation whenever the League of Nations had to watch over the implementation of regulations of the Versailles Peace Treaty. On the one hand, Switzerland was not a signatory to the Treaty of Versailles and could thus feel free of all obligations. On the other hand, being a member of the League, she was obliged to display solidarity in her actions. Switzerland attempted to define her neutral position clearly in view of this ambivalent situation, which had to lead to compromises.

It was a natural consequence of her neutrality that Switzerland concerned herself primarily with those tasks of the League of Nations devoted to the expansion of international relations under international law, and that she stayed aloof from everything pertaining to the system of sanctions against those States which violated the League's Covenant. The League of Nations had established a complicated process of arbitration for the settling of disputes, but its arbitration was not binding. Switzerland, however, regarded binding arbitration as the best guarantee for a lasting peace. The Swiss delegation tirelessly promoted the concept of obligatory settlements of international conflicts on the basis of established arbitration procedures. Above all, Switzerland endeavored to sign bilateral agreements with other States on the question of arbitration. She was thus the first member State of the League of Nations which, in 1920, signed agreements on obligatory arbitration with Denmark and with Poland.

Her attitude in the so-called Vilna Conflict is characteristic of the position of neutral Switzerland within the League of Nations. In 1920 Polish irregulars had occupied the city of Vilna, in violation of the cease-fire agreement with Lithuania. In order to settle the dispute, the Council of the League of Nations intended to hold a referendum in Vilna under the supervision of international troops. The Belgian, British, and Spanish contingents were to march to Vilna via Switzerland, Austria and Czecho-slovakia. On the basis of the London Declaration, Switzerland categorically refused any passage of the troops. She thus avoided a potentially dangerous precedent and demonstrated unambiguously that the League of Nations could not set foot on Swiss soil in any of its military operations, regardless of their purpose.

When neighboring Austria, threatened by financial ruin, needed financial assistance, Switzerland did emerge from her political reserve; as was dictated by her neutrality, however, avoiding any international obligations. It is also understandable that Switzerland, on the question of Germany's accession to the League of Nations, departed from her usual political reservations. It was most desirable for Switzerland to see her most powerful neighbor as a member of the great international peace organization of which she herself was a member. Switzerland regarded as one of her most important tasks in the League of Nations to work for its universality. Subscribing to an international agreement such as the Kellogg Pact, which declared war an invalid means of national policy, was not in violation of her neutrality, for the principles of this declaration of peace were the very ones that Switzerland represented.

Switzerland was, of course, able to participate fully in all humanitarian endeavors of the League of Nations without compromising her neutrality. She was a member of the Commission on Hygiene as well as of the Commissions on Intellectual Collaboration, the Restriction of Drug Traffic, the White Slave Traffic, and the Repatriation of Prisoners of War from Russia and Siberia; she was active in the International Labor Office and in a number of economic and cultural undertakings. Furthermore, Switzerland provided the League of Nations with a number of outstanding experts for the solution of difficult problems. These persons acted and carried out their assignments on an unofficial, personal basis, and not as official representatives of Switzerland.

The withdrawal of Hitler's Germany from the Disarmament Conference and from the League of Nations in 1933 upset Switzerland in her participation in the League. Although she was not directly affected by Germany's step, it did mean a new menace to her, if only for geographical reasons. She sought to meet it by a strengthened national defense. Her relations with Germany remained correct, but were overshadowed by a press conflict in the following year, when the German government banned the major Swiss newspapers from Germany. Switzerland protested passionately, citing freedom of the press, and resisting too extensive an interpretation of her neutrality. The responsible leader of Swiss foreign policy supported this point of view in the following significant statement: "Neutrality does not refer to individuals, but to the State. Neutrality means the intention not to side with any of the belligerents. The question of individual or even collective sympathies or antipathies has no relevance to the problem of neutrality."

A major concern of the Swiss Federal Government was maintaining good relations with neighboring Fascist Italy. In late 1924 it signed an arbitration agreement with Italy. But relations with Italy were put to the test during the Ethiopian conflict. The question was whether or not Switzerland would join in the blockade that the League of Nations imposed against Italy in 1935. On the one hand, as a member of the League of Nations, Switzerland was bound by its Covenant to participate in economic sanctions. On the other hand, to take politically non-neutral measures against a friendly neighbor seemed unwise, not only for reasons of state, but also because of a deep-seated respect for neutrality rooted in a long tradition. This situation presented Swiss foreign policy with one of its most delicate tasks. The Swiss Delegate to the Assembly of the League of Nations stated that, in principle, Switzerland recognized her obligation to participate in economic and financial sanctions, but that she also must live up to her axiom of neutrality. In accordance with this point of view, the Confederation joined in the embargo on the export of arms; but following the old Swiss tradition, she imposed the embargo on both belligerent parties, that is on Ethiopia as well. Switzerland also participated in the refusal of credits to Italy and in the export embargo on goods vital to the war effort; but she refused to participate in the boycott of Italian goods and the interruption of trade relations.

Concerning her relations with Russia, Switzerland had persistently refused to establish diplomatic relations with the Soviet Republic ever since the latter had been founded. However, starting in the mid-thirties, she did indicate on various occasions that it would be desirable to see the situation come to an end soon.

The Spanish Civil War was indicative of the interpretation of neutrality held by large portions of the population. It showed that many groups did not yet understand the policy which prohibited the neutral Confederation from taking an official stand on the conflicts of foreign nations. Many Swiss demanded that the Federal Council maintain diplomatic relations only with the Spanish Republic as the sole legitimate government of Spain, and not with Franco's regime. This interpretation echoes the nineteenth-century ideology of the solidarity of peoples. However, the responsible leaders of Swiss foreign policy did not let domestic trends interfere with their strictly neutral course.

During the thirties, the initial signs of disintegration of the League of Nations increased in number and frequency. The League's failure in the Sino-Japanese conflict and the dismal outcome of the Disarmament Conference of 1932-1934 were the early harbingers of impending doom. The more this disintegration progressed, the less could the small Swiss nation expect protection from the international organization. Therefore, Switzerland had to be increasingly careful not to be drawn into any international entanglements, to remain strictly neutral in respect to the political blocs which had begun to form among the great Powers, and to rely primarily on her own resources. This attitude meant the abandonment of differential neutrality and a return to integral neutrality.

In 1937, after the sanctions against Italy had been lifted, the Swiss generally began to suspect that the League of Nations could not, in this crisis of its basic tenet of collective security, give sufficient protection to the small Swiss nation. This view was confirmed by statements of such foreign statesmen as the British Prime Minister Neville Chamberlain. It is obvious that the *Anschluss* of Austria by Germany in 1938 only served to accelerate Switzerland's endeavors to return to her absolute neutrality. Thanks to Motta's wise and painstaking preparations, this goal was reached on May 14, 1938. On this date, the League of Nations adopted a resolution stating, in part: "The League of Nations . . . taking into consideration the unique position of Switzerland which derives from her perpetual neutrality . . . accepts and acknowledges the intention proclaimed by Switzerland that, on the basis of her perpetual neutrality, she will henceforth cease to participate in the implementation of sanctions, as regulated by the Covenant, and declares that she will not be required to do so." After an eighteen-year journey in the increasingly stormy waters of collective security, Switzerland thus withdrew to her original harbor, a mountainous island of absolute neutrality. There, in a position of her own choosing, relying solely on her own resources, she awaited the oncoming ill tides.

Preparing to Defend Neutrality

At the outbreak of World War II, Switzerland was better prepared, economically and spiritually, than she had been in 1914, but not militarily. For some years, the Confederation had been forced to note with growing disappointment that no one in the world truly believed in collective security and that, therefore, no one dared make decisive armament reductions. The failure of the Disarmament Conference seemed to indicate that the right of the stronger would once again prevail in the world, triumphing over written guarantees. When Switzerland's neighbors to the north and south both transformed themselves into gigantic military camps, pervaded by a nationalistic spirit of aggressiveness, the Swiss people had to accept the painful truth that strengthening their national defense was one of the country's foremost tasks. The federation bought weapons and ammunition, extended in 1935 the period of basic training for recruits (which met with general approval): requested considerable credits for further acquisitions of material, and promulgated new military regulations in 1938. Two years earlier, the Swiss people had already subscribed to a defense loan in the amount of 322 million Swiss francs and had thus expressed their unequivocal will to defend their country. These were enormous sacrifices, considering that the small population was plagued by economic crises. These plebiscites were regarded everywhere as an expression of an unconditional readiness to defend the country, a feeling to which the Social Democrats subscribed as well.

Economic and military preparations were closely linked. The experience from World War I indicated that the landlocked country, poor in raw materials and surrounded by belligerents, would suffer severe limitations. Hence, government warehouses and private pantries were stocked up. These measures of an economic "die-hard policy" in preparation for an economic siege made it possible for Switzerland to survive the duration of the war. It was the head of the Economics Department who said, after the German invasion of Austria, "Let it be known to all nations: Whoever honors our sovereignty and leaves us in peace, is our friend. But whoever should attack our independence and our national integrity, will provoke war. We Swiss will not go begging."

National defense was also activated at the intellectual level as the pan-German ideology of National Socialism grew ever stronger. Switzerland's Constitution, which had been taken for granted for all too long, was reconsidered, and its basic elements re-examined. This led to a process of serious national self-examination. The people descended into the depths of the past in order to find the bond linking Yesterday with Today and to see where fresh energies could prepare for the future. The Swiss form of democracy was seen as a fusion of Swiss liberties with the modern, rational concept of freedom. The Swiss democracy, which had grown organically close to the people, was thus separated from the other continental democracies. Federalism—uniting the individual States, different in culture and size, granting equal rights to each, and thus greatly facilitating a solution to the minority problems—was regarded as the form of government most closely related to the essence of the Swiss nation as founded by the will of the people: unity in diversity. When it became known that Switzerland was considered part of the German Reich in German training regulations, and that official German maps incorporated Switzerland into the Reich territory, the Confederation doubled its efforts to battle this impudence. The various groups of the population were united in this struggle, and the people's moral resistance was mobilized. The German Chancellor's solemn declaration in the spring of 1937, which guaranteed Switzerland's inviolability, was received with unconcealed mistrust; the German *Führer* had discredited himself by too many broken promises. The Alemannic Swiss cultivated their dialect and their native literature with increased consciousness and care. Romansh, designated an Italian dialect by nationalistic Italian linguists, was elevated to be the fourth national language of Switzerland by a plebiscite in 1939. The most striking manifestation of the national spiritual resistance must have been the great National Exhibit in Zürich in 1939. Here, the person in the street could study pictures from Switzerland's past, could sense a meaningful connection between the Christian Cross, the Swiss Cross, and the Red Cross, could find pleasure in the value of the fruits of Swiss labor, and find solace in the pictures of the Swiss soldier donning his tunic with grim determination. It was as if the country's living traditions were once again reaffirmed.

Neutrality During the Second World War

When the war broke out, the Federal Assembly elected the General with only a few dissenting votes.[2] It seemed like a rejection of German militarism that Henri Guisan, from Canton Vaud (Waadt), was elected Supreme Commander of the Swiss Armed Forces with 204 out of 229 votes.

---

[2] The Swiss army is without a General except in times of war. On such occasions, when military preparations are required for defense of the nation against any threat to her security, a General is elected by the Federal Assembly.

Throughout the period of mobilization General Guisan was able to retain the sympathies of all parts of the country and of all classes of the population. To the Swiss people he was the embodiment of their will to defend themselves. The Federal Assembly announced the Confederation's determination "to maintain neutrality by all means and under any circumstances." Late in August 1939 the Federal Council issued a declaration of neutrality to all nations, which had almost the same wording as the one of 1914, and ordered mobilization. Two days later, a decree on general industrial conscription followed. Switzerland was firmly determined not to be drawn into any conflict.

At the outbreak of the war 400,000 men were under arms. The number of soldiers increased in time to 850,000, including members of the Auxiliary Forces and the Local Guards.[3] There were never less than 100,000 men mobilized, a very impressive figure in view of a total population of only 4 million. The other nations began to realize that Switzerland would give her utmost in any battle that might be forced upon her. At the beginning of the war, the situation was similar to that of 1914: Switzerland was surrounded by belligerents and by countries which had not yet taken sides. Accordingly, Switzerland concentrated her troops on her northern and western borders and stationed smaller contingents in the south and the east. The general military situation changed drastically with the collapse of France (bringing to Switzerland the internment of approximately 50,000 French and Polish troops) and with Italy's entry into the war. Switzerland now found herself encircled by a single belligerent, the Axis Powers. Startled, the Confederation wondered how to hold in check the gigantic armies of tanks which rolled over any artificial obstacle, what to put up against the incredible numbers of fighter aircraft that the Axis Powers employed, and against the paratroops and the airborne troops. The civilian population of a few particularly exposed areas began to flee to the interior, but neither disorder nor panic ensued. It was generally known that should one of the belligerents violate Swiss neutrality, it had been hoped to find an ally in the other party at war, and that the national defense could be linked up to a European front. But this possibility existed no longer.

Within a short time, General Guisan totally reorganized the Swiss defense plan, abandoning traditional concepts and incorporating innovative ideas. He assembled the core of the troops in the interior in order to be able to defend Swiss independence for as long as possible in the Alps, while

---

[3] Thus the Swiss put over 40% of their entire male population, of all ages, under arms at their peak mobilization, a truly astounding figure. A comparable figure for America today would be over 55 million men under arms. - LB Rohrbach.

temporarily giving up the borders and the plains which were regarded as the country's ramparts. The so-called redoubt (*réduit*): a concept from the theory of fortification, signifies a fortress which is established in the interior of another one, with the purpose of increasing the defense possibilities of the main fortress and enabling the defenders finally to drive out the aggressor. In a battle with such a superior enemy as the Axis powers, it was a realistic concession to give up a part of the country in order to save the whole in the end. That was the purpose of a relatively weak outer defense on the borders, and a much stronger inner defense in the *réduit national*. The idea of the *réduit*, which was never put to its final test, gave courage to many faint-hearted in the darkest hours. The population viewed the fortress in the Alps with pride and confidence and believed in its invincibility. No one abroad doubted the Swiss army's determination, or its readiness to fight. Only when the German armies returned home defeated, and a desperate, last-ditch defense effort was begun in Germany, did the Swiss troops leave the mountains and once again protect the borders against possible invaders.

The German army command repeatedly worked out detailed plans for an invasion of Switzerland. It was intended that the German troops should advance across the Rhine, occupy the capital, Bern, and take the entire country from there. In the spring and early fall of 1940, the danger of the implementation of such plans seemed the greatest. After the Germans had successfully invaded France and had started the Russian campaign, the invasion of Switzerland was no longer of interest to Germany. General Guisan's repeated threats to blow up the Gotthard and Simplon rail links were effective, for these links were indispensable for the Axis partners' coal-supply lines. The Germans also had to consider what an invasion would cost them: As matters stood, the Swiss were supplying them with war materials and granting them large credits, as well as taking care of their own food supplies. After an invasion, the Swiss would not be able to supply the Germans with arms, due to destroyed factories and ensuing raids by Allied bombers. Switzerland would no longer receive food supplies from the Allies and would have to rely for food on the Germans, who hardly had enough for themselves. An invasion would thus bring neither military nor economic advantage. After the American and British armies landed in France and in North Africa, Germany was totally absorbed in her defense and could not afford yet another enemy, however small.

A final incident bringing military danger occurred at Switzerland's northern border toward the end of the war, in the spring of 1945. It was feared that mutinous troops, separated from the main body of the German army, would try to invade Switzerland. The French army commander, de

Lattre de Tassigny, who had been marching up the Rhone Valley with his troops, came to the rescue. He marched along Switzerland's northern border to Lake Constance and thus gave the country a feeling of security, both from the German soldiers and from the Russians who were advancing toward Lake Constance. It seemed dangerous to have Russian military forces in the immediate neighborhood, as Switzerland still did not maintain normal relations with the Soviet Union. But this danger passed, and Swiss independence was maintained throughout the entire war. The neutrality of Swiss air space was violated many times: at first, mainly by German fighter aircraft, but later, predominantly by British and American bombers. Several air raids caused considerable damage, the worst case of this kind claiming 40 lives in Schaffhausen in 1944. Switzerland, too, was familiar with total blackouts and air-raid sirens.

As during World War I, Switzerland again had to struggle hard for economic survival. With all her might she sought to stay out of the blockades and counter-blockades of the belligerents and to keep out of their economic regimentation. Threatened with economic suffocation by the Axis Powers, she had to supply them with food, industrial goods, and, above all, war materials. But even under the most severe pressure she did not abandon the neutral principle of mutuality and of equal treatment of the belligerents. In spite of an increasing shortage of means of transportation, she insisted on being allowed to export goods vital to the war effort into Allied countries through German-occupied territories. It was only through such services to both sides that Switzerland was able to obtain the raw materials required to keep her industry going and to overcome economically critical situations. Her trade with foreign countries was regulated by increasingly complex treaties, but Switzerland was never compelled to make political concessions or to export a male work force. The battles of that time were not fought by the army in the field, but by Swiss delegates at the conference table in tough economic negotiations with other nations. The end of the war brought proof that Switzerland's attitude, approved of by both belligerent parties and consonant with international law, was beneficial not only to herself but all of Europe. After the cease-fire, Switzerland could immediately place her undamaged economic potential at the disposal of the European reconstruction that was so urgently needed.

In order to survive economically, the Swiss had to open up new sources of food production at home. A complete change of emphasis in agricultural production had become necessary. Switzerland's export-oriented production had to be changed to a versatile system of farming and cattle husbandry to serve domestic needs. Under the systematic guidance of the Agricultural Commission headed by F. Wahlen, pastures were converted into meadows and meadows into fields; forests were cleared, and the yield of the soil was increased. It was said the Swiss had to kneel in the furrow if he were not to kneel to a foreign master. *Cultiver la terre, c'est sauver la patrie* ("Cultivating the soil means saving the country") people said in French-speaking Switzerland. All men who could be spared by the military were assigned to agricultural production. By producing exclusively for domestic use, agriculture succeeded in providing food for the population of the Swiss industrial State. Of course, food allocations for the individual citizen were strictly rationed, just as they were in the countries at war. Soon a large part of the economy was controlled by Federal and cantonal authorities—a control which extended to even the smallest detail. A large majority of the Swiss population favored this state-controlled economy. Through this system, which permitted private enterprise in a limited scope, the government not only protected citizens from the dire hazards of wartime, but it also banned the threat of social upheavals such as the National Strike of 1918. Compensations for wage deficiencies paid to soldiers on active duty and to their families also helped to preserve social peace. The farmers and laborers fought this economic battle together. Although the industrial population was most severely affected by price increases, the contrast between city and country was never as sharp as it had been occasionally in the past. An alienation between these two basic elements of the Swiss population did not occur.

Although there had been a deep rift between German-speaking and French-speaking Switzerland during World War I, the two linguistically different parts of the country stood united in their resistance to the racial delusions and power concepts that pressed in upon the country during World War II, from whichever side they might come. The Swiss people clung to their federal structure, firmly rooted in their belief in the individual destiny of the part within the whole, and in their insight into the profound significance of the federal constitutional organization. The diversity of their cultural existence had made the Swiss aware of the great values of individual riches. The Confederation did not wish to standardize these diversified forces; she saw her task as uniting them in a common consciousness of being Swiss. The spiritual and cultural ties between German-speaking Switzerland and neighboring Germany, which heretofore had been so close, began to slacken. The passionately democratic Canton of Ticino let its relations with neighboring Fascist Italy cool, and since the establishment of the Vichy regime in France, French-speaking Switzerland turned away from her western neighbor. This cultural and material self-reliance was not regarded as a permanent ideal, but only as a temporary emergency measure.

National Socialism tried everything in its power to infiltrate Switzerland with its ideals in preparation for the *Anschluss*. Organizations covertly distributed prohibited propaganda material; so-called "officials" of the German consulates kept records on the political attitudes of Swiss citizens; and spies ferreted out military and economic secrets. However, because of Switzerland's healthy resistance, National Socialism, which was systematically organizing treason, could win very few followers in the Confederation. Blinded by the false glitter of the new German ideals, or possibly enticed by the promise of a traitor's reward, a few stray souls did condescend to do henchman's duties for the enemy by preparing acts of sabotage. Seventeen traitors were court-martialed and executed by firing squads. In comparison with such other countries as Holland, Belgium, Denmark, and Norway, Switzerland had a much smaller number of traitors. Switzerland did have a very dangerous fifth column such as had been present in all the countries Hitler had overrun and which had prepared the way for his takeover. But all parties publicly declared their abhorrence of these foreign doctrines and their adherence to the ideals of their own country. Its liberties seemed to be the best shield against dictatorships of any form or origin. The truce among the parties and their willingness to cooperate was manifest in the admission of the Social Democrats to the Swiss executive organ, the Federal Council. The citizens concerned themselves more and more seriously with the further development of social reform, promoting progress toward a welfare state in the Confederation. Thus all parties were engaged in constructive cooperation. This united front within the country was the most effective defense. As history shows, Switzerland succumbed to a foreign aggressor only when domestic squabbles disturbed her defense, when Swiss citizens maintained treacherous contact with the enemy.

In order to remove any doubts at home and abroad as to the attitude of the governmental and military authorities, the following declaration was issued in 1940: "Should news be disseminated by radio, leaflets or any other means, which cast doubt upon the determination of the Federal Council and the Army Command to defend the country, such news is to be considered inventions of enemy propaganda. Our country will defend herself again any aggressor and to the bitter end." In spite of this official reinforcement of the people's psychological resistance, quite a few Swiss citizens succumbed to the shock evoked everywhere by Hitler's *blitzkriegs,* especially the one in western Europe. In the unfortunate summer of 1940 the situation of the world seemed desperate: France, to whom Switzerland had planned to turn in case of a German attack, was overrun from the outside, defeated from the inside by rapidly deteriorating circumstances, and forced to surrender;

Holland, Belgium, Luxembourg, and Denmark were overrun, Poland and Norway conquered; Italy had entered the war at the side of her Axis partner, and Russia was in alliance with Germany. Only England continued to fight, but she was retreating to her island. Some influential personalities already raised their defeatist voices and advocated economic and political readjustment. Evil rumors spread through the country, intensifying this war of nerves and having a discouraging effect. An unfortunate radio address by the President of the Confederation, M. Pilet, disconcerted the citizens even further. However, the strong reaction evoked by all these adversities is a worthy testimony to the steadfastness and soundness of popular feeling in the Confederation. This attitude was also supported by the unshakable determination of the General. In late July, General Guisan summoned the high-ranking troop commanders to the Rütli for a report, "to listen to the mysterious call which emanates from this place." In a courageous speech he drove an attitude of unyielding resistance into the minds of his listeners. The General's words seemed like the people's answer to the somewhat defeatist effect of the President's speech and to the impertinence of the cocky conquerors. Subsequently, the mass phenomenon of defeatism all but disappeared. In 1942, in a special decree, the Federal Council made subject to punishment any propaganda "aimed at sacrificing the neutrality of the country."

Only reluctantly, under the pressure of the gigantic German armies, did Switzerland submit to a number of restrictions on her freedom. Although it is natural that in times of crisis, a democracy will delegate certain rights to a small group of men authorized to act quickly, it is dangerous to relinquish one's liberties for a long time. How two-edged such a defensive weapon can be, was shown when the freedom of the press was limited by the introduction of censorship. Its purpose was to prevent provocation of the Germans through attacks in the Swiss newspapers, which freely expressed their opinions. But this also held the danger that the people's will to defend themselves would be weakened if news about German military operations was suppressed. So the restriction of this freedom as well as the measures taken by the censorship authorities repeatedly caused passionate discussions. In spite of the censorship, the press of all political parties related all significant news items to the public. It was generally acknowledged that in a democracy such as Switzerland, foreign policy must not be excluded from public discussion, and that the neutral country, too, should claim the privilege of forming her own opinion on world events.

The prohibition of the Communist party (which was promulgated before the outbreak of the war) and of the Fascist front met with almost unanimous approval. In these times of national struggle for existence, political parties that counted on foreign assistance to achieve power seemed to be guilty of moral treason. Even the democratic and neutral State must use repressive measures to protect its rights and liberties.

There were, however, differences of opinion in Switzerland with regard to the exercise of the right of asylum. The number of immigrants, which had already been considerable in 1933, now took on unprecedented proportions. The Swiss population would have liked to open up the country's borders to take in the many who merely wanted to save their lives, if nothing else, from the atrocities of their persecutors. Yet the authorities already warned of the "overcrowded boat" and pointed out the "limits of what is acceptable in admitting refugees." But during the most difficult times, Switzerland gave shelter to more than 100,000 immigrants, in spite of threats of the German tyrants.

The Confederation regarded it as her special duty and the privilege of the Neutral to alleviate suffering inflicted by the war, as much as she could and as was possible within the scope of the general principles of international law. Next to numerous private charities, next to the Red Cross and its various auxiliary organizations, in particular the Children's Relief Organization[4], mention should be made of the services rendered by Swiss authorities to the belligerents, especially the representation of numerous foreign interests in enemy territory. Here Switzerland faced some very difficult tasks.

The crowning glory to Swiss charitable activities was the creation of the "Swiss National Fund for the Relief of War Victims." The members of the Federal Council unanimously approved an initial contribution of 100 million Swiss francs to the Fund; it reached 250 million Swiss francs by 1948. Faithful to the traditional principle of neutrality, this aid benefited victims from all the nations at war: France, Italy, Austria, Germany, Belgium, Holland, Luxembourg, Norway, England, Finland, Poland, Czechoslovakia, Hungary, Yugoslavia, Albania, Greece, Rumania, and Bulgaria. Food, clothes, shoes, medication, tools, building supplies, agricultural tools, and seeds were distributed; emergency shelters and workshops were constructed; veterinary, surgical, orthopedic and technical missions were organized; and tens of thousands of tubercular adults, as well as children threatened by the disease, and invalids, were hospitalized in Swiss sanatoria.

When in 1945 the weapons finally fell silent in the world, a sigh of relief could be heard throughout the country. Switzerland could say that she had kept the promise made in her declaration of neutrality in 1939. She

---

[4] *Kinderhilfswerk.*

welcomed the end of the war with a feeling of having been freed from a nightmare, the pressure of which had oppressed her for years. Now she could come out of her forced isolation and gradually resume her natural, close relations with the free nations. The resumption of her relations with Russia, which had been interrupted since 1921, was in accordance with the neutral principle of equal attitudes toward all nations and also took into account the gigantic shift of power in Europe. Switzerland was ready and willing to cooperate sincerely in the new community of nations which was to be established in a world that had just undergone an ordeal; for she hoped that the ultimate purpose of the new world order would not mean that a few great Powers would subjugate the world and that the small nations would have to give up their sovereignty and their own way of life. Fully aware of the high value of neutrality, both the government and the people agreed that the political maxim of Swiss independence, tested and proven through the centuries, should not be relinquished under any circumstances. Switzerland would join the new security organization, the United Nations, while maintaining her perpetual neutrality. In fact, there is hardly a European State whose foreign policy contains such an old principle.[5]

However, neutrality had a bad name. In a battle for life or death, the neutral State cannot do right by either of the belligerents; it is threatened and mistreated by both. Switzerland found it very difficult to make other nations realize the national and supranational meaning of the principle on which her foreign policy is founded. But during the postwar years, she gradually succeeded in breaking out of her isolation and in regaining her international prestige.

Translated from the German by Ulrike E. Lieder. Reprinted by permission from *Modern Switzerland*. Edited by Murray Luck (Palo Alto, CA: The Society for the Promotion of Science and Scholarship, 1978): 419-438.

---

[5] For secondary sources see Edgar Bonjour, Swiss *Neutrality Its History and Meaning*. 2nd edition. London 1952. Edgar Bonjour. *Geschichte der schweizerischen Neutralität*. 9 vols. Basel 1970-76. 1st-6th editions. Daniel Frei, *Neutralität—Ideal oder Kalkül?* Frauenfeld 1967.

VI: BETWEEN HAMMER AND ANVIL

Neutrality and the Necessities of Trade

Heinz K. Meier

Switzerland depended on its foreign trade not only for the feeding and clothing of its inhabitants but also for the employment of its labor force. Swiss industries could offer work only if they received from abroad all those raw materials which were unavailable in the country itself and if they could sell a considerable part of their products in foreign countries. Without employment the workers would lose the means for maintaining their families and become discouraged, dissatisfied, and politically unruly. On the other hand, as long as steady work was available, hardships such as the stringent rationing of food, clothing apparel, and fuel, the blackout of the country, increased military service, and rises in prices, could be taken in stride. The Federal Council remembered well that widespread unemployment had been an important contributing factor to the general strike at the end of World War I, and it was determined to do its utmost not to let things drift toward a similar crisis. To maintain full employment in the country was one of the foremost objectives of Swiss trade policy during World War II, at least equal in significance to the objective of securing an adequate supply of food and fodder.

Neutrality Applied to Commerce

The best way to achieve that goal was to maintain commercial relations which were as normal as possible with both belligerent camps. Although foreign trade is not an integral part of neutrality in a technical sense, since neutrality is a political-military concept and not an economic one, it is obvious that a country in Switzerland's position could not afford to indulge in any favoritism. Favoring one side at the expense of the other would not only interfere with the Swiss claim of strict neutrality, it would also endanger its independence. The Swiss maintained that they fulfilled their obligations of economic neutrality as long as deliveries made to either belligerent were met by concessions of equal value by that belligerent, so that the Swiss services did not substantially surpass the economic performance of the other nation in favor of Switzerland. That was the basic principle to which Switzerland tried to adhere throughout the war. It did not aspire to maintain the same volume of trade with the Allies as it did with Germany. That simply was not possible. What it did was to make sure that the value of its exports to Germany was not substantially higher than the value of German exports to Switzerland and that its exports to the Allies were compensated for by Allied goods.

The Swiss clung to that ingenious interpretation of the word "normal" for a long time. The overall war trade balance of Switzerland showed that imports from Axis countries reached the value of 7.1 billion francs, while exports to those countries had the considerably lower value of 5.3 billion francs. The corresponding figures for trade with the Allies showed 2 billion francs worth of imports and 1.7 billion francs of exports.[1] For the Allies, there was nothing "normal" in the fact that the Swiss war trade volume with the Axis countries increased considerably over what it had been in the immediate prewar years and that it was so much greater than the Swiss trade volume with them. They came to see Switzerland's export policy as a clear case of aiding and abetting their enemy and eventually closed their ears to the Swiss claim that Switzerland received more goods from the Axis countries than it delivered to them.

War conditions made existing trade agreements and tariff regulations obsolete. Blockade and counter blockade took their place. The Allies used the means of blockade first and foremost to control and restrict imports to Switzerland. By imposing all kinds of conditions on the granting of export licenses and navicerts, they tried to reduce Swiss trade with their enemy. That represented a new twist in economic warfare, an attempt by their own blockade to put pressure on a neutral government to persuade it to modify its policy toward Nazi Europe. The Axis powers responded by putting up a counter blockade. Switzerland was very sensitive to that, especially after June, 1940, when it was almost surrounded by Axis controlled territory. Germany as it turned out, was much less preoccupied with economic warfare than the Allies and made a suprisingly ineffective use of its stranglehold.

Nevertheless Switzerland, caught between the two belligerent camps, was in a very precarious position. With extraordinary skill the Swiss managed to navigate between this modern-day Scylla and Charybdis by

---

[1] Heinrich Homberger, "Minister Dr. Hans Sulzer zum Gedächtnis", in *Schweizer Monatshefte,* 39 Januar, 1960): Sonderbeilage, 7-8. The general remarks are based on Hanspeter Brunner, *10 Jahre schweizerisch-amerikanische Handelsbeziehungen 1936-1945* (Zürich, 1946): 22-33.

keeping up an almost uninterrupted series of simultaneous trade negotiations with both belligerent camps. As the war progressed, mistrust of Swiss actions and policy increased on both sides. The fear that concessions granted to Switzerland might help the enemy in one way or another grew and so did the demands made on the Swiss.

The fall of France in June, 1940 markedly increased Switzerland's economic dependence on Germany. Before the collapse of France, Swiss exports of weapons and ammunitions, for example, were almost equally divided among the warring camps. Of the 64 million francs worth of weapons exports estimated for 1939, 42 million went to France and Great Britain. In 1940 the figures were, in millions of Swiss francs, France 26, Great Britain 21, Germany 33, and Italy 34; in 1941, Germany 122, Italy 61, and the Allied countries 0.[2] The figures demonstrate the fateful consequences of the German victories in the West. Since Germany controlled the supply and delivery of raw materials and fuels indispensable to Swiss industry, the Swiss were forced to tie their economy more closely to that of the main Axis power. Despite this fact, Britain continued to treat the Swiss Confederation gently. A working agreement based on the war trade agreement of the preceding April was negotiated in London in October, 1940; by it Britain agreed to relax the blockade and to allow Switzerland to import certain essential commodities under the "navicert" system. Navicerts were a kind of commercial passport issued by British officials to certify that goods sent to European neutrals were not destined for Germany. They were granted on a scale which would allow the neutrals to import sufficient quantities for their own domestic requirements. The concessions granted to Switzerland in October, 1940 were to be canceled if it became evident that the Swiss re-exported imported goods, or if the goods were retained in Italy or Vichy France. Under certain conditions Switzerland was permitted to export to the Axis powers goods which were manufactured from raw materials that had come from abroad with navicerts. The Swiss had argued in London that a disregard of their needs would mean the loss of all bargaining power with the Germans. If they were not allowed to trade with other countries they would inevitably succumb completely to German economic domination. In London the belief persisted that "it was on balance advantageous to maintain an economic link with the Swiss." Thus "the proposal to sever economic connections with Switzerland and to

---

[2] W.N. Medlicott, *The Economic Blockade*, I (London, 1952): 585-592. Medlicott has the figures from Jakob Ragaz, "Die Ausfuhr von Kriegsmaterial aus der Schweiz während des Zweiten Weltkrieges", in *Der Aufbau,* April 8, 1949, 118-119.

include her in the blockade of the Axis was frequently considered, and always postponed."[3]

Continuing Trade with the United States

The arrangements, surprisingly enough, permitted the continuance of a lively U.S.- Swiss trade in both directions until 1942 and for the exporting of Swiss goods to the United States all through the war. The figures of Table 1 (next page) are instructive, although the fact must be kept in mind that transportation and insurance costs rose rapidly, accounting for a considerable part of the money paid for raw materials and manufactured products. The ability of Switzerland to continue exporting its goods throughout the war sometimes caused astonishment in the United States. Yet most of the goods exported—watches, textiles, and chemicals—were of little bulk and transporting them was a relatively minor problem. In the early months of the war most of the goods were transported to Savona, near Genoa, where they were loaded on Greek ships chartered by Switzerland. After the occupation of Greece, the Swiss took over the chartered vessels and added tonnage from ships of Honduran, Panamanian, and other registry, creating a merchant marine of more than 60,000 gross tons. Both belligerents, including the United States, declared that they would respect the immunity of those ships. With the Allied invasion of North Africa late in 1942 the Mediterranean ports of Savona and Marseilles became unusable, and the Swiss had to ship their goods by rail and truck through Vichy France and Spain to the Portuguese ports of Lisbon, Oporto, Faro, and Bilbao. A fleet of one hundred diesel trucks, converted so that they could use charcoal for fuel, and ninety thousand railroad cars, well marked with large Swiss crosses, carried on the trade against many obstacles and great odds. In the Portuguese ports the goods were loaded on Swiss owned merchant ships. The Germans were relatively generous in giving permission to let the goods pass through their counter blockade, though their restrictive measures frequently bothered the Swiss negotiators in Berlin and Bern.[4] Thus it was possible for Macy's department store to sell typewriters made in Switzerland in the midst of war and for many other retailers to deal in

---

[3] Arnold and Veronica M. Toynbee, eds., *The War and the Neutrals. Survey of International Affairs 1939-1946* (London, 1956): 76, 19-20, 217-218. See also Adolphe Vaudaux, *Blockade und Gegenblockade. Handelspolitische Sicherung der schweizerischen Ein- und Ausfuhr im Zweiten Weltkrieg* (Zürich, 1948).

[4] Paul Erdman, *Swiss-American Economic Relations, Their Evolution in an Era of Crises* (Basel: Kylos Verlag, 1959), 90-91, describes the measures taken by Switzerland to keep its goods moving through blockade and counter blockade.

Swiss watches and clocks. When a Burbank, California, jeweler announced the sale of a stock of five hundred Swiss alarm clocks, people gathered before dawn to await the opening of the shop. The clocks were gobbled up within an hour and the jeweler had the sale of his life.[5]

Table 1: U.S.-SWISS TRADE DURING WORLD WAR II[6]

Years	American products imported to Switzerland (millions of Swiss Francs)	Swiss products exported to the United States (millions of Swiss Francs)
1931/35	SwF 102.8	SwF 60.1
1936/40	131.0	108.6
1941/45	120.2	177.8
1949	132.7	129.7

	Total	Raw Material	Manu-factures	Foods-stuffs	Total	Watches	Chemicals	Textiles
1940	199.2	136.5	41.7	21.0	139.9	50.8%	16.7%	15.4%
1941	151.3	28.9	91.6	30.7	108.0	53.7%	23.7%	10.5%
1942	235.3	18.8	8.9	207.6	102.2	73.6%	11.8%	7.5%
1943	56.4	14.3	3.9	38.2	152.8	74.5%	5.2%	12.5%
1944	21.2	12.2	1.5	7.4	140.8	71.7%	5.6%	16.8%
1945	136.8				385.3			

(Figures in millions of Swiss Francs}

The procedure for importing Swiss products was actually quite complicated. If a United States manufacturer needed a certain kind of Swiss product, he first had to make sure that nothing comparable to it could be found on the American market. He then had to make an application for the product and submit it to the War or Navy Department or any of the other government agencies concerned. The agency discussed the purchase with the Foreign Economic Administration, which supervised the trade agreement with Switzerland. If FEA decided that the product was essential, it informed the British Ministry of Economic Warfare of the intended purchase and notified the American legation in Bern to the same effect. The actual order was then placed through ordinary commercial channels. In

---

[5] "Goods Still Move", in *Business Week,* Aug. 14, 1943, 49-50.
[6] Erdman, *Swiss-American Economic Relations,* 88 and 93; Bolli, *L'aspect horloger, 123.*

Switzerland the Swiss manufacturer would check with the American legation to find out whether the particular deal was permitted by the allied authorities and whether his sale came under the quota of products of stipulated money value for the given period. The American officials would then issue a "Certificate of Origin and Interest", attesting to the fact that the "enemy content" of materials and labor did not surpass a fixed tolerated percentage of the total value of the product. Next, the Swiss trading partner had to get the necessary German papers, the *Geleitschein,* the German equivalent of the navicerts, which authorized the transit of the goods through the counter blockade. Only when and if all those papers had been secured could the product be sent on its way.[7]

Adapting to Economic Warfare

The intricacies, difficulties, and complications inherent in Switzerland's economic position were clearly revealed in the prolonged negotiations which took place almost continually from the middle of 1941. Even before the United States entered the war, it undertook steps which set it well along the road to economic warfare. The most important step was that of blocking the funds of individual countries as part of the establishment of measures of exchange control. An initial, limited foreign exchange control was established in April, 1940, by an executive order. Under it all assets in the United States belonging to persons who resided in occupied Norway and Denmark were frozen. In the next fifteen months President Roosevelt arranged similar measures involving a total of thirty-two countries and seven and a half billion dollars.[8] Executive Order 8785 of June 14, 1941 declared the assets of all continental European countries frozen. The purpose of that sweeping measure was "to prevent the liquidation in the United States of assets looted by duress or conquest", "to prevent the use of the financial facilities of the United States in ways harmful to national defense and other American interests", and "to curb subversive activities in the United States."[9] The measure created considerable consternation in Swiss circles.

---

[7] "Hands Across the Sea", in *Fortune,* 29 (Feb. 1944): 46-47.

[8] Judd Polk, "Freezing Dollars Against the Axis", in *Foreign Affairs,* 20 (Oct. 1941): 112; William L. Langer and S. Everett Gleason, *The Undeclared War 1940-1941* (New York, 1953): 193-194.

[9] White House, Press Release, June 14, 1941, quoted in Erdman, *Swiss-American Economic Relations,* 94.

Felix Somary, the banker and financial expert who had been delegated by the Federal Council to prepare large purchases of American goods in 1938 and 1939, felt strongly that the Swiss government itself was to blame for being included in the measure. He pointed out that Switzerland had made a mistake when it officially took a stand in protecting I.G. Chemie of Basel, a holding company suspected of having intimate ties with the powerful German dye trust I.G. Farben. I.G. Chemie owned a 90% interest in the American firm of General Aniline & Film Co., the second largest United States manufacturer of photographic equipment and the third largest firm making dye-stuffs. Because of its suspected ties with the chemical industry of Nazi Germany the United States government sequestered General Aniline, which led to the diplomatic intervention of the Swiss minister in Washington. Somary contended that although the Basel firm was owned on paper by Swiss citizens, the Americans had a strong case and that the Federal Council had acted unwisely when it decided to intervene. That intervention had given ammunition to certain officials in the Treasury Department who had previously made strenuous efforts to establish exchange controls over all Swiss assets in the United States.[10] There may be considerable truth in this view. The Treasury Department, under Secretary Henry Morgenthau, Jr., had been pressing for the adoption of general measures of exchange control for months, but had been held back by the Department of State which felt that the Treasury was intruding upon its jurisdiction. Obviously, measures such as those advocated by the Treasury were bound to strongly affect the foreign relations of the United States.[11] Yet whether Switzerland would have had a chance to escape inclusion in the executive order of June, 1941 if the Federal Council had not moved in support of the I.G. Chemie of Basel is doubtful.

As it was, the measure had no crippling effect upon Swiss exchange in the United States, because, strictly speaking, it did not freeze the one and a half billion dollars worth of Swiss assets in the United States.[12] What it did was subject those assets to licensing by the Treasury Department. The foreign owners no longer had complete freedom in disposing of their assets, but if such assets were positively identified as neutral, their owners could apply for a "special license" and receive permission to use them under

---

[10] Felix Somary, *Erinnerungen aus meinem Leben,* (Zürich, 1960): 276-277, 280-281.

[11] Langer and Gleason, *The Undeclared War,* 193; John Morton Blum, *Years of Urgency 1938-1941. From the Morgenthau Diaries* (Boston, 1965): 326-337.

[12] Figure of Swiss assets from the table "Property Frozen under Foreign Funds Control as of March 13, 1942", World Peace Foundation, *Documents on American Foreign Relations, 1941-1942,* 752.

Treasury control. A substantial number of the frozen Swiss assets were held by Swiss banks in anonymous numbered accounts. The banks, adhering to Swiss bank secrecy laws, did not reveal the identity of the owners of the accounts despite repeated requests by the Treasury Department. As a consequence the accounts were treated like enemy assets and no privileges regarding their use were extended to them.

General License No. 50 allowed the Swiss government and the Swiss National Bank to perform financial transactions for Swiss nationals with domicile in Switzerland, subject to certain controls. That burdened the exchange with a great deal of red tape, but in practice permitted the continuance of business almost as normal. The main difficulty stemming from the American measure was actually an internal one and had to do with the transfer of funds. In the course of the ensuing years the Swiss National Bank accumulated large amounts of American dollars with which it could do very little since they were not convertible into other currencies. The Swiss franc, on the other hand, became scarce and rose steadily in value as compared to the dollar. In order to retain liquidity of financial assets the Swiss banks under the direction of the National Bank had to devise careful and elaborate schemes of "managing the dollar" *(Dollarbewirtschaftung).*[13]

A little over a month after the announcement of the executive order freezing the assets of continental European countries, the American government issued a blacklist as a further instrument of trade control. Officially called "Proclaimed List of certain Blocked Nationals", it listed the names of people and firms in neutral countries who were dealing with Axis countries and therefore were to be excluded from trade with U.S. firms. Eventually some 1,100 Swiss persons and 1,330 Swiss firms were listed, and the Proclaimed List, together with its British counterpart, the Statutory List, became one of the most effective and most feared tools of economic warfare.[14]

The entry of the United States into the war in December, 1941 had no immediate effect on the volume and character of its trade with Switzerland. The United States had cooperated closely with Great Britain even before the

---

[13] Brunner, *10 Jahre,* 40-55; also Rudolf J. Ernst, *Die schweizerischen Kapitalanlagen in den Vereinigten Staaten* (Zürich, 1943).

[14] Text of Presidential Proclamation of July 17, 1941, in World Peace Foundation, *Documents, 1941-1942,* 752-756; figures from *Neue Zürcher Zeitung,* No. 396, March 6, 1945. In addition to the blacklist the U.S. government maintained an even more voluminous "gray list" containing names of firms *suspected* of trading with the enemy. In contrast to the blacklist the strictly confidential graylist was never made public. It proved to be even more of a nuisance to the neutrals. (Victor Nef to the author, Dec. 13, 1968.)

attack on Pearl Harbor. All that was left to do was to work out the details of administrative arrangements between Washington and London. In view of the experience accumulated by the British Ministry of Economic Warfare, it was decided to make London the center of global economic control. The Board of Economic Warfare in Washington, later renamed the Foreign Economic Administration, would refer applications for export licenses to the Ministry in London which in turn would make its decisions in consultation with representatives of the American embassy.[15] As a consequence, the important and long drawn out negotiations between Switzerland and the Allies, or United Nations as they began to call themselves in the course of the year 1942, took place in London, with Bern and Washington being of secondary importance.

Negotiating in London

In the early spring of 1942 the Swiss sent a mission to London led by Minister Dr. Hans Sulzer and Professor Paul Keller, delegate of the Federal Council in charge of trade agreements and formerly professor at the St. Gallen School of Economics. Sulzer, of the important firm of Sulzer Brothers, had gathered his experience in wartime negotiations during World War I as Swiss minister in Washington, while Keller had served on earlier wartime missions in London. The purpose of the trip was to eliminate obstacles which the British had raised in the wake of the German-Swiss agreement of July 18, 1941. In that fateful agreement Switzerland had received coal, iron, seed potatoes, and other vital goods from Germany and was promised supplies of mineral oils and other important materials from eastern Europe. Furthermore, Switzerland succeeded in loosening the counter-blockade against some of its exports, especially watches for the United States. As a price for those German concessions, Switzerland had to extend clearing credits to Germany for the purchase of Swiss manufactures, a kind of "political life insurance premium" for Switzerland, amounting to 850 million francs by the end of 1942.

The agreement, looked upon as a great achievement by the Swiss, which it was, became a target of criticism and attack by the British.[16] They stopped issuing navicerts for industrial raw materials unless Switzerland

---

[15] A. and V. Toynbee, eds., *The War and the Neutrals,* 59-60.

[16] Homberger, "Minister Dr. Hans Sulzer", 5-7; W.N. Medlicott, *The Economic Blockade,* II (London, 1959): 206-213. See also the confidential report on the domestic situation in Switzerland in *Documents on German Foreign Policy, 1918-1945*, Series D, XIII, 1941, 331-335. This report by an unknown informant stated that popular sentiment in Switzerland "overwhelmingly would like to see an English victory."

furnished them strategic war manufactures. In order to be able to do that, the Swiss had to bargain for German *Geleitscheine,* transit permits, which they did indefatigably. After German willingness in principle had been secured, the matter needed to be finalized with the British. Preliminary talks in the Mixed Commission, a group made up of Swiss officials and Allied representatives in Bern, led to the conclusion that a Swiss mission should be sent to London. The mission became urgent when the British government ruled that no "Certificates of Origin and Interest" for Swiss goods to be exported through the blockade were to be issued in the future if the "enemy content" of those goods, i.e. the Axis material and labor invested in their manufacture, amounted to more than five per cent of their value. That condition dealt a crippling blow to Swiss exports outside Europe, since most Swiss products contained German raw materials. Up to that point the enemy content had been restricted to twenty-five per cent of their value, a condition Switzerland could live with.[17]

The Swiss delegation, which traveled to London by air via Lisbon, expected to have to do much explaining and hard bargaining, but was fairly confident of success. To their dismay, weeks of negotiating stretched into months without producing any tangible results. Hope changed into discouragement as the Allies continuously brought up new points and arguments. By Christmas 1942 the delegates returned to Switzerland, their mission having ended largely in failure. What had happened during those nine long months spent in the bomb-threatened British capital?

When Sulzer and his delegation began their official discussions with the British, headed by Dingle Foot, Parliamentary Secretary of the British Ministry of Economic Warfare (B.E.W.) on March 28, 1942, they knew that American representatives had also been invited to participate. The British had felt that American representatives should attend the talks since the United States would have to furnish some of the supplies desired by the Swiss.[18] The chief American figure was Winfield Riefler, "an outstanding economic expert" who, with the rank of minister under Ambassador John J. Winant, was in charge of the rapidly expanding Economic Warfare Division in the American Embassy in London. Riefler and the other

---

[17] Homberger, "Minister Dr. Hans Sulzer", 8-9.
[18] Matthews (Chargé d'Affaires, U.S. Embassy, London) to Secretary of State, March 26, 1942, *FR, 1942,* 111, 376-377.

Americans present at the first meeting remained largely passive since they had no instructions on the American position.[19]

Riefler described those first discussions as follows: The Swiss presented a list of manufactures valued at two and a half million francs which they wanted to export each month to the United States and the United Kingdom and the British Commonwealth. Among the goods were watch parts, machine tools, dynamo-electric machines, motors, precision tools, and screws and nuts. They were negotiating in Berlin and Rome for Axis approval and permits of passage. In return for those exports the Swiss desired to obtain imports of equal value from the United States and the British Commonwealth, particularly quantities of iron and steel and certain non-ferrous metals. They hoped to receive guarantees of actual supply of those goods rather than merely navicerts or export licenses. That was to be the so-called "compensation deal." Furthermore, they sought restoration of quotas for goods which they were able to buy and asked that the Blockade Committee's recent reduction of the permissible enemy content in Swiss exports to five per cent be revised. Although the chances for coming to an agreement along those lines were slim or, as Riefler wrote, "subject to considerable skepticism", the British conferees set a series of conditions, among them the categoric demand that none of the Allied materials should be used for the manufacture of goods for the Axis. The Swiss delegates agreed, in principle, with that stipulation, but pointed out that too rigid an adherence to it might be damaging to the Allies themselves, for "they feared that if nothing containing any component however small of imported ingredient were exported to Germany, the Germans would say that no coal could be allowed to Switzerland for operating any factory that made goods for export to the Allies." The freedom of the Swiss to use imported materials for the manufacture of goods for export to Germany, permitted in the War Trade Agreement of April 1940, accounted according to Sulzer for the fact that the Germans were willing to give their approval to the present proposals.[20]

This particular problem was at the heart of the difficulties encountered by Switzerland. As the weeks went by in London, Sulzer and Keller became aware of the fact that concessions had to be made in this respect. That was brought home to them at a meeting on May 6, 1942, when for almost two hours they were grilled by the British. Riefler reported that for the first time

---

[19] David L. Gordon and Royden Dangerfield, *The Hidden Weapon* (New York, 1947): 44-45; Matthews to Secretary of State, March 26, 1942, and Welles (Acting Secretary of State) to Matthews, March 28, 1942, *FR, 1942,* III, 377-78.

[20] Matthews to Secretary of State, March 28, 1942, *Ibid.,* 378-381.

since his arrival he felt he was "getting near to the heart of the Swiss problem." The pressure on the Swiss for reductions in exports of machinery to Germany "was absolutely relentless." Every possible contingency came under discussion, with the British never conceding the objective. The Swiss, "visibly very worried", indicated that they wished nothing more than to be able to find ways of lessening German penetration of their economy, yet they feared that Switzerland would lose its independence if it should stop or even limit its exports of machinery. Keller stated:

> We cannot have unemployment in the metal industry, particularly that employing highly skilled labor. It is impossible politically for us to tell our people they must go on relief because we will not let them manufacture for Germany, especially when Germany is willing to furnish all of the materials and we furnish only the employment. You can cut down on our food if you want to go that far and we can tighten our belts and still remain free, but if you force us to throw our skilled workers into unemployment, they will either go to Germany to work and we won't dare to stop them under the circumstances, or they will force us to come to terms with Germany completely.

Riefler cabled his government that he was "impressed with sincerity of Swiss and with the potency of their arguments."[21] In his search for a solution to the problem he picked up an idea brought up by Sulzer during the meeting, namely to decrease Swiss dependence on Germany by promoting the purchase of Swiss manufactures and financing a preemption program for the storage of goods in Switzerland for postwar delivery, thus providing employment for skilled Swiss workers.[22] He further developed the plan in a detailed dispatch to his superiors on the Board of Economic Warfare. The Axis powers were much more successful "in diverting a huge proportion of the Swiss economy to manufacture for their benefit" than the Allies because they offered the Swiss as much employment as they would accept, while the Allies tried to force unemployment upon the Swiss. On the basis of that analysis Riefler proposed that the United States and Britain change their approach to the Swiss problem by adopting a positive program

---

[21] Riefler to Perkins (Executive Director, BEW): May 6, *Ibid.,* 382. This report, like the other communications from Riefler to the BEW and back, was transmitted through the official diplomatic channels. It is therefore technically an embassy telegram from Ambassador Winant to the Secretary of State and filed as such in the State Department files with the notation "From Riefler for Perkins." I will indicate throughout the actual sender and the intended receiver.

[22] *Ibid.,* 381-383.

to work out plans to divert Swiss industrial potential in such a way as to "leave a minimum of free resources available to work for the Axis." In addition to supporting an increase in orders for Swiss exports on the free list, Riefler especially emphasized a program of "building up the strongest possible army within Switzerland", as a means of absorbing manpower within Switzerland. It took Washington a month to answer Riefler. Its answer consisted of a detailed series of objections which indicated that it did not think his ideas could be implemented.[23]

In the meantime Sulzer began to grow restless. As the head of an important firm he was used to tackling difficulties and to proceeding energetically to solve them. As minister in Washington, a quarter century earlier, he had run into the obstacles and intricacies of wartime negotiations and yet had been able to bring about results despite great odds against his mission. The London experience was therefore doubly frustrating; it just was not possible to achieve any positive solutions. His letters expressed growing concern and discouragement. Late in April he complained of the narrow-minded second and third rate people with whom he had to deal. In July he argued with his Swiss counterparts that they had to make some concession, only to receive an absolutely uncompromising reply from Bern. He was told that Switzerland just could not afford to restrict its economic relations with Germany and Italy. It was a fact that with the aid of the Axis powers the economic existence of Switzerland was relatively assured, while the help of England and America could not even reach Switzerland if relations with the Axis deteriorated.

Sulzer felt and stated strongly that Switzerland paid a high price for German goods by furnishing Germany with a huge supply of strategic war material and that in doing so it was endangering its neutrality. The Allies had become aware of the exploitation of Swiss industrial potential by the Axis, and if they now made efforts to counteract it they could not be blamed entirely or be reproached for attempting to compromise Switzerland. In Sulzer's opinion it was wrong to demand that all concessions be made by one side only, the Allies, who were already at a disadvantage with regard to the economic services of Switzerland. Sulzer's sense of fairness and straightforward honesty, traits which had been evident already in his work in World War I, forced him to take such a stand with his government in Bern, even though he found little understanding there. He felt isolated in London, where, despite his private opinion, he presented the official Swiss

---

[23] Riefler to Perkins, May 8, 1942, and Perkins to Riefler, June 8, 1942, *Ibid.,* 384-385 and 388-389.

viewpoint as strongly as he knew how.[24] He would have liked to return to Switzerland, but war conditions made traveling back and forth dangerous and time-consuming. In October he wrote to Bern: "This mission has become for me a real time of pain. Never in my life was I burdened with a heavier one."[25]

The Weapon of Blacklisting

In September the Swiss negotiators in Berlin succeeded in obtaining the agreement of the Germans to accord transit permits for priority supplies offered by the Swiss to the Allies. Thus they were in a position to be able to guarantee the execution of their part of the compensation deal. The Allies wondered what price the Swiss had had to pay for the German agreement. They were informed that the only condition imposed by the Germans was the demand that the Allies should refrain, for the duration of the plan, from interfering with Swiss firms and should not force them to abandon or reduce the execution of German or Italian orders. That sounded rather vague and the Department of State desired a clear definition of the type and scope of Allied efforts that were to be discontinued. The Swiss refused to hand over the text of the German agreement, nor would they describe in certain terms the exact nature of the German conditions relating to Allied efforts to make Swiss firms reduce shipments to the Axis.[26] Under those circumstances the Americans were not interested in concluding any deals with the Swiss. They were not tempted much by what Switzerland had to offer them; the essentials Switzerland could furnish, they would receive anyhow. In the course of the summer and fall of 1942 the American position crystallized. It was expressed in simple and straightforward terms in one of the State Department's telegrams: "In other words, if we are to abandon our present policies, the Swiss government must satisfy us that they are actually effecting a decrease in exports of machinery and arms to Germany."[27] In 1942 the United Nations were not yet in a position, militarily and strategically, to force the Swiss to stop trading with the enemy, nor were the Swiss willing, ready, or able to make any substantial concessions in that

---

[24] See the long "Memorandum of the Swiss Trade Delegation to the British-American Delegation" of July 31, 1942, *Ibid.,* 390-396.

[25] Excerpts from the correspondence of Sulzer and Heinrich Homberger of the Swiss Commission for Supervision of Imports and Exports, in Homberger, "Minister Dr. Hans Sulzer", 10, 13, 15-20, 21-23, and 24 (quote).

[26] Harrison to Secretary of State, Sept. 9 and 19, 1942; Hull to Harrison, Sept. 12 and 28, 1942, *FR, 1942,* III, 397-401.

[27] Hull to Harrison, Sept. 28, 1942, *Ibid.,* 401.

direction. Therefore the London negotiations ended in a stalemate and neither side achieved its objectives.

When Sulzer returned to Switzerland in December he brought home with him at least the semblance of a compensation agreement, contained in an exchange of five letters between himself and Foot and Riefler. The letters stipulated that Switzerland would deliver during the first four months of 1943 exports of a specific nature of the approximate value of two and a half million Swiss francs. In return, the British and American governments would make available specific quantities of toluol, copper, rubber, nickel, tinplate, and steel sheets, all for the exclusive use of the Swiss army. If the Swiss so desired, they could substitute oats for iron and steel.[28] That was indeed a meager result for the Swiss, yet not an insignificant one. For one, the principle of compensation deals was saved for the time being. Secondly, during 1942 and for another few months in 1943 the Allies desisted from cutting Switzerland off completely from its supply centers and markets outside the blockade. Finally, the talks had clearly revealed the key to the thinking of the Allies and in consequence the means by which Switzerland could keep open the channels of trade with them. Recognition of and respect for the uncompromising attitude of the Allies toward Swiss exports to Germany induced the Swiss to bargain even harder with Germany during the ensuing months and to initiate a slow reduction of exports of war materials and machinery to the Axis powers.[29]

Periodic talks between Switzerland and the Anglo-American Allies remained inconclusive during 1943. Switzerland depended upon Germany for its supply of vital raw materials, most importantly coal and food, which the Allies were in no position to replace and, therefore, continued to maintain its close economic ties with its northern neighbor. As a consequence, the Allies began to instigate more retaliatory measures. In April 1943 the Department of State instructed Minister Harrison to deliver a note to the Swiss government which announced that the Allies had suspended the issuance of navicerts and export licenses for imports through the blockade for an indefinite period of time. The note also threatened the resumption of blacklisting as well as a reduction in the permitted enemy content of Swiss exports. Harrison was most reluctant to deliver the note and cabled Washington that the Swiss had indicated a great deal of good will toward the Allies and could be counted on to be entirely sincere in their

---

[28] *Ibid.*, 401-405. Toluol is an ingredient used in the dye and drug industry.
[29] Homberger, "Minister Dr. Hans Sulzer", 25; Medlicott, *The Economic Blockade*, II, 219-35, "The Sulzer Mission."

efforts to wrestle important concessions from the Germans. "They are now in midst of negotiations with Germans. They have given every indication of standing to their guns. If we now impose sanctions, I fear this will create a situation which can be used by Germans to our disadvantage . . .".[30]

Harrison, in concert with his British colleague, was able to postpone the delivery of the note for a few weeks, but late in May the final instructions from Washington arrived in only slightly modified form. When Harrison handed the revised note to Federal Councilor Marcel Pilet-Golaz, chief of the Federal Political Department, on May 26, he found the Swiss magistrate in a rather resigned mood. Switzerland, Pilet-Golaz stated, "invariably complied to the full with her obligations." He was sure that the war would end with an Allied victory and that as soon as a second front was established in the west Switzerland would be cut off from contact with the west and "would have to live on its own fat." For that contingency Switzerland was trying to accumulate reserves and the new restrictive move by the Allies was a real blow. Pilet-Golaz saw great difficulties in meeting Allied demands because of Swiss dependence on German coal. He also mentioned that Germany had voiced complaints about the intelligence facilities the Allies enjoyed in Switzerland and wondered whether "these and other important factors had perhaps been overlooked" when the Allies decided on their new measures. In any case, Switzerland's position was, in Pilet-Golaz's words, "that of a small country being slowly strangulated." Harrison, who must have heard those complaints many times before, transmitted the content of the audience without adding any comments of his own.[31]

The ball was now in the hands of the Swiss government again and it was up to them to find a way out of the new impasse. In order to put even more pressure on them and to induce them to give in to Allied wishes, Britain and the United States made still another threatening move by proceeding to revise their policy of blacklisting Swiss firms. Blacklisting banned a listed firm from doing business in or with the United Nations. Such a boycott was thought to hurt a firm and to reduce its ability of helping the Axis cause. However, that did not necessarily apply in the case of Switzerland. Important firms there could execute orders without the Allies having a chance to interfere, and blacklisting them did not necessarily interpose a ban upon their ability to manufacture for the Axis.

---

[30] Hull to Harrison, April 27, May 6 and 14, 1943; Harrison to Hull, April 29 and May 17, 1943, *FR, 1943*, II, 830-836.

[31] Harrison to Secretary of State, May 27, 1943, *Ibid.*, 842-43.

The overseas business such a firm would lose might be made up by additional business with the Axis.

These arguments against blacklisting were used by the Swiss legation in London, and they had their effect upon Riefler. In February 1943 he wrote to the Department of State: "When we threaten to list such firms, therefore, we simply force them to choose between Axis orders which they have the ability to fill and overseas orders, the continuation of which are uncertain because of Germany's counter-blockade. . . . Under these circumstances a firm listed in Switzerland is in a sense a firm lost to us. It represents a defeat because it means that the firm has chosen to commit itself entirely to the Axis and to turn its entire capacity to the use of the Axis."[32] Nevertheless, the threat of blacklisting had a certain effectiveness because the firm involved lost its overseas export outlets and its established trade connections.

More important than that was the fact that the stigma attached to blacklisting increased steadily as the war progressed. Apprehension over the future availability of assets in Allied countries rose and so did the fear that blacklisting might be carried over into the postwar period, which would allow non-listed firms to gain competitive advantages. In order to reach Swiss firms trading with the Axis, Riefler proposed to rely more on these aspects, particularly "to raise the fear that the lists will be maintained in certain cases for a period after the close of hostilities."[33] After some hesitancy the Department of State agreed to follow that line. It instructed its diplomatic representatives in the neutral European countries to use the threat of possible postwar consequences on individual, carefully selected, firms.[34] The British agreed that "selective word-of-mouth approaches by our missions to individual firms . . . constitute the best tactics in the plan for creating uncertainty regarding the possibility of post-war listing." Such a program by the diplomatic missions should be supported "with judiciously placed press articles and related publicity to the fact that in the last war the blockade and black-listing did not become inoperative with the Armistice."[35] In October 1943, after the various points of policy and procedure had been cleared between Washington and London, Foot put it in even more graphic terms in a note to Riefler: "It appears that we are now agreed on the action to be taken in Switzerland, Sweden, Spain and Portugal, namely, that

---

[32] Riefler to Acheson (Asst. Secretary of State): Feb. 24, 1943, *FR, 1943,* V, .309-312.
[33] *Ibid.*
[34] Hull to Winant, June 3, 1943, and Acheson to Riefler, June 19, 1943, *Ibid.,* 329-336.
[35] Winant to Secretary of State, Sept. 3, 1943, *Ibid.,* 336-337.

warnings are to be given in suitable cases to neutral firms and individuals and that there is to be a whispering campaign on the subject."[36]

By that time "the whispering campaign" and the pressure approach on individual firms was in full swing in Switzerland. Britain and the United States were upset because Swiss exports to Nazi Germany had reached unprecedented heights during the first half of 1943. Since Germany had made up its huge arrears in coal deliveries to Switzerland, the Swiss were obliged to furnish the guaranteed exports contracted before January 1943. Until those orders were carried out there would be a substantial increase in exports rather than a reduction. It was all quite embarrassing, especially to Sulzer, but to the Allied representatives it looked as if the Swiss manufacturers were trying to sell as many of their products as possible before the door was closed. Harrison and Riefler expressed disappointment at what appeared to them to be a calculated gambit of staging long drawn-out negotiations with innumerable delays "at which they are past masters" while going full steam ahead in selling their products to the enemy."[37] As a consequence, Riefler and Foot urgently called for the resumption of listing. The Swiss reacted sourly to the new twist in Allied tactics. Rather than voicing their dissatisfaction in the Mixed Commission in Bern and at the London trade negotiations, the Federal Council instructed its ministers in Washington and London to officially protest the revival of pressure on Swiss firms as being a breach in the Allied undertaking under the compensation agreement of the preceding December. Both Riefler and Foot refused to accept the Swiss point of view that approaches to individual firms were inconsistent with the Allied commitments. They reiterated:

> If a neutral firm takes advantage of the war situation to increase its sales to Germany or her satellites, it is in effect choosing to assist the German war effort, and thereby helping to postpone the eventual liberation of Europe, an event which is as much in the interest of the neutral European countries as it is in that of the United Nations. In our opinion such a firm has no genuine cause for complaint if it finds itself placed upon the Statutory and Proclaimed Lists, and thereby prevented

---

[36] Quoted in Riefler to Secretary of State and OEW (Office of Economic Warfare): Oct. 7, 1943, *Ibid.,* 342.

[37] Harrison to Secretary of State, April 8, 1943, *FR, 1943,* II, 900, contains Sulzer's statement of regret about the unforeseen development. Riefler to Secretary of State and OEW, Aug. 22, 1943, *Ibid.,* 866-869, contains statistical materials, furnished by the Swiss, about the substantial increases in Swiss exports to Germany during the first half of 1943. Comments on Swiss tactis in Riefler to Secretary of State and OEW, Oct. 27, 1943, *Ibid.,* 883-884.

from trading with the British Empire and the United States, and with other countries overseas.[38]

Forced Concessions

The "very vigorous pressure campaign on individual Swiss firms, particularly the large and most powerful ones", showed results in that the Swiss government was "showing extreme anxiety to stop the pressure campaign." Tangible concessions were, however, slow in coming. Riefler hoped that the leading Swiss firms would force the government to offer substantial concessions in order to induce the Allies to refrain from further pressure. A group of Swiss firms agreed to drastically limit their export of fuses to Germany in return for their removal from the list. Other firms followed suit by individually undertaking to reduce exports to Germany. In October the firm of Sulzer Brothers, Winterthur, a large manufacturer of diesel engines and other heavy machinery, was threatened with blacklisting unless it agreed to reduce its exports to the Axis to prewar levels. On October 22, Sulzer Brothers replied that it refused "to sign an undertaking so 'humiliating' in character", whereupon the Allies decided to put the firm on the blacklists to be made public on October 30. The measure had some drastic effects. The Federal Council issued a decree making it illegal for Swiss firms to enter into an undertaking with foreign governments with regard to their exports. But it also sent Professor Keller to London, for the fourth time since the outbreak of the war, with new proposals for Swiss concessions. This time satisfactory terms were reached in a much shorter time than usual.[39]

The December 19, 1943 agreement, in the form of an exchange of letters, fixed ceilings on Swiss exports to Germany to "be revised at least every six months in order to consider which of those exports shall be further reduced." The ceilings were expressed in terms of value, with the year 1942 being the basis. The Swiss had to guarantee not to reduce the prices of their export goods. The increase in the price level of goods from Axis Europe had to be met by a corresponding increase in the prices of Swiss exports. Due to the general increase in prices since 1942 the ceilings established by the agreement actually reduced Swiss exports to Axis Europe by more than half. In order to prevent the Germans from concentrating their limited

---

[38] Text of letter of Foot to Walter Thurnheer (Swiss Minister in London) enclosed in Riefler to Secretary of State and OEW, Oct. 15, 1943, *Ibid.*, 879-881.

[39] Riefler to Secretary of State and OEW, Oct. 21, 1943, *Ibid.*, 883-886. Medlicott *The Economic Blockade*, II, 509-513 and 518-519, gives a detailed account of the Sulzer blacklisting affair and its implications.

buying power on the specific items of greatest value to them, individual ceilings were put on each product, in particular on arms and ammunition, fuses, airplane parts, ball bearings, and machine tools. Thus the Germans could not compensate for quotas that had not been exhausted by transferring their funds to other manufactures. Furthermore, the Swiss agreed to stop repairing vehicles and other war equipment for Axis Europe and to restrict drastically the processing of goods. The Allies, in return, restored the blockade quotas for food, tobacco and fodder, but no guarantees were given that scarce items would actually be supplied. They promised not to pursue their blacklisting policy except when specific firms violated the limits provided by the agreement. Firms which already had given pledges to the Allies regarding the reduction of their exports were not to be bothered by the Swiss government and, finally, Sulzer Brothers was to be unlisted upon signing a satisfactory undertaking on its exports.[40]

The December 19, 1943 agreement marked a turning point in Switzerland's economic struggle during World War II. The restrictions imposed on trade with Germany were drastic without being compensated for by equivalent increases in trade with the Allies. As the victory of the Allies, desired and prayed for by the vast majority of Swiss citizens, came closer, the bargaining position of the Swiss government became weaker. Some interesting differences with the situation in World War I are apparent. In World War I the Swiss government, in its relationship with the United States, worried mainly about the supply of bread cereals. The scarcity of supplies in the United States and the absence of available shipping had raised the specter of a famine during the early months of 1918. Food was not a prime concern during World War II. Due to excellent planning both before and during the war and a rigorously enforced rationing system which imposed considerable privation on the Swiss population, Switzerland came through the war years without fear of hunger.[41]

The Unique Character of World War II

The problem during World War II was not the scarcity of supplies abroad or the lack of tonnage for shipping. Switzerland had purchased large quantities of goods not only in the United States but also in Argentina and

---

[40] Foot and Riefler to Keller, Dec. 19, 1943, and Keller to Foot and Riefler, Dec. 19, 1943, *FR, 1943,* II, 888-892.

[41] See the careful study by Josef Rosen, *Wartime Food Developments in Switzerland.* (Stanford University, California, War-Peace Pamphlets No. 9, May 1947); also Ernest S. Hediger, "Switzerland in Wartime", in *Foreign Policy Reports,* XVII 1, No. 20 (New York, Jan. 1, 1943): 267-268.

other countries of Latin America, as well as the Near East, and had stores in Portugal and Spain. Shipping, though not plentiful, was made adequate by chartering and the creation of the Swiss merchant marine. The real difficulty arose from the fact that the character of World War II differed from that of World War I. Though the latter had been bloody enough and toward its end had involved the mobilization of all available resources among the belligerents, the former was prosecuted on an even more intensive and all-inclusive scale, making it a truly total war in which everything was subordinated to the single objective of eliminating the enemy. Therefore the situation of the neutrals was more precarious in World War II than in World War I.

On the other hand, the peculiar features of World War II also offered special opportunities for a flexible, imaginative, and skilled neutral, especially one as experienced as Switzerland. What Switzerland did during World War II demanded a great deal of nerve and skill. At all times it attempted to set off the demands of one side against those of the other and for a long while it succeeded surprisingly well in winning concessions from both. It was able to convince both belligerent camps of the importance of its remaining neutral and then exploited the great powers' interest in keeping it from joining the other side. That was one of the strongest points used, time and again, by the Swiss diplomatic representatives in London and Washington.

The task of balancing one side against the other was easier during periods of relative equilibrium in the world power constellation. As soon as one side or the other had a clear preponderance, the situation for a small neutral nation like Switzerland became more difficult to handle. From the summer of 1940 to about the middle of 1943 Germany had an unquestionably dominant position in Europe. During that period Switzerland could maintain its position of independence only by making important concessions to its powerful neighbor through a conciliatory approach for which it received much criticism later on, most of it undeserved. In the course of the year 1944 the Allies achieved a position of dominance in the war and Switzerland had to bend to their demands, which were often no less galling and peremptory than those of the Germans before. But at no time did Switzerland give up the really basic symbol of its independence. No foreign troops entered the country without being disarmed and interned, and Switzerland's soil was not used for the passage or deployment of foreign armies. The point was unmistakably clear to both sides that Switzerland had the will and determination, as well as the capacity, to resist an attack upon its territory. Though the eventual outcome of such an attack could hardly be doubted, victory would have to be bought dearly.

During World War II, as on other occasions before, Switzerland proved to be adept in the art of procrastination. It substituted for its lack of military power and political weight most of the following tactics, which have been catalogued as being typical for small states in a study of World War II neutrals, namely: holding out the possibility of concessions at some price and then making the price exorbitant, distracting the demanding state by such means as reference to cheaper alternatives, increasing the demanding power's fear of retaliation from the other side, trading off individually trivial concessions to avoid making vital ones, taking advantage of conflicts within the demanding side, giving 'informal' and secret understandings to avoid open declarations fixing policy and to counteract favors to the other side, insisting that compensation be tangible and immediately receivable, and otherwise avoiding a decision until its timeliness disappears.[42]

Fortunately for Switzerland, it also had assets other than wide experience in negotiating out of weakness. As a highly respected member of the family of nations with a long tradition of neutrality and humanitarian services, it had accumulated a store of moral credit on which it could draw. That, and the substantial services Switzerland continued to provide to the warring powers as a neutral nation, goes a long way in explaining why Switzerland was able to successfully withstand the pressure exerted on it by both sides during World War II.

Reprinted by permission, from Heinz K. Meier, *Friendship under Stress. U. S.—Swiss Relations 1900–1950* (Bern: Herbert Lang, 1970): 272-293. Subtitles added by the editor.

---

[42] Annette Baker Fox, *The Power of Small States: Diplomacy in World War II* (Chicago, 1959): 185. Fox dealt with Turkey, Finland, Norway, Sweden, and Spain. She exluded Switzerland, the "most famous neutral of all", because she considered it to be unique to the extent that it had "become so fixed a feature in the thinking of European diplomats that there was a psychological obstacle to invasion possessed by no other neutral." *Ibid.,* 5. The study of Switzerland's problems during World War II shows, however, that it had experiences which were very similar to those Fox describes as characteristic for the neutrals she dealt with.

VII: "LINKING THE HIDEOUSLY-SUNDERED NATIONS"

Neutral Switzerland as 'Protecting Power'

Leo Schelbert

Few people know of Switzerland's role as a 'Protecting Power' during the Second World War, and even fewer are familiar with the meaning of the term and its related concepts of 'good offices' and 'mediation'. Yet these concepts point to a vast range of tasks Swiss diplomats have undertaken on a world-wide scale during the war years, often under difficult and, at times, perilous conditions and benefiting especially those hard-hit by the impact of war. The following sketch of this little known aspect of Switzerland's role intends to show that Swiss neutrality during those trying years did not mean standing aloof from, but rather being intensely involved in, the events; and was designed, in Winston Churchill's words, to help by "linking the hideously-sundered nations", to shield those in danger, and to mitigate suffering.

Good Offices, Mediation, and Protecting Power Defined

The notion 'good offices' dates from a provision of the Hague Convention of 1899 and 1907 that addresses "the pacific settlement of international disputes." Article 2 of the 1907 version states: "In case of serious disagreement or dispute, before an appeal to arms, the contracting Powers agree to have recourse . . . to the good offices or mediation of one or more friendly powers." The latter must be "strangers to the dispute", as Article 3 put it, and they may be asked to provide their 'good offices' by "the States at variance". The parties neutral to the conflict may also offer their 'good offices' on their own, a step, however, that legally could not be interpreted by the potential belligerents as "an unfriendly act."[1]

---

[1] See Carnegie Endowment for International Peace. Division of International Law. Pamphlet No. 4. *The Hague Conventions (I) and 1907 (I) for the Pacific Settlement of International Disputes* (Washington, DC: The Endowment, 1915): 3. A concise sketch is Edgar Bonjour, *Geschichte der schweizerischen Neutralität. Vier Jahrhunderte eidgenössischer Aussenpolitik*, Vol. 6: *1939–1945* (Basel: Helbing & Lichtenhahn, 1970):105-154. See also Denise Bindschedler-Robert, "Les bons Offices dans la Politique étrangère de la Suisse", in: *Handbuch der schweizerischen Aussenpolitik*. Herausgegeben von Alois Riklin, Hans Haug und Hans Christoph Binswanger (Bern: Paul Haupt, 1975):

The distinction between the notions of 'good offices' and 'mediation' has not been sharp and at times the two terms are used interchangeably.[2] Yet strictly constructed 'good offices' mean to facilitate the solving of conflicts between nations by suggesting helpful *procedural* ways in conflict resolution; 'mediation', in contrast, implies "to take part actively in the search for a negotiated solution" that involves addressing the *substantive* issues.[3]

The return to 'total' war in the twentieth century, however, in which the distinction between soldiers and civilians as well as between battlefields and non-combatant zones collapsed, necessitated a vast expansion of the activities implied in 'good offices' and 'mediation'. Thus the institution of 'Protecting Power' emerged, meaning a selected nation was being "charged with safeguarding the interests of the belligerents" in an enemy country, especially in relation to enemy property, prisoners of war, and interned civilians.[4] It was found to be helpful if the same nation served as Protecting Power concerned with the interests of two opposing belligerents. The "Protecting Power became almost an 'umpire', enabling it to use the

---

679-691; also Martin Schärer, "L'activité de la Suisse comme puissance protectrice durant la seconde guerre mondiale", *Revue d'histoire de la deuxième guerre mondiale* 31 (January 1981): 121-128. An authoritative study of the institution is Raymond Probst, *'Good Offices' in the Light of Swiss International Practice and Experience.* Dordrecht: Martinus Nijhoff Publishers, 1989. Chapters I to V discuss the notion and workings of 'good offices', VI to VII of 'Protecting Power', and VIII "new forms of general 'good offices'." For a recent example see David D. Newsom, "The Sensitive Link. The Swiss Role in the U.S.—Iran Hostage Crisis", in: *Einblick in die schweizerische Aussenpolitik. Zum 65. Geburtstag von Staatssekretär Raymond Probst.* Herausgegeben von Edouard Brunner et al. (Zürich: Verlag Neue Zürcher Zeitung, 1984): 291-303. During that crisis D. Newsom was U.S. Undersecretary for Political Affairs from 1978-1981, R. Probst Ambassador of Switzerland in Washington. See also David D. Newsom, ed., *Diplomacy under a Foreign Flag. When Nations Break Relations.* New York: St. Martin's Press, 1990 for other case studies since World War II; ibid. also Newsom's essay "Sensitive Link", 32-43 and a brief survey by R. Probst, "The 'Good Offices' of Switzerland and Her Role as Protecting Power, 18-31."- All translations into English of German or French texts are by L Schelbert.

[2] H. G. Darwin, "Mediation and Good Offices", in: *International Disputes. The Legal Aspects* (London: Europa Publications, 1972): 85. Bindschedler-Robert, "Les Bons Offices", 680.

[3] Bindschedler-Robert, ibid.; Darwin, "Mediation", ibid.

[4] See Article 86 of the "International Convention Relative to the Treatment of Prisoners of War", Geneva, July 27, 1929; also "International Convention for the Amelioration of the Condition of the Wounded and Sick in Armies in the Field;" both are reprinted in French and in English in *The Statutes at Large of the United States of America from December 31, 1931 to March 1933.* Vol. 47, Part 2 (Washington, DC: Government Printing Office, 1933): 2021-2073 and 2074-2101.

argument of mutual advantage to obtain the desired improvement."[5] It was a difficult role to play since the Protecting Power needed to gain the trust of both belligerents it was mandated to serve. It had to be, as Werner Rings felicitously put it, "an advocate for the enemy" within the context of the "adventure of political neutrality."[6] The state which a Protecting Power consented to represent, however, could not assign to that Power any task or make any demands that could jeopardize the power's neutral stance or endanger its own interests.[7]

Switzerland's Protecting Power Mandates
   During the Second World War Switzerland emerged as the most widely chosen Protective Power by the nations at war. Its perpetual neutrality, internal stability, location in the heart of Europe, multi-ethnic composition, and relative insignificance in Great Power politics as well as the extensive experience it had gained in World War I made Switzerland a preferred choice, rivaled only by Sweden.[8] When Germany started the war on September 1, 1939, Switzerland had only a few 'protecting power' mandates, but these increased rapidly with the fall of France on June 14, 1940 and with the entry of Japan and the United States into the conflict on December 7 and 8 in 1941. The Swiss government assumed all mandates

---

[5] Probst, *'Good Offices'*, p.126.
[6] Werner Rings, *Advokaten des Feindes. Das Abenteuer der politischen Neutralität.* Wien: Econ-Verlag, 1966. The richly illustrated work contains the "original interviews" of a program Rings created for Swiss television. He is a naturalized Swiss citizen and author of several works relating to the Second World War, among them *Life with the Enemy. Collaboration and Resistance in Hitler's Europe 1939–1945.* Translated by J. Maxwell Brownjohn. Garden City, NY: Doubleday, 1982; biographical note ibid., 352.
[7] See Antonino Janner, *La Puissance protectrice en Droit internationale d'après les expériences par la Suisse pendant la seconde guerre mondiale.* Juristische Fakultät der Universität Basel. Institut für internationales Recht und internationale Beziehungen. Schriftenreihe, Heft 7 (Basel: Helbing & Lichtenhahn, 1948): 14.
[8] Konrad Walter Stamm, *Die guten Dienste der Schweiz. Aktive Neutralitätspolitik zwischen Tradition, Diskussion und Integration* (Bern: Herbert Lang, 1974): 166. For Sweden see Wilhelm Carlgren, "Die Mediationstätigkeit in der Aussenpolitik Schwedens während des Zweiten Weltkrieges", and Bengt Åkerrén, "Schweden als Schutzmacht", in: *Schwedische und schweizerische Neutralität im Zweiten Weltkrieg.* Herausgegeben von Rudolf L. Bindschedler et al. (Basel: Helbing und Lichtenhahn, 1985), 97-110 and 111-119. According to Åkerrén, 116, Sweden held 114 official mandates for 28 different nations in the Second World War.

previously held by the United States so that by the end of 1943 the Swiss administered 219 single mandates for 35 nations.[9]

The following selective listing indicates the geographic range of the mandates accepted by Switzerland and to be implemented by its diplomats abroad. The Swiss representatives were to 'protect'

> *Germany's* interests in Great Britain, the United States, Yugoslavia, Turkey, and Dutch Indonesia;
> *Great Britain's* interests in Germany, France, Italy, Hungary, Rumania, and Japan;
> *Vichy France's* interests in Great Britain, the United States, Italy, Egypt, and Brazil;
> *Italy's* interests in Egypt and Brazil;
> *United States'* interests in Germany, France, Italy, Japan, China, and Denmark;
> *Japan's* interests in Great Britain, the United States, Egypt, and Argentina.[10]

Once a nation had severed diplomatic relations with a given state, it technically meant that they had become potential enemy powers. According to Article 2 of The Hague Conventions of 1899 and 1907 each signatory state was expected to seek a peaceful solution of the contested issues that had caused the rupture of diplomatic relations before the resort to arms, yet unfortunately this provision lacked the force of a contractual obligation.[11]

If a state chose Switzerland to serve as a Protecting Power in an enemy nation, it transmitted that intent to the Swiss Foreign Office in Bern. In turn, the Swiss government then informed that enemy nation of the request received and formally asked its consent to accept Switzerland as Protecting Power for the nation that had made the request. If the answer was positive, Swiss diplomatic and consular offices then assumed the mandate with the numerous tasks it implied. If a sudden rupture between states occurred, this process of assuming a mandate could be drastically shortened so that Switzerland could implement its role as Protecting Power even before all the formal steps had been taken.[12]

---

[9] Stamm, *Die guten Dienste,* 166; Rings, *Advokaten,* 21, gives the number of 43 states by including so-called de facto representations which lacked the full juridical status of a Protecting Power and reduced activities mainly to consular issues.

[10] See Rings, *Advokaten,* for an inclusive table, p. 20; also Janner, *La Puissance protectrice,* 68-70.

[11] Bindschedler-Robert, "Les bons Offices", 680; she points out that also article 33 of the Charter of the United Nations maintains the status quo.

[12] Janner, *La puissance protectrice,* 18-19.

Given the numerous mandates it accepted during the Second World War, Switzerland was forced to create a special division "for foreign interests" in its Department of Foreign Affairs in order to coordinate effectively the resulting obligations. This special division was organized into five subsections: One for Germany's interests in 12 nations, one for Italy's in 16 nations, one for Great Britain's in 14 nations, one for the United States' and Japan's in 18 nations, and one for all other countries, with Switzerland protecting their interests in 38 nations. Although generally the already-established embassies and consulates were entrusted with the tasks implied in a Protecting Power mandate, because of the heavy workload connected with several mandates special offices were created also abroad, that is in London, Berlin, Vichy, Washington, and Bucharest. The central office in Bern had over 150 employees, the offices abroad over a thousand, two-thirds of whom were non-Swiss.[13] As a result, Switzerland was present as Protecting Power in 56 capitals and was entrusted with safeguarding 219 foreign embassies and consulates. The center in Bern was in constant telephone contact with 1,108 Swiss diplomats and consular officials abroad, received over 500,000 reports and 54,000 telegrams, and maintained 69,000 dossiers. It also supervised the exchange of some 35,000 civilians between the belligerents.[14] Switzerland provided the already existing infrastructure free of charge to the powers it represented, the salaries for the specially appointed staffs excepted.[15]

The Protecting Power's Range of Tasks
A mandate's duties to be assumed by Swiss officials representing Switzerland as Protecting Power were numerous. At times they were administratively routine, at other times complex, dangerous, and frustrating "since the neutral who watches over enemies is [also] counted as an enemy."[16] Officials had to maintain a triple loyalty, that is to safeguard the interests of Switzerland, of the nation they represented as Protecting Power, and of the belligerent in whose territory they fulfilled their mission for the enemy.

William Preiswerk, for instance, took over the German Embassy in London. To gain the confidence of the British, the Swiss representative immediately changed all the locks to the German Embassy in order to assure his exclusive access to the building. He was to safeguard the interests

---

[13] Stamm, *Die guten Dienste*, 167.
[14] Rings, *Advokaten*, 22.
[15] Stamm, 168.
[16] Rings, *Advokaten*, 24.

of Germany, Italy, Japan, Bulgaria, and Thailand in Great Britain, British India, New Zealand, Canada, Australia, and South Africa.[17] Individuals, furthermore, could pursue their tasks in a manner strictly circumscribed by protocol or they could maximize their activities in order to get leaders to the negotiating table, to protect foreign nationals in enemy country, to prevent bloodshed, and to help those in dire need.[18]

The activities undertaken by the functionaries of a Protecting Power may be divided into consular, diplomatic, and combat-related tasks. Although the three categories are not sharply separated, a listing of the duties of officials implementing the Protecting Power's role according to those categories may be helpful:

Consular:
Issue of passports and other legal papers to civilians of an enemy nation; notarization of documents;
protection of the civil rights of members of an enemy state;
protection of their property and businesses;
transmission of assistance from public or private agencies;
visits to camps of interned enemy aliens;
initiation and supervision of the exchange of civilians between belligerents.

Diplomatic:
Initiation and supervision of the safe return to their home countries of diplomatic and consular officials, their families, and staffs after the declaration of war, including the charter of ships and accompaniment on the return voyage;
protection of embassy grounds, buildings, and diplomatic and consular depositories;

---

[17] Ibid., 26.

[18] The efforts of Carl J. Burckhardt, Walter Stucki, and Max Waibel, for example, seem at times to have transcended the radius of officially sanctioned tasks. See for instance Herbert S. Levine, "The Mediator: Carl J. Burckhardt's Efforts to Avert the Second World War", in *Journal of Modern History* 45 (1973):439-455, a rather critical appraisal; also Paul Stauffer, "Friedenserkundungen in der Anfangsphase des Zweiten Weltkrieges: Carl J. Burckhardt und Birger Dahlerus", in: *Einblick in die schweizerische Aussenpolitik*, 375-399; and *Zwischen Hoffmannsthal und Hitler: Facetten einer aussergewöhnlichen Existenz*. Zürich: Verlag Neue Zürcher Zeitung, 1991; Stauffer views Carl J. Burckhardt's account such as *Meine Danziger Mission 1937–1939*. Zürich: Fretz & Wasmuth, 1960, as a form of self-promotion. Max Waibel's efforts to achieve a capitulation of the German Army in Northern Italy without bloodshed in the spring of 1945 are described by Bonjour, *Geschichte* 6, 125-133; also by Allen Dulles, *The Secret Surrender* (New York: Harper and Row, 1966): passim; for Stucki and Lutz see below.

transmission of messages between belligerents if their wording was deemed
    proper in form;
transmission and promotion of peace initiatives between hostile nations.

Combat Related:
Periodic supervisory visits to prisoner of war camps as regulated by the
    1929 Geneva Convention;
protection and care of the severely wounded and sick enemy soldiers in
    conformity with the 1929 Geneva Convention;
prevention of bloodshed through mediating negotiation between
    belligerents;
initiation and supervision of the exchange of the sick and severely wounded;
initiation and supervision of the exchange of prisoners of war.[19]

Tasks Accomplished
    Many of these activities were performed quietly and were little
noticed, others such as the *exchange of civilians* demanded complex and
extended negotiations. In the Second World War some fifty such exchanges
were accomplished by the 'good offices' of Switzerland as Protecting
Power. Among them were the following:

1940	A large number of women between Germany and Great Britain, generally civilians below age 18 and above 65
1940:	Interned civilians between Germany and France
	Some 2,000 interned civilians between Germany and countries of the Western Hemisphere
1942-44:	Some 1,700, about half of them Jewish, between Germany and Palestine
1943:	Some 28,000 Italians, mainly women and children, repatriated from Ethiopia and Erythrea in three voyages
1943:	Some 1,500 between the United States and Canada with Japan
1944:	Some 900 Germans in South Africa with British citizens in Germany
1944:	Some 600 diplomats and civilians exchanged between Germany and Turkey.[20]

    The *financial assistance distributed* by Swiss officials as Protecting
Power agents reached about 245 million Swiss francs, about 2.5 billion
Swiss francs in today's value ($1.5 billion U.S.). In dealing with enemy
aliens in a belligerent's country, the representatives of the Protecting Power

---

[19] See Janner, *La puissance protectrice*, 39-59; Schärer, "L'activité de la Suisse", 123.
[20] Ibid., 45-46; see also Bonjour, *Geschichte*, Vol. 6, 140-141.

were to give them the same services and tutelage as were due Swiss citizens.[21]

As to *peace feelers* by the belligerents, the Swiss government observed "official abstinence", especially after the Allies had declared that they would accept only an unconditional surrender by the Axis powers, so that this aspect was left to "private initiative." The question of making peace was in the view of the Swiss government "a matter of the belligerents, not of the neutrals."[22]

A special diplomatic duty of the Protecting Power was to ensure the proper treatment of *prisoners of war*. On July 27, 1929 the principles of the Hague Convention of October 18, 1907 had been further developed.[23] Sections dealt with issues such as capture, captivity, camps, food and clothing, intellectual and moral needs, labor to be performed, and disciplinary matters. Given conditions after battles, the destruction of towns and installations, and especially the scarcity of provisions, the Convention set a high standard not easily reached. Under the dire conditions of total warfare the temptation was omnipresent to take revenge on the prisoners of war and to feed them the least and last. Of special importance was Article 86 of the 1929 Geneva Convention which stated:

> Representatives of the protecting Power or its accepted delegates shall be permitted to go any place, without exception, where prisoners of war are interned. They shall have access to all places occupied by prisoners and may interview them, as a general rule without witnesses, personally or through interpreters.

This task of the Swiss representatives was demanding and time-consuming. In 1944, for instance, they made 350 reports, the result of 42 rounds. These reports were not shared with the detaining power and dealt with 150 camps, lazarets, and military prisons that housed thousands of Allied prisoners of war in Germany. In May 1945 there were 140 camps with some 350,000 German prisoners of war in the United States which were also under the jurisdiction of Switzerland as a Protecting Power. In Japan and in the territories it controlled, the work of Swiss officials was seriously hampered by the refusal of Japanese authorities to disclose the

---

[21] Ibid., 142, 141.

[22] Ibid., 123, 107; ibid., 105-124 deal with the official restraint concerning peace initiatives.—As to unconditional surrender see Günter Moltmann, "Die Genesis der Unconditional-Surrender-Forderung", in: *Probleme des Zweiten Weltkrieges*. Herausgegeben von Andreas Hillgruber (Köln: Kiepenheuer & Witsch, 1967): 171-198.

[23] See above, footnote 4.

whereabouts of about two-thirds of their prisoners of war, who had to endure the most deplorable living conditions and treatment. One Swiss representative and his wife were killed; another disappeared under mysterious circumstances.[24]

The reports on the prisoner of war camps addressed in detail the provisions stated in the 1929 Geneva Convention and answered questions about accommodations, the prisoners' state of health, their degree of safety, especially near combat zones, their treatment, work assignments, and general well-being. They contained answers about the posting of the Geneva Convention in the proper language and place in the camp as well as about religious services, pay, grievances, and opportunities to fill their free time meaningfully.[25]

As to combat-related tasks, the functionaries of a Protecting Power had above all to deal with the *severely wounded*. The 1929 "Convention for the Amelioration of the Wounded and the Sick in Armies in the Field", which was "to perfect and complete the provisions" of the 1864 and 1906 Geneva Conventions, provided in Article 1 that "they shall be treated with humanity and cared for medically, without distinction of nationality, by the belligerent in whose power they may be." According to Article 4 armies in retreat were to leave "medical personnel and material" behind and they were to exchange the names "of the wounded, sick, and dead" with the enemy. An "Annex" to the Convention also envisioned "hospitalization in a neutral country" if captivity was likely further to aggravate the physical or mental health of wounded soldiers.[26] Agents of the Protecting Power were to make sure that the provisions of the Convention were implemented, often a daunting and difficult task.

A Case of Protecting Severely Wounded Enemy Soldiers

An incident reported by Walter Stucki, the Minister of Switzerland in Vichy France and in charge of the Protecting Power mission, may highlight what the implementation of the Geneva Convention regarding the severely wounded involved.[27] In the afternoon of Friday, August 25, 1944, "two

---

[24] Janner, *La puissance protectrice*, 53.; Stamm, *Die guten Dienste*, 170; the Swiss delegate was Robert Bossert; the Basel physician Matthäus Vischer, delegate of the International Committee of the Red Cross and Protective Power delegate was executed with his wife in December 1943; see Stamm, ibid., 244-245, endnote 20.

[25] Janner, *La puissance protectrice*, 71-73; the questionnaire is given in full in German.

[26] See above, footnote 4.

[27] See Walter Stucki, Ministre de Suisse. *La fin du régime de Vichy* (Neuchâtel: Editions de la Baconnière, [1947]): 178-180; originally published in German as *Von Pétain zur IV. Republik*. Bern: Herbert Lang, 1946.—Vichy was the capital of that part of France's

high-ranking German officers of the health service" approached Minister Stucki "visibly nervous, but in a most correct manner" and asked whether he would take into Swiss tutelage some twenty to thirty severely wounded German soldiers soon to arrive in Vichy who were too ill to be transported any further. "I accepted", Stucki wrote, "under condition that each individual case was examined and appraised by officers of the French Health Service." But if the arriving SS forces should try to requisition cars and gasoline in the possession of the Swiss legation or should attempt to disarm members of the French police or military stationed in Vichy, he immediately would have to cancel the agreement. The German officers agreed with the conditions and, visibly relieved, thanked Minister Stucki. Stucki without delay formed a team of French physicians and nurses and had Hôtel Radio prepared to accept the soldiers. "My chancellery", he wrote,

> created for each of the German soldiers taken into my care a personal identification card to be attached to each bed, with the seal and signature of the [Swiss] Legation. I ordered a Swiss flag raised at the entrance of the hotel. I visited briefly with the chief physician and asked to be informed once the wounded had begun to be remitted or in case of an incident.

Later that evening Walter Stucki received another visit, this time in secret from a captain of the F. F. I., that is the partisans called French Forces of the Interior. Stucki told him of his decision to accept the German soldiers into his care as well as of the conditions he had set. The greatly disturbed visitor told him that it would be difficult to "prevent his men from committing acts of reprisals" since the German forces had heartlessly killed the F. F. I.'s severely wounded and the "battle between the F. F. I. and the S. S. . . . had been waged with unusual ferocity and brutality."[28] Referring to the Geneva Convention Minister Stucki impressed upon his visitor that

---

Southwest the Germans had carved out as a semi-independent remnant of the nation. Although the government, headed by Marshall Pétain, was supposed to have been sovereign, it became increasingly a puppet regime reduced to aspects of protocol and being subjected to ever greater restrictions; see Michèle Cointet, *Vichy capitale 1940–1944*. Collection Vérités et Légendes. Paris: Perrin, 1993; of special interest in this context are the chapters "Communiquer avec le monde: Les ambassades", 224-254, and "La fin du régime", 255-277. Stucki had been a witness of the forced removal of Pétain; Cointet observes that Stucki's book, which he approached critically, "appeared to be very solid", 280. Cointet, 251, observed: "The ambassador of Switzerland Walter Stucki played a role appreciated by all, Pétainists and those of the 'résistance'."

[28] Stucki, *La fin*, 179-180.

"he could not allow under any circumstances that the severely wounded under Swiss protection be harmed." If need be, he would "defend them with revolver in hand and would not recoil no matter what the consequence." His insistence was successful. In a later note he added with satisfaction: "The behavior of the F.F.I. regarding these people was henceforth irreproachable."[29]

About 10 o'clock that evening the German convoy marked with the Red Cross carrying the wounded to Vichy began to arrive. "I will never forget", the Swiss representative noted,

> the impact of horror with which those two hours left me. The soldiers arrived, the belly torn by bullets, the two eyes burst, the lungs punctured, legs and arms barely attached to the body. They were fully or mostly naked, soaked in blood, covered with dust. All, one after the other, were washed by the [French] physicians and nurses, sedated, carried to bed, and during all that time not a cry, not a complaint, hardly a sigh. . . . The hospital physicians and nurses who with great devotion took care of these severely wounded enemies all night long deserve very special praise.[30]

Incidents such as these show that the tasks involved in implementing a given mandate could mean "an immense amount of work that demanded total devotion and often forgetfulness of self."[31]

The Swiss Protecting Power's Private Arm: The ICRC

As Protecting Power, Switzerland had one special advantage: Geneva is the seat of the International Committee of the Red Cross (ICRC), a purely Swiss institution, which is to be distinguished from its offspring, the International Red Cross, the umbrella organization of national Red Cross groups such as the American or Swiss Red Cross.[32] The ICRC resulted from a memoir published in 1862 by Henri Dunant, titled *Un souvenir de Solférino,* and was established the following year under the name "International and Permanent Committee for Relief to Wounded Military Personnel", yet the tasks it assumed greatly expanded over the next decades.

---

[29] Ibid., 181-181 and footnote 1.

[30] Ibid., 184-185.

[31] Martin Schärer, "L'activité de la Suisse", 122.

[32] See David Forsythe, *Humanitarian Politics. The International Committee of the Red Cross* (Baltimore: Johns Hopkins University Press, 1977): 4-5; see ibid., 6, a graph that highlights the complex structural relationship between the ICRC, the International Red Cross, the national Red Cross organizations, and national governments.

The Committee, furthermore, "remained a private institution, governed by Swiss law, whose members are elected by co-optation among Swiss citizens." Although it is therefore "national in character", it is "free to act in the international field, given the fact that 'Swiss law is not interested in the international activity of the ICRC'."[33] The emblem of the institution (as well as of the International Red Cross and of its member groups) is the Swiss flag in reverse colors, and the 25 members of the Committee are Swiss nationals. Seventy-five percent of its budget is provided by the Swiss government and is supplemented by an annual fund drive in Switzerland. The Committee has been the driving force behind the so-called Geneva Conventions and, although politically guided by the tradition of neutrality, pursues humanitarian assistance to victims of war, civil strife, and internal upheavals. The creation of new weaponry and forms of combat demand a constant adaptation of the Geneva Conventions signed into law by numerous states which after ratification are deposited with the Government of Switzerland.[34] The ICRC's maxim is aptly stated by Werner Rings: "Political neutrality, yes; but never neutrality in questions of humanitarian concern."[35] This principle is far more easily stated than applied in practice, however, and the lines may become blurred, especially if conflicts derive from opposed ideologies.

During the Second World War the activities of the ICRC, so to speak the private arm of the Swiss government as a Protective Power, were many and wide-ranging. It had 137 delegates in the field, maintained 39 million registration cards, searched for 40,000 missing persons, 30,000 of whom it was able to locate, made 11,000 visits to camps of interned civilians and prisoners of war, chartered some 12 ships that brought 200,000 tons of provisions to prisoners of war in Germany in what would equal 500 railroad trains of 40 cars each. When by the fall of 1944 a desperate Hitler ordered

---

[33] See Georges Willemin and Roger Heacock under the direction of Jacques Freymond, *The International Committee of the Red Cross*. International Organization and Evolution of World Society, Vol. 2. The Graduate Institute of International Studies, Geneva (Boston: Martinus Nijhoff Publishers, 1984): 20; 19-26 give a concise "History of the ICRC, 1863-1945."

[34] Ibid., 23-25. Since the Cross derives from the Christian tradition, in 1929 "Red Crescent" organizations in Muslim nations were officially accepted as members of the umbrella organization of the International Red Cross; ibid., 21.—The connection with Switzerland is evident, for instance, in the remarks after the title of the "Convention between the United States of America and Other Powers, Relating to Prisoners of War" : "Signed at Geneva, July 27, 1929; ratification advised by the Senate, January 7, 1932; ratified by the President, January 16, 1932, ratification of the United States of America deposited with the Government of Switzerland; proclaimed August 4, 1932."

[35] Rings, *Advokaten,* 86; the statement is attributed to a Genevan diplomat.

that, given Allied bombing of German cities and the increasing scarcity of provisions, Allied prisoners of war should be left to starve, ICRC delegates prevailed with Heinrich Himmler and SS-General Gottlob Berger to ignore the order and to allow 474 trucks with 137 trailers to make 3,000 trips to Germany and to transfer 23,000 people. When in October 1944 Budapest fell into the hands of the Hungarian Arrow Cross, a brutal right-wing and anti-Jewish party, ICRC delegates protected 6,000 children and distributed daily 450,000 meals to people trapped in the Jewish ghetto.[36]

In March 1945, some 15,000 starving prisoners of war had been forced to march for three weeks from Karlsbad westward in sub-zero weather. René Bovey, the ICRC delegate led a convoy with provisions to meet them, of whom some 12,000 were British, some 3,000 were Russian nationals. The food distributed was crucial for their survival and although Soviet Russia had refused to sign the Geneva Convention and forbade that provisions be given to Russian prisoners in German hands, R. Bovey ignored that injunction in the name of humanity. When in 1945 Allied forces moved towards the concentration camp Mauthausen that housed 40,000 inmates, the implementation of the order to dynamite it before it could be liberated by the Allies was prevented by successful ICRC intervention.[37]

The following document illustrates the complexity of the work the ICRC might be called upon to shoulder. It contains the "substance" of a reply Carl J. Burckhardt, then President of the ICRC, gave to a telegram he had received from Minister Leland Harrison, the representative of the United States in Switzerland. On February 16, 1945, Burckhardt had been urged "to take the following action:"

1. Increase to greatest possible extent visits of its delegates to places of detention of all categories of 'Schutzhäftlinge';
2. Augment number [of] committee's representatives in Germany as substantially and rapidly as possible;
3. Instruct its delegates to take every advantage of mounting confusion within Germany to mitigate [the] lot of all civil detainees and dissuade German officials from last minute excesses.

---

[36] A detailed, in part critical study of these activities is Arieh Ben-Tov, *Facing the Holocaust in Budapest. The International Committee of the Red Cross and the Jews in Hungary, 1943–1945.* Henry Dunant Institute, Geneva. Dordrecht: Martinus Nijhoff Publishers, 1988.

[37] Data given in the above paragraphs are based on Rings, *Advokaten*, 28, 32, 34, 80, 127, 200; see also Bonjour, *Geschichte* , Vol. 6, 151-152 and Jacques Meurant, "Le comité internationale de la Croix-Rouge et la protection des civils", in: *Revue d'histoire* 31 (1981): 129-138.

To these requests Carl J. Burckhardt answered:

> Replying to your letter of February 16 I must in first place stress fact that in their memorandum to us dated February 1 German Government stated: 'Visits to camps and places of detention where alien detainees ("Schutzhäftlinge") are confined are unfortunately not feasible at the moment for imperative reasons of national defense.'
>
> In a recent communication our delegate Dr. Schirmer reported: 'Headquarters of German Security Police have informed us that permission to visit concentration camps of alien detainees must be secured in each particular instance from Himmler himself.'
>
> This [is the] present situation. I am awaiting an answer from Himmler concerning place and date I can see him personally. I shall spare no endeavor should interview take place to do my utmost to secure best possible result. You are aware how difficult that will be.
>
> We are anxious to send as many delegates (to Germany) as possible. They must be men of character. Five new delegates are accordingly leaving for Germany within next few days. We shall send others as soon as we can manage.
>
> Decisive problem is and remains question of transportation. Within 4 days thousands of prisoners and detainees can starve. . . .
>
> There is not a moment to be lost. Our delegates can only get into camps if they bring something with them and if they have gasoline and can still manage to travel on the roads (with trucks). Should it be found impracticable to except two railway lines in north and south from aerial bombardment, then any number of freight cars placed [at] our disposal will be useless. All this is most extremely urgent. Large scale methods of action and sweeping decisions alone can secure any results.
>
> We are often expected to do miracles. That, of course, is impossible; but by exerting every nerve and applying our will we can do something provided certain indispensable means for execution of our task be furnished us.[38]

Carl J. Burckhardt's reply dramatizes how agents of the Protecting Power were caught between the demands and conditions of two belligerents. On the one hand he was pressured by the United States to act decisively and quickly, on the other hand authorities of the German Reich put every possible obstacle in his way. The realities of war such as bombing raids, scarcity of fuel, and impassable roadways further severely limited what could be accomplished. The diplomat was, however, no stranger to

---

[38] Foreign Relations of the United States. *Diplomatic Papers. 1945.* Vol. II. *General: Political and Economic Matters* (Washington, DC: United States Printing Office, 1967): 1133-1134.

this predicament. As High Commissioner of the League of Nations in Danzig between 1937 and 1939 and as delegate of the ICRC he had been engaged before in what he called "a neckbreaking assignment." After persistent, yet diplomatically astute maneuvering with Reinhard Heydrich, Chief of the German Security Police, he could finally visit the concentration camp Esterwegen near Wilhelmshaven where, as he put it, he "got a look into the abyss."[39] Hitler's government had insisted and kept doing so throughout the war that, in contrast to prisoner of war camps concentration camps, were not war-related, thus were not covered by the Geneva Convention and were outside the jurisdiction of the mandate of a Protecting Power as well as the ICRC.[40]

Besides the International Committee of the Red Cross, the Swiss Red Cross also was engaged in mitigating the suffering created by war. Since 1942 that organization had devoted its efforts mainly to helping children, and collected some 55 million Swiss francs for that cause. It enabled some 81,000 children mainly from France—Germany rejected the organization's efforts—to spend three months in Switzerland where they received needed medical care, were provided with new clothing, and could recover from their deprivations. The Swiss Red Cross also managed homes for some 10,000 children in France and Belgium and distributed food, clothing, and medications in war-ravaged regions. Towards the end of the war, furthermore, Switzerland established a special fund named "Swiss Assistance for the War-Damaged [*Schweizerspende an die Kriegsgeschäd-igten*]" which reached some 145 million francs so that the total of Swiss assistance programs for those in distress abroad represented about 2% of the national income.[41]

If most of the tasks involved in the Protecting Power mandate demanded quiet, detailed, and little-noticed work, there were moments of unusual complexity which received some wider attention. Three of them are briefly sketched below.

A Unique Challenge in Vichy, France

On August 20, 1944 Marshall Pétain had been forced by the German government to leave Vichy, an event witnessed by Minister Stucki.[42] The

---

[39] See *Danziger Mission*, 54-63; also above, footnote 18, the references to H. Levine's and P. Stauffer's essays.

[40] Janner, *La puissance protectrice,* 43.

[41] Bonjour, *Geschichte,* Vol. 6, 152, 154.

[42] See *Diplomatische Dokumente der Schweiz 1848–1945.* Vol. 15: *1943–1945*(Bern: Benteli Verlag, 1992): 553; Pétain had told Stucki: "I request of you the great sacrifice to be at my disposal at all times, day and night, in case I or my collaborators should find it

"whole town of Vichy was in a feverish state", the Swiss representative reported, "caused by fear and anxiety, fear of the Germans, and especially fear of the Maquis."[43] Although he had been asked by the Swiss Foreign Minister Pilet-Golaz to return to Switzerland right away, at least for consultation, Minister Stucki replied that he found it impossible to leave until two conditions had been met: "We will return", he wired back to Bern on August 25, "as soon as

1 the roads are passable;
2 my incessant efforts to save Vichy from the spilling of blood have led to certain success.
Both might take some days still . . . ."[44]

The situation was complex. German troops were still firmly entrenched in the region, with near-by Clermont-Ferrand serving as their headquarters. They were supported by the French 'miliciens', noted for their lawlessness and violence. In the mountains the anti-German F. F. I., that is the French Forces of the Interior, were in control and moved their forces towards Vichy. Another group of the resistance which had served in the Spanish Civil War hoped to establish in Vichy a Marxist workers' commune. Given these conditions, people were afraid of a carnage and believed that Walter Stucki, the Swiss agent of the Protecting Power mandate, should stay in Vichy "in order to protect the town from heavy turmoil and great bloodshed."[45] He accepted the task and decided to negotiate with both the German and the underground leaders in broad daylight.

On August 22, 1944 he had his chauffeur drive him in the legation's car marked with the Swiss flag, first to the German command post in Clermont-Ferrand. He openly informed the stunned officers of his intention

---

necessary."—The sketch given above follows Stucki's vivid account in *La fin,* 100-124; see ibid., 106-108, General Alexander Neubronn von Eisenburg's moving statement in answer to Stucki's plea not to implement orders to take Pétain captive; the General explained that he, too, found the assignment repulsive; but he was also aware that, if he were to refuse orders, he would risk not only his own life, but also that of his wife and children.

[43] *Diplomatische Dokumente*, Vol. 15, 584.

[44] Ibid., 562.

[45] Ibid., 584; see ibid., 562, where Stucki notes: "The miliciens, robbers and criminals of all kinds have left Vichy;" he also requested that the miliciens' notorious leaders not be given asylum in Switzerland. The miliciens' activities especially after August 25, 1944, during their retreat to Germany are described by J. Delperrie de Bayac, *Histoire de la milice, 1918–1945.* 2 vols. Collection marabout université. [Verviers?]: Arthème Fayard, 1969, Vol. 2, 248-250. They summarily executed any one suspected to belong to the 'résistance' the members of which retaliated by similar measures.

to visit the headquarters of the F. F. I. hidden in the mountains, the leaders of which had let him know in secret that "they would be grateful for his visit and mediation." Stucki requested a pass through German-held territory, a request granted by the German commanding officer with some apprehension for Stucki's safety. Neither he nor his car might ever return, he commented. But the representative of Switzerland was unwavering in his resolve. "I drove high up into the mountains of the Central Massif", Stucki wrote to Bern, "in an adventurous drive which will remain unforgettable to me." Almost all bridges had been blown up, and at a German checkpoint he was nearly shot. The guard had taken the Swiss flag to be that of the Red Cross, and only the day before a car with the Red Cross emblem had passed by, opened fire, and killed five German soldiers. Yet Minister Stucki, who was forced at gunpoint with raised arms into the army post, quickly regained his composure and sharply protested that this was no way to treat an ambassador plenipotentiary; if he were harmed, he declared, such action would create a serious international scandal. Finally he could move on unmolested and reach F. F. I. headquarters at Mont Dore. "In a five-hour meeting with the civilian and military leaders of the F. F. I. movement in Central France I discussed in detail", Stucki explained,

1) the guarantees for the return of my legation to Switzerland;
2) the guarantees for the [proper] treatment of the diplomatic corps;
3) the modalities of the transition of Vichy from the old to the new regime.
I was able to gain the full confidence of these people who on the whole made quite a good impression.[46]

On his return, the Swiss Minister needed to convince the German commanding officer that it would be in the Germans' best interest to quit Vichy without a fight. During the night of August 23 the German elements, the Gestapo included, did indeed leave, but they were partially replaced by German SS troops which, as the Swiss Legation's military attaché reported to Bern, had brought with them heavy military equipment. These "were troops who came from the South of the Massif Central, via Clermont-Ferrand and Thiers, also from Chateauroux. In the course of the afternoon [of August 24 also] a substantial detachment of the SS took quarters in Vichy."[47] (It was that very evening when Walter Stucki had received and

---

[46] Ibid., 584; Stucki, *La fin*, 143-165, dramatically describes his journey.
[47] *Diplomatische Dokumente*, Vol. 15, 573, R. de Blonay to R. Masson.

accepted the request of taking the German soldiers into Swiss protection who had been heavily wounded in a fierce encounter between the SS and the F. F. I.[48]) The Swiss military attaché de Blonay then went to meet with the German commander Colonel Krämer and requested that he confer with Minister Stucki which the colonel did in the afternoon of August 25. Perhaps in consequence of that meeting the German troops stationed in Vichy quit the town that night, leaving behind ammunitions, provisions, and all sorts of equipment.

The following day Minister Stucki had leaders of the F. F. I., intent on taking control of the town, meet with the local representatives of the then defunct Vichy government in order to promote an orderly transition. On that afternoon of August 26, 1944 the F. F. I. solemnly marched into Vichy under a banner that read: "Vive les Alliés, Vive de Gaulle, Gloire aux F. F. I."[49] The Swiss representative then telephoned the German commander General Ottenbach in Clermont who "seemed to desire his intervention in case of an eventual capitulation."[50] On August 28, 1944 at 11:30 p.m. Minister Stucki was finally able to send the following message to the Swiss Foreign Minister in Bern:

> Thanks to my incessant mediation efforts the departure of the Germans and the handing over [of the administration of Vichy] to the F. F. I. has occurred without a single shot and without serious incidents.
>
> All sides have thanked me and Switzerland for this in a touching manner, and the town of Vichy has made me its honorary citizen. Our flag is hailed everywhere.
>
> Because yesterday afternoon German troops have moved out also from the further environs, especially Clermont-Ferrand, my efforts of mediation have ended.[51]

Stemming the Tide of Murderous Terror in Budapest

A second unusual situation engaging representatives of Switzerland as Protecting Power occurred in Hungary. The country had been divided between those who sought help from Germany in regaining territory lost after World War One and those who rejected any alliance with the Third Reich. In April 1941 Lászlo Bardossy, Premier from 1941 to 1942, involved Hungary in the war against Russia.

---

[48] See above, footnote 27 and corresponding text.

[49] Stucki, *La fin*, picture opposite p. 160: "Long live the Allies, long live de Gaulle, glory to the F. F. I."

[50] *Diplomatische Dokumente,* Vol. 15, 573, R. de Blonay to Masson.

[51] Ibid., 571.

Until March 19, 1944 Jewish Hungarians could live "almost normal lives." Although anti-Semitism in Hungary was also a dangerous force, during the war years it had led only to one if most destructive event, the deportation of some 18,000 Jews, the majority of whom perished in Kamenetz-Poldosk.[52] Despite its being in the Axis orbit, numerous Jews actually had found refuge in Hungary from the Third Reich's infamous policies, so that their numbers, 404,000 in 1939, had grown to 680,000 by March 1944.[53] But from March 19, 1944 onward when German troops occupied Hungary, and especially after October 15 when the Arrow Cross Party took control, Hungarian Jews were victims of an immense catastrophe which continued until January 18, 1945, when Russian troops liberated Pest and by mid-February Buda. On April 3, 1944 a decree forced Jews to wear a yellow star, on April 16 their property had to be reported for eventual confiscation, on April 27 Jewish Hungarians of the provinces were driven out. On the same day some 50,000 were deported to forced labor camps in Germany and on June 24 Jews were rounded up in Budapest and forced into so-called yellow star houses.[54]

An international storm of protests erupted once reliable news had been sent secretly to Geneva and widely disseminated from there. In June 1944, for instance, 383 articles and newsreports appeared in the Swiss Press alone within just 18 days and widely advertised religious services were held by Swiss churches.[55] Leaders of the Western world were urged to put pressure on the Hungarian government to stop its criminal persecutions. President Roosevelt, Prime Minister Churchill, the Queen of Holland, the Pope, and

---

[52] Quotation from Robert Rozett, "Child Rescue in Budapest, 1944-5", *Holocaust and Genocide Studies* 2,1 (1987):56, endnote 1. The sources, primary and secondary, are voluminous; see the 2479 entries given by Randolph L. Braham, *The Hungarian Jewish Catastrophe. A Selected and Annotated Bibliography*. Second Edition. Revised and Enlarged. New York: The City University of New York, 1984. Two surveys of the events are, for example, Margit Szöllösi-Janze, *Die Pfeilkreuzler Bewegung in Ungarn. Historischer Kontext, Entwicklung und Herrschaft* (München: R. Oldenbourg Verlag, 1989): 283-432; Raphael Patai, *The Jews of Hungary. History, Culture, Psychology* (Detroit: Wayne State University Press, 1996): 578-595.

[53] The numbers given vary; those above are from Sergio DellaPergola, "Between Science and Fiction: Notes on the Demography of the Holocaust", in *Holocaust and Genocide Studies* 10,1(1996): 35, and Rozett, "Child Rescue", 56-57, note 3. Szöllösi-Janze, *Pfeilkreuzler*, 432, gives these numbers computed by R. Braham: In March 1944 there were 762,000 Jews in Hungary, in 1945 255,000 were liberated, 437,000 had been deported to Auschwitz.

[54] For a helpful chronology of the complex events see Jenö Levai, *Hungarian Jewry and the Papacy. Pope Pius Did Not Remain Silent*. Translated by J. R. Foster (London: SANDS, 1968): 117-119.

[55] Rings, *Advokaten*, 146, 148.

the Archbishop of Canterbury lodged sharp protests with the Hungarian government.[56] In July the Swiss Foreign Minister Pilet-Golaz searched for ways to save as many Jews as possible, especially some 6,000 Jewish children sheltered in houses under Swiss or Swedish protection, who were to be given visas to Switzerland. Heinrich Rothmund, the Chief of Police in the Swiss Department of Justice "was wholly committed to our initiative". Karl Th. Stucki of the Swiss Foreign Office also reported that Rothmund "is truly happy with our initiative and is considering our plans with greatest readiness. . ."[57]

Several neutral states such as Switzerland, Sweden, and the Vatican acted individually or in concert directly on the scene, especially in Budapest. Switzerland was represented on three levels. Minister Maximilian Jaeger was the head of the Swiss Embassy, supported by Anton Kilchmann, the Legation's secretary, and his staff. Carl Lutz who resided in the British Embassy was in charge of Switzerland's activities as Protecting Power for Great Britain, the United States, El Salvador, and their enemy Germany. He was assisted by men such as Karl Hofer, Ernst Vonrufs, and Peter Zürcher. Friedrich Born was the chief delegate of the Swiss International Committee of the Red Cross (ICRC): helped by Robert Schirmer and Alex Weyermann. Thus Switzerland was active as a state on the official diplomatic level, as the Protecting Power of foreign interests, and as supporter of the ICRC, a Swiss institution.[58] The Swedish nation was represented by Raoul Wallenberg whose intrepid activities became widely known and admired.[59]

---

[56] The U.S. protest is given in *Diplomatische Dokumente*, Vol. 15, 444, note 1, in French translation.

[57] *Diplomatische Dokumente,* Vol. 15, 481; report by Karl Th. Stucki, ibid., 482: Er "ist von unserer Initiative geradezu beglückt und geht mit grösster Bereitschaft auf unsere Absichten ein."

[58] *Diplomatische Dokumente*, Vol. 15, richly document the three-leveled involvement of Switzerland. On Carl Lutz see the monographs of Alexander Grossmann, *Carl Lutz und seine Budapester Aktion: Geschichte und Porträt.* Wald: Verlag im Waldgut, 1986 and of Theo Tschuy, *Carl Lutz und die Juden von Budapest.* Vorwort von Simon Wiesenthal. Zürich: Verlag Neue Zürcher Zeitung, 1995; forthcoming English version to be published by W. B. Eerdmans, Grand Rapids, Michigan.

[59] R. Braham, *Hungarian Jewish Catastrophe* gives 30 entries for Wallenberg, but only 2 for Lutz and none for Born, although the combined efforts of Lutz and Born far surpassed what Wallenberg was able to accomplish. See Elenore Lester, "Raoul Wallenberg: The Righteous Gentile from Sweden", in: *The Holocaust in Hungary Forty Years Later*. Edited by Randolph L. Braham and Bela Vago (New York: The City University of New York, 1985): 147-160; the essay, however, describes Wallenberg's efforts isolated from those of others.

Also Angelo Rotta, the papal representative, energetically did his part to stop the atrocities.[60]

The Swiss representatives collaborated closely with leaders of the various Jewish organizations. Moshe (or Miklos) Krausz, until March 19, 1944 secretary of the Palestine Office in Budapest then under British jurisdiction deriving from a League of Nations mandate, became indispensable to the efforts of Carl Lutz. Otto Komoly, President of the Zionist Association was central to the work of the ICRC undertaken by Friedrich Born.[61] Lutz called Moshe Krausz "the soul of this enterprise", that is the establishment of numerous houses in Budapest which were put under Swiss diplomatic protection, and Krausz wrote of Lutz in his important letter of June 19, 1944 to the merchant George Mandel Mantello who served in Geneva as first secretary of the Consulate General of El Salvador: "[Lutz] is a wonderful person who spares no effort to achieve anything in the interest of Jewry. . . . I myself am a personal friend of Consul Mr. Lutz."[62] Per Anger called the delegate of the ICRC Friedrich Born "a daring man" who unhesitatingly undertook dangerous missions.[63]

What did the efforts of the Swiss representatives achieve in close cooperation with others, especially the Zionistic groups? On the diplomatic level Minister Jaeger put constant pressure on the Hungarian government and was in especially close contact with the Regent Admiral Horthy; although the latter was an anti-Semite, he strove to extricate Hungary from German as well as potential Soviet domination. Minister Jaeger had the support of the Swiss Foreign Minister Pilet-Golaz, who sought ways to enable the persecuted to find refuge in Switzerland.[64] The embassies of

---

[60] See Yehuda Bauer, "Conclusion", in: *Genocide and Rescue. The Holocaust in Hungary 1944*. Edited by Cesarani (Oxford: Berg, 1997): 205; also Per Anger, *With Raoul Wallenberg in Budapest. Memories of the War Years in Hungary*. Preface by Elie Wiesel. Translated from the Swedish by David Mel Paul and Margareta Paul (New York: Holocaust Library, 1981): 58.

[61] Asher Cohen, "Resistance and Rescue in Hungary",, ibid., 128; see Rozett, "Child Rescue", 49, note, for an identification of the various groups.

[62] See facsimile in Rings, *Advokaten*, 143; the letter moved Georges Mantello to provide important assistance.

[63] Anger, *With Raoul Wallenberg*, 82; in this instance Born drove unprotected into the ghetto to rescue two Swedish Jewish women. "This bold stroke succeeded", Anger comments, "and the two were released" (83).

[64] Bucher, *Zwischen Bundesrat und General*, 591; the chapter is perhaps too optimistically titled "Pilet's erfolgreiche Massnahmen zur Rettung ungarischer Juden", 590-595. On the supposed relationship between the Swiss Foreign Minister Pilet-Golaz and the diplomats in the field see Neville Wylie, "Pilet-Golaz and the Making of Swiss Foreign Policy: Some Remarks", in *Schweizerische Zeitschrift für Geschichte* 47 (1997): 608-620.

neutral states officially issued the following numbers of passports to Jews: Switzerland 7,800, Sweden 4,500, the Vatican 2,500, Portugal 698, Spain 100.[65] In addition these numbers were greatly increased by Swiss Protection Letters, promises of visas, emigration permits, and baptismal certificates, since at times Christianized Jews received greater protection. Carl Lutz's office issued no less than 50,000 Swiss protection letters and was also the conduit for some 20,000 El Salvadoran passports provided on the initiative of Georges Mantello in Geneva. This task, which derived from Switzerland being also El Salvador's Protecting Power, Lutz wrote, "created for us an awkward situation", since of course everybody knew that there were no Salvadoran Jewish citizens in Hungary. "Yet the distressful situation outweighed all reservations. . . . Within some weeks there were numerous El Salvador citizens in Budapest so that I needed to appoint a special official for this new matter." Also Honduran passports arrived so that a collective passport was finally created by Lutz's office.[66] As Per Anger put it: ". . . what was involved was continually trying to find new ways to save human lives, and the Swiss, after long negotiations, succeeded in getting the Hungarian ministry to approve the 'citizens of El Salvador.'"[67] It has been estimated that the representatives of neutral states issued some 120,000 protective documents, perhaps some 80,000 of them via Lutz's Protecting Power office. These had been physically created with the dedicated help of Jewish groups of Budapest. It is not surprising, therefore, that a general of the German Wehrmacht complained on November 21, 1944: "The Swiss Embassy continues now as before to put itself to a high degree *disruptingly* before the whole Jewish action by issuing protective passes."[68]

The disastrous rise to power of the Arrow Cross Party on October 15, 1944 shattered a relative calm that had been achieved since early July by the June protests and led to renewed brutal measures such as the creation of a central ghetto and the impressment of thousands of Jewish men and women to work under horrendous conditions on the fortifications of Budapest.

---

[65] Rings, *Advokaten,* 199.

[66] Quote in Bucher, *Zwischen Bundesrat und General,* 592; Anger, *With Raoul Wallenberg,* 59, comments: "It is also well known that the Swiss [as Protecting Power], by taking over the interests in Hungary of San Salvador at American request, succeeded in furnishing several thousand Jews with papers ... . Actually, San Salvador had no citizens in Hungary ... ."

[67] Anger, ibid.

[68] Quoted in Rings, *Advokaten,* 152; from *Eichmann in Ungarn. Dokumente.* Edited by Jenö Levai (Budapest: Pannonia Verlag, 1961): 193: "Schweizer Gesandtschaft stellt sich nach wie vor in hohem Masse durch Erteilung von Schutzpässen *störend* vor die ganze Judenaktion."

Thousands of others were deported, still others brutally attacked by Arrow Cross gangs. In response Friedrich Born, Carl Lutz, and Raoul Wallenberg established special houses marked by the Swiss or Swedish flags so that in December 1944 there were 23,000 owners of various forms of protective papers at least somewhat shielded from attacks in 77 houses, 26,000 in the ghetto, 10,000 in private homes, and 3,000 in Swiss consular buildings.[69] The ICRC was especially anxious to protect Jewish children. Parents brought them to numerous protected shelters, some provided by Hungarian non-Jews, and "Friedrich Born and his assistant Weyermann maintained contact with Jewish leaders from all factions of the community . . . and their offices became points of convergence for ICRC, VH and Zionist Youth activities."[70]

At times Carl Lutz found himself in difficult situations. On December 8, 1944, for instance, he was "threatened by an Arrow Cross man with a cocked revolver", but able to escape to his car and alert the Chief of the Hungarian Cabinet Bagossy. "When he arrived on the scene, the Arrow Cross men surrounded him on four sides with machine guns and tore from him his revolver and legitimization papers." On another occasion Lutz got caught in a traffic jam. "Immediately I was surrounded by a rowdy whistling mass of people", he reported, "which . . . used many slurs such as 'the Jew-protecting Swiss rabble shall get out of Budapest right away or else.'" With the Russians approaching the city, he observed further, the tasks of protecting foreign interests became ever more difficult. Yet "I like the numerous tasks. I find great satisfaction in being able to save human lives and to mitigate suffering."[71] The achievements of the Swiss, Swedish, Papal, and other representatives who in close cooperation with various Jewish organizations did their utmost to stem the tide of deportations, attacks, forced labor, and murders is concisely summarized by Raphael Patai's chapter heading: "How Half of Budapest Jewry Was Saved."[72]

The Rescue of Prominent Allied Captives Held in Germany

In contrast to Walter Stucki, who valiantly strove to prevent bloodshed in Vichy, and to Carl Lutz and Friedrich Born, who struggled together with the representative of Sweden Raoul Wallenberg and others to save as many Jewish lives in Budapest as possible, Swiss Minister Peter A. Feldscher who

---

[69] Rings, ibid.

[70] Rozett, "Child Rescue", 51; the article describes impressively events and protective measures taken, especially also by Otto Komoly; VH stands for Vaad Ezra Vehatsala.

[71] *Diplomatische Dokumente*, Vol. 15, 772-773, passim.

[72] *The Jews of Hungary*, 578.

represented Switzerland as Protecting Power in Berlin faced among his numerous duties a different, if also challenging, task. The Germans held a number of notables as captives of war, among them Giles Romilly, nephew of Winston Churchill; Captain John Elphinstone, nephew of the Queen of England; Lord Lascelles of the Grenadier Guards, son of the Princess Royal and Lord Harewood; Michael Alexander, nephew of British Field-Marshal Sir Harold Alexander, the British commander in charge of the Allied invasion of Italy; John Winant, son of the American ambassador in London; and Tadeusz Pelczinski, Chief of Staff of the Polish Army.[73] These and other prized captives were actually hostages, to be executed in case of an Axis defeat.

Gottlob Berger, SS Commander and since October 1, 1944 Chief of the Prisoner of War Camps in SS Headquarters, claimed that the Hitler regime observed the 1929 Geneva convention in the first phase of the war.[74] When in late 1944, however, the fortunes of war had turned and provisions in Germany had become scarce, 'non-productive' prisoners were to be left starving or to receive only minimal rations insufficient for survival. After mid-March 1945, when Allied victory had become a certainty, a third phase was to begin, that is annihilation of the detainees, including of the notable captives who were held in the castle Colditz in northern Germany. Giles Romilly had been brought there on November 11, 1941, was watched day and night under most stringent security measures, and a constant log was kept of his every move. Then other notables arrived who met a similar fate. "We wrote countless letters to the [Swiss] protecting power about the way they had been treated", G. Romilly recalls. "But where it was all up to I don't know, but later on they were allowed a little bit more freedom during the daytime, but they and the other prominente when they arrived—that Charley Hopetoun and the others—were all locked up at night in that same particular block."[75]

When American forces approached the region of Colditz, the prisoners were transferred on April 11, 1945 to the castle of Königstein, then moved again to a prison in Laufen. Urged on by a British message, Minister Feldscher, the Swiss Protecting Power Plenipotentiary in Germany, went with "six cars densely packed with provisions and gasoline" to that place, preceded by his assistant Rudolf A. Denzler who had found out where the

---

[73] Rings, *Advokaten,* 36-37; the sketch given here follows Rings, 36-58, who states, 38: "These prominent [captives] have been liberated under dramatic circumstances; for the first time the story of their liberation is being told here in their own words."

[74] See ibid., 57-58; 183-184 a biographical sketch of Berger.

[75] Quoted ibid., 42. G. Romilly is quoted in English by Rings.

prisoners were kept and had gained access to them. Minister Feldscher then opened formal negotiations with the commander in charge of the prisoners in the presence of John Elphinstone and General Bor and gained the concession that the captives would not be moved again. "It was then that we knew for the first time", Sir Michael Alexander attests, "that the Swiss representatives were interested in us. We thought we were lost, we thought that nobody knew where we were."[76] Minister Feldscher then asked his deputy R. A. Denzler, who rented a room in plain view of the prison, to keep the German captors under constant surveillance as to their dealings with the hostages. Only two days later Denzler was informed that despite the previous promise the captives were to be moved again, this time to camp Markt-Pongau. He immediately drove to Salzburg, to Fuschl, and to Königsee to lodge a protest with the authorities in charge, yet without success. He then rushed back to Laufen where in late April the transfer took place. "As we left the camp, in the company of some very sinister looking SS and other rather strange people in long leather-coats", Sir Michael Alexander reported, "we happened to notice in the square of the town Laufen, we saw standing behind a tree or we thought we saw . . . behind the tree Mr. Denzler himself looking out from behind and observing our departure. So we said oh well let's go, he knows . . . ", with Sir Alexander later adding, "it was a conspirational wave, a life line was still out."[77] The Swiss Protecting Power representative then trailed the convoy through remote forest roads and reached Markt-Pongau at the same time as the captives.

Also Minister Feldscher arrived in Markt-Pongau and requested immediate access to the camp commander. He demanded that the prisoners be transferred to Swiss sovereignty, yet his request was refused and he was told to see Gottlob Berger who alone had the authority to allow such a transfer. Late that night the Swiss plenipotentiary located Berger who had received orders to kill the captives. Minister Feldscher impressed upon him to prevent such a crime in his own self-interest since after the soon-to-be-expected armistice he would have to pay for it with his life. The next morning Berger agreed to the transfer. He approached the prisoners himself, gave them "whisky and cigarettes and promised to do all he could to help" them.

That very evening a convoy left Markt-Pongau marked with the Swiss flag and, after a dinner in a farmhouse that had been arranged by Berger, it drove on. "We saw the American forces coming up the plain", Sir

---

[76] Ibid., 48.
[77] Ibid., 51.

Alexander wrote, " very slowly in great 'panzers' coming, creeping slowly forward and the advanced scouts coming up. We saw the two sides. It was very interesting and then we were through to the Americans who were expecting us perhaps, I don't know. Anyway, we had the Swiss flag flying on the [vehicles] . . . and they let us through."[78] Thus ended another unusual task that had fallen to the representatives of Switzerland as Protecting Power.

On Monday, May 7, 1945 a headline of the *Times of London* announced: "Lord Lascelles Released. Group of Prisoners Reach Americans."[79] The next day Captain John Elphinstone sent the following handwritten note to Rudolf Denzler from Buckingham Palace:

> Dear Mr. Denzler
> I feel I must write to you—as a free man once more—to thank you for all the help to us—and to tell you briefly how all went! Your Minister and Mr. Buchmutter continued your splendid work and arranged everything with the Obergruppenführer and after a most exciting and not un-anxious trip we drove unto the American lines—You can imagine our feelings!
> Unfortunately it became impossible to carry out the original intention of going through to Switzerland and we were appropriated by the U. S. Army who were however most kind.
> From Innsbruck Lord Lascelles, John Winant, de Hamel and myself went to Gen. Patch's H. Q. and flew from Augsburg to London yesterday. Lord Lascelles and I came straight on here where we had a magnificent welcome.—It really seems too good to be true, and I still feel its all a wonderful dream. However what I want to do is to tell you how more than grateful we all are to you and your Legation for the absolutely splendid way you arranged things.
> Please accept my deepest thanks and best wishes for the future.
>
> Yours sincerely, John Elphinstone.

Shortly after this Minister Feldscher received mail from London; a book that contained a personal letter of thanks from Sir John Elphinstone and from Princess Mary, the King's sister.[80]

---

[78] Ibid., 54; a headline of the *Times of London* announced on Monday, May 7, 1945, p. 4: "Lord Lascelles Released. Group of Prisoners Reach Americans."

[79] *The Times*, p. 4.

[80] Rings, *Advokaten,* 182, a facsimile of the letter; 183, reference to the gift for Minister Feldscher.

Switzerland's Activities as Protecting Power Assessed

While most tasks of Swiss officials engaged in performing the duties of a Protecting Power were barely noticed in the media and soon faded from memory, the treatment of American prisoners of war in contrast to that of German captives in the United States briefly emerged as a contentious issue and indirectly also criticized Switzerland's performance. With Allied victory becoming a certainty in April and May 1945, members of the United States Congress went to Germany, visited concentration camps such as Buchenwald, Belsen, and Dachau, and talked with Americans freed from prisoner of war camps. Somehow the two quite different experiences of concentration camp victims and of war captives were merged into one, and some legislators began to question the 1929 Geneva Convention and, by implication, Switzerland's usefulness as a Protecting Power.

On April 26, 1945, furthermore, Congressional hearings were initiated that "coincided with a considerable degree of popular indignation aroused by revolting revelations of German brutality in civilian prison camps overrun by our troops advancing in Germany."[81] At the hearings Representative Richard F. Harless claimed that for the nearly 400,000 German prisoners in the United States—as of April 25, 1945 there were 340,407 Germans, 50,302 Italians, and 3,260 Japanese detained in 490 camps[82]—the "Geneva Convention had been stretched." A *New York Times* headline stated that "Nazi Prisoners 'as Fat as Hogs' Are Reported at Arizona Camp."[83] This contrasted with an "inexcusable treatment of prisoners overseas", the newspaper claimed, and that every month 75,000 Axis prisoners of war were still arriving in the United States.[84] Although a later headline announced "1,975 Arrive Here from Nazi Prisons. Soldiers Homeward Bound and Recovering Rapidly, Tell of Abuses in German Camps", the article itself clarified that "their stories varied." It also quoted Sgt. William B. Bubuiser, age 27, of Burlington, Vermont, who declared: "I am glad the way we treat the German prisoners over here. I am sure that helped us over there. It would have been much worse if they thought we were mistreating their own men."[85] A later report further announced that there had been "no massive atrocities or torture, but much brutality." Items such as watches or identity papers occasionally were stolen by the guards

---

[81] See "Investigations of the National War Effort", June 12, 1945, in: *House Reports.* 79th Congress, 1st Session (January 3–December 21, 1945): No. 728, p. 1.

[82] Ibid., 6.

[83] *New York Times*, April 23 (1945): 3.

[84] Ibid., April 27, 7.

[85] Ibid., April 29, 16.

and food was generally scarce.[86] Yet German prisoners of war in the United States were "pampered" and members of Congress demanded that the Geneva Convention should be, if not fully abrogated, at least modified.[87]

Such demands and criticisms of "the [U. S.] War Department's method of handling enemy prisoners of war interned in this country" were rejected at the hearings by witnesses such as Brigadier General R. W. Berry, Deputy Assistant Chief of Staff, who insisted that the 1929 Geneva Convention was "the supreme law of the land."[88] A representative of the State Department further observed that it "cannot be denounced in time of war. It can be denounced, but the denunciation must be filed with the Swiss Federal Council 1 year before it becomes effective."[89] In his prepared statement Edwin A. Plitt, the representative of the State Department, quoted Articles 86 and 87 of the Geneva Convention in full that outlined the Protecting Power's duties in regard to the treatment of prisoners of war. He observed that the duties of the State Department included dealing with the protecting powers in all such matters.[90] Switzerland's performance as Protecting Power was then officially assessed in words that acknowledged its difficult, yet properly fulfilled mission:

> The Swiss government acts as the protecting power for both Germany and the United States in the matter of prisoners of war abroad and it has given us good representation, as also has the International [Committee of the] Red Cross.
>
> From the very beginning reports have been received from the Swiss Government on maltreatment of American prisoners, but all were of a minor nature and none as serious as those received between the early part of December 1944 and just prior to VE-day.
>
> It must not be forgotten that at the time those acts occurred, the German armies were being cut to pieces and that the Swiss Government was unable to get its reports or supplies through because of the destruction of communication facilities by our armed forces.
>
> As our allies, the Russians, came in from the east, Germany was forced to move vast numbers of prisoners to the west. As our armies came in from the west, they were forced to move the other way. The only possible inference is that many of the prison camps must have

---

[86] Ibid., April 30, 5.

[87] Ibid., May 1, 9.

[88] "Investigations", *House Reports* (1945): No. 728, p.1, 3; Berry and Plitt both invoked "the law of the land."

[89] Ibid., 6.

[90] Ibid., 4-5.

been overcrowded. Perhaps in many places they did not even have camps or lodgings sufficient to take care of their people.

Protest is lodged immediately upon our learning of ill treatment to Americans. The protecting power is asked to get in touch with the German Foreign Office and have that office assist the Wehrmacht in bringing about a better compliance with the provisions of the Geneva Convention. Results were not always satisfactory, but some good has been accomplished and the treatment improved. If the commanding officer of a German prison camp is a Wehrmacht officer, it is possible to get somewhere; but if he is a Gestapo or an Elite Guard officer, it is quite another story.

Under ordinary circumstances the Swiss Foreign Office orders its representatives to make an inspection after a formal protest, but when a particular territory is completely overrun, it is often impossible to find out exactly what did happen. Naturally, the Germans deny many of the accusations made against them, and it is true, as stated above, that corrective measures have been taken by them in a number of instances.

When the protecting power sends one of its representatives to an American camp, he is generally accompanied by a Special War Problems Division man in order to keep the State Department fully informed. This is not compulsory, but is rather a courtesy extended by the protecting power.

At the time of the alleged shooting of 100 Americans taken prisoner . . . the State Department protested in the most vigorous terms against such acts.

On the other hand, the German Legation at Bern has registered many complaints against our treatment of German captives. One allegation is that prisoners of war were used as shields by United States troops, the truth or falsity of which has not yet been determined by the committee.[91]

This sober assessment was echoed by the American Secretary of State Cordell Hull. He acknowledged the work of Switzerland, "representing us diplomatically in enemy countries", as

our sole link with them. We had to depend on her representatives to ensure the welfare of American prisoners of war. We were keenly gratified by the conscientious manner in which Switzerland had endeavored to fulfill this task, even though her efforts in the Japanese

---

[91] Ibid., 5-6.

area had been largely ineffective because of the uncooperative attitude of the Japanese military authorities.[92]

Cordell Hull could have added that efforts to protect people in concentration camps and especially Jewish victims of unimaginable atrocities were only partially successful. Disregarding the complexities of the times and Switzerland's beleaguered state, some scholars have questioned the commitment in this regard not only of official Switzerland, but also that of the Swiss International Committee of the Red Cross.[93] Supposedly both had been too much concerned with legalities in situations where only quick and resolute action could avert disaster. One may counter that the benefits of hindsight should not be underestimated and, also, that every action taken had to be tested not only against the demands of international law, but also against the very real danger that every help, as limited it may have been, would be totally eliminated by the hostile powers.

Perhaps the words of David Newsom, American Undersecretary for Political Affairs during the 1979 Iranian hostage crisis, in which Swiss representatives again served as a link between two nations in conflict, may pertain also to Switzerland's service as Protecting Power in the Second World War: "Unassuming in claiming credit, professional in conduct and assessment, and totally reliable in objectivity and discretion."[94]

---

[92] Quoted by Meier, *Friendship under Stress*, 309; from Cordell Hull, *The Memoirs of Cordell Hull* Vol. 2 (New York: Macmillan, 1948), 1348-1349.

[93] See, for instance Yehuda Bauer, "Conclusion", in: Cesarani, ed., *Genocide and Rescue*. 205; the author belittles the neutrals' efforts as basically self-serving and resulting from "positive anti-Semitism", that is trying to get on the good side of the victorious Allies. A. Ben-Tov, *Facing the Holocaust*, 387 criticizes the Swiss government and claims that the ICRC was too dependent on it, following the government's too limited approach. "When it [ICRC] abandoned its narrow interpretation of its principles and accepted the fact that its delegate in Hungary, Friedrich Born, had taken the practical steps, subsequently with the help of Dr. Schirmer, then the institution's achievements in Hungary were truly great."

[94] Brunner et al., eds., *Einblick*, 303; D. Newsom refers specifically to the 'Good Offices' especially of R. Probst, then ambassador of Switzerland in the United States.

VIII: THE SPIRIT OF RESISTANCE

The Swiss *Wochenschau* and *Armeefilmdienst*

Stephen P. Halbrook[1]

Prologue: Total Resistance

"National Defense and the *Ortswehren* (Local Forces)" is the title that flashes across the screen as you sit in a movie theater in Switzerland in August 1943. The newsreel looks back with the words: "May 1940: Attack on Belgium and Holland; breakthrough of Panzer forces far into the hinterland. Paratroopers, saboteurs, evacuation of the civil population . . . . Call of the General for the formation of the Ortswehren (Local Defenses)."[2]

Three long years have past since Western Europe collapsed and the small Swiss republic has been surrounded by German Nazi and Italian Fascist forces. Under General Henri Guisan's capable leadership, all of Switzerland is ready to resist invasion, right down to each local village.

The drama begins with an urgent call to a Swiss military officer. He sends three young men in Scout uniforms rushing off on their bicycles with old Model 1889 rifles on their backs. One bursts into an office where an older man is dictating to a secretary. The old man reaches for the hatrack, grabbing an old military coat with armband and holstered pistol. The alarm spreads like wildfire.

A young boy alerts a man at home, and instantly he and his wife run out, both in uniform. Men sprinting with rifles in hand: one positions himself at a window to shoot toward railroad tracks, two others take sniper positions at a bridge, still others await on high ground behind obstructions. Barricades of heavy logs are thrown up on roads. A crane-like device on wagon wheels positions concrete tank obstructions. Women and children are warned away. A tent hospital is readied.

An alarm signal sounds and a room full of *Ortswehr* men grab their rifles and run out, secreting themselves along a barricaded road, Molotov cocktails or other explosive devices at the ready. An enemy vehicle appears,

---

[1] The author wishes to thank the following persons who assisted in obtaining copies of films used for this study: Cdmt. Jean Abt, Centre d'histoire et de prospective militaires; M. Markus Meister, Chef Sektion Armeefilmdienst; Dr. Yves-Alain Morel; Peter Baumgartner-Jost.

[2] *Landesverteidigung und Ortswehren*, August 1943. **C.** Note: Bolded capital letters used in the footnotes herein refer to the source in the Videotape Bibliography at the end of this article.

the devices are lit, and several are hurled at the vehicle, which explodes. Nightfall comes as the sound of heavy weapons fire abounds. Ortswehr members camouflaged with branches and leaves lurk in the shadows. Finally the army is mobilized in large numbers and marching down the road.

The voice admonishes that total war requires total defense, commitment, and engagement. The lessons are: Don't evacuate! Remember the bad experiences from France and Belgium. The *Ortswehren* are essential for our freedom.

The above is a typical example of the Swiss newsreels made during World War II. The message could not have been lost on anyone: the entire Swiss population would offer total resistance to any Nazi invasion. This episode was calculated to give the people confidence that resistance was not only possible but would be pursued relentlessly. That was an important message given the demoralization which contributed to the quick collapse of Western Europe in 1940 in the face of the German Blitzkrieg. This particular film was especially directed to the boys and old men constituting the *Ortswehr*, encouraging maximum participation and the will to stand firm and to fight to the end, should invasion come.[3]

It goes without saying that the only invader could have been the German Wehrmacht. Based on a leak from Hitler's own headquarters, Swiss Intelligence believed that an attack would take place in March 1943. While an assault did not materialize then, in early July 1943 the Anglo-American invasion of Sicily began, and before long Mussolini was deposed and Hitler hurried troops to Northern Italy.[4] Thus, when the above film was shown in August, the Swiss had every reason to anticipate a possible Nazi invasion. Moreover, while not wishing to provoke German aggression, the Swiss were intent on sending the message that an onslaught would be stoutly opposed. It was common knowledge that German intelligence viewed the Swiss newsreels.

The German Wochenschau
An ideological weapon of Josef Goebbels' propaganda ministry, the German *Wochenschau* (weekly news) was loud, boisterous, and arrogant.[5]

---

[3] At the very time, Federal Councilor Karl Kobelt, head of the Swiss military department, issued a message encouraging every Swiss to join an official organization such as the *Ortswehr* in order that, in event of invasion, any persons captured would not be shot as guerillas. See Stephen P. Halbrook, *Target Switzerland* (Rockville Centre, N.Y.: Sarpedon, 1998), 181.

[4] Halbrook, *Target Switzerland*, 179-181, 189-190.

[5] *Die Deutsche Wochenschau* is available in the Bundesarchiv, Koblenz, Germany. Most of the newsreels have been reproduced with English subtitles on videotape under the designation *Through Enemy Eyes: A Newsreel History of the Third Reich at War* (Chicago:

Headed by Reichsfilmintendant Fritz Hippler, each edition of the newsreel was meticulously approved by Goebbels and then sanctioned by Hitler personally.[6]

A typical edition, shown in May 1940, entertained viewers with the Wehrmacht attacks on Holland, Belgium, and France. Enemy soldiers are always dead or in the process of surrendering, while Wehrmacht soldiers rarely get a scratch. Civilians happily greet the German tanks, except that posters are put up demanding that they surrender all firearms within 24 hours or face the death penalty. Hitler promises that this great war will be harbinger of the 1,000-year Reich. A patriotic song mixed with the images and music of artillery barrages, Luftwaffe bombings, and tank assaults compose the grand finale.[7]

After the attack on the Soviet Union was launched in 1941, the German *Wochenschau* shows lots of dead Soviets and not one dead German. There is a rare wounded man walking with the help of a comrade, and an occasional elaborate state funeral of a high leader; but no dead German bodies, even after Stalingrad.

The German regime made special *Ausland Wochenschauen* (Foreign Weekly News) which included local topics for each country it sought to influence. In the final report of *Heer und Haus* (Army and Home) at the end of the war, Swiss Major Roland Ziegler noted about the German newsreels: "The purpose was to prove to the Swiss that the German Wehrmacht could not be stopped from crushing every enemy while the Swiss were still under a kind of idyllic Seldwyla illusion regarding their defense readiness." (Seldwyla is an imaginary Swiss town in a novel by nineteenth century Swiss author Gottfried Keller.) In order to have the desired effect on the Swiss, it was necessary for the German propaganda "to show as little as possible about things that the Swiss had available in excellent quality and which they particularly trusted." Ziegler explained:

> For example the infantry. While the newsreels intended for Germany showed infantry battles at length, they were almost completely missing on the newsreels destined for Switzerland. On the other hand, the Swiss were shown in detail what they did not have because they did not need it. This procedure included for example the showing of newsreels with the following potpourri: (i) huge bombers bombarding cities and train stations followed by the "Zibelemärit" [November onion festival] in Bern, followed by attacks of large tanks, (ii) submarines in attack mode

---

International Historic Films, various dates).

[6] Paul Alexis Ladame, *Une caméra contre Hitler* (Genève: Editions Slatkine, 1997), 101-102.

[7] *Die Deutsche Wochenschau*, No. 506, 15 May 1940, UfA, Ton-Woche.

followed by the *Knabenschiessen* [annual boys' shooting match] in Zürich followed by dive bombers, (iii) large tanks followed by a miniature train installation built by a man in Aarau followed by pictures from the air war with numerous airplanes and paratroops. The purpose was clear: Swiss movie-goers should leave the theater with the impression that nothing could be done against the German army and all the Swiss were doing was play.[8]

However, the Swiss not only developed their own newsreels to counter German propaganda, but also showed newsreels from Britain and other Allies on a regular basis in Switzerland. The radio waves brought the encouraging words of Winston Churchill as well as the frightening threats of Adolf Hitler. Swiss anti-Nazi sentiment was exhibited at the movie theater. In 1941, when the United States was still neutral, reporters for *Fortune* magazine returned from Germany via Switzerland and observed the following rather humorous phenomenon:

> There are 360 movie houses in Switzerland . . .. The movie houses show both American and German newsreels. The Nazi reels move with a peculiar jerkiness, a result of the removal of all "*heil*ing" for the Swiss market. The Germans are still puzzled, but they found that Swiss audiences laughed uproariously at every sight of a grim-faced German shooting up his hand like a railroad signal and grunting "*Heil, Hitler!*" One theater had to stop the film to restore calm after a scene in which Hitler himself had said "*Heil, Hitler!*"[9]

In a recent interview, Paul Ladame, the first director of the Swiss *Wochenschau*, confirmed the accuracy of the above report. He added that at the time, the American newsreel was not well liked because it was not against Hitler. The United States was not in the war yet. This changed after Pearl Harbor, and American films along with those of the British were smuggled into Switzerland and shown for the rest of the war.[10]

The Swiss Wochenschau
Two official Swiss entities produced films: the civilian *Schweizer Film-Wochenschau* or *Ciné Journal Suisse* (Swiss Weekly News) and the military *Armeefilmdienst* (Army Film Service). The films of both entities

---

[8] Major Roland Ziegler, *Geschichte der Sektion Heer und Haus 1939-1945* (AHQ Bern 1945), 47-48.
[9] "Switzerland Sits Tight", *Fortune* 24 (September 1941), 74, 112.
[10] Interview with Paul Alexis Ladame, Geneva, 29 May 2000.

were shown to the populace throughout the entire country. Both sought to present facts, to give hope, and to engender the spirit of resistance. They would engage in a David and Goliath battle with the mighty German *Wochenschau*.

Paul Ladame, the first *Wochenschau* director, recorded his experiences in *Une caméra contre Hitler.*[11] When talkies began in Europe in 1929, Ladame acted in several movies and learned script writing, casting, and directing. He earned a diploma in Berlin at the Reimannschule. When he returned in 1936 to cover the Olympic Games, his school had been closed and its Jewish professors expelled. He was watched by the SS.

Mobilized into the Swiss army when World War II erupted, Ladame's prewar experience would lead to his appointment as *Wochenschau* director. "I was in my gray army uniform at 3000 meters guarding a pass when I was called and offered the task of being director of the newsreel. I signed the contract the day the Germans captured Paris."[12] Ladame writes: "My civilian job was to counteract, and if possible to neutralize, the shrewd German propaganda. In theory my job was simple: the Nazis fomented fear and hopelessness with their films. Their army appeared so strong, young, well-armed, and well-trained that any resistance seemed doomed. My job was to instill hope, courage, and confidence."[13]

With only Ladame, two cameramen, and a secretary, they began by producing short documentary films. The budget was low, equipment minimal, and only three meters of raw film could be used for each meter projected in the cinemas. Films could not be made abroad, in military areas, or in refugee camps. The first edition of the Swiss *Wochenschau* was shown in Bern on August 1, 1940 to members of Parliament, the press, and various dignitaries. A great success, it included five subjects: passage over the border by a column of the French army, including Polish and African soldiers; daily life of these internees in a camp in central Switzerland; 1,600 volunteers sorting out thousands of letters at the prisoner-of-war agency in Geneva; a speech of International Committee of the Red Cross President Max Huber; and a spectacular explosion of mines in Valais.[14]

---

[11] Paul Alexis Ladame, *Une caméra contre Hitler* (Genève: Editions Slatkine, 1997). Further information was obtained in an interview with Ladame by the author, Geneva, 29 May 2000. See also Paul Alexis Ladame, *Defending Switzerland* (Delmar, NY: Caravan Books, 1999), 10-11, 45-46, 50.

[12] Interview with Paul Alexis Ladame, Geneva, 29 May 2000.

[13] Ladame, *Defending Switzerland,* 45-46, 50.

[14] Ladame, *Une Caméra contre Hitler,* 41-42.

The *Wochenschau* was shown in all cinemas of the country in the German, French and Italian languages. About 35 copies of each edition were produced. The typical episode had three to five subjects, including sporting events and documentaries. At the beginning, the newsreel had a duration of three minutes, but was extended to six minutes. All cinemas of Switzerland were obliged to show the presentation.

The Swiss newsreel effectively countered the German one; viewers cheered the former and booed the latter. Funding shortages led in March 1941 to a meeting of concerned citizens with the common theme: "Wir kämpfen gegen die deutsche Propaganda wie mit einer Korkpistole gegen Panzerwagen (We fight against the German propaganda as with a cork gun against armored vehicles)."[15] The assembly passed a resolution to the Federal Council demanding more funding, which would be forthcoming. Ladame served as head of the newsreel, making 200 films, until 1944, when he was succeeded by Hans Laemmel, who then remained head until 1961.[16]

The Armeefilmdienst

The *Armeefilmdienst* (Army Film Service), a component of *Heer und Haus* (Army and Home), extended its message from the army to civilians, including the pupils of elementary and secondary schools and attendees of private cinemas, beginning in late summer 1940.[17] The acting head of the *Abteilung Presse und Funkspruch* (Department of Press and Radio), Fueter, had pointed out to the Chief of the General Staff in April 1940 that the German newsreel sought to create an impression that any resistance to superior German power would be senseless. Switzerland's neutrality precluded a prohibition on the German films, but something had to be done to counter this massive stream of propaganda. The films of the Armeefilmdienst contained military themes, complementing the predominantly civilian themes of the *Wochenschau*.

Colonel Oscar Frey wrote to the Adjutant General in May 1941 that the Swiss films must confront the German films directly and as quickly as possible. "Example: The German newsreel shows a tank attack. Answer:

---

[15] Ibid., 49.

[16] Hans Laemmel, "Missverständnisse um die Filmwochenschau", in *Neue Zürcher Zeitung,* January 24, 2000, 11.

[17] On the *Armeefilmdienst*, see Yves-Alain Morel, *Aufklärung oder Indoktrination? Truppeninformation in der Schweizer Armee* (Zürich: Thesis Verlag, 1996), 162-70; Oskar Felix Fritschi, *Geistige Landesverteidigung während des Zweiten Weltkrieges* (Winterthur: Fabag + Druckerei AG, 1971), 174-75; Major Roland Ziegler, *"Heer und Haus", Die Schweiz in Waffen* (Murten: Vaterländischer Verlag, 1945), 190-192.

Swiss Ik. [Infanteriekanone, infantry antitank cannon] exercises, going in position, shoots. Final picture: a shot-through tank armor." The will to resist and confidence in the army would be confirmed when Swiss civilians left movie theaters making comments such as "Did you know that we also have flame-throwers? The medical service and avalanche-dog service take care of our soldiers."[18]

Such short films of no more than five minutes—"Answers" to the German newsreels—began to appear, sometimes in two-week intervals, and were shown in all cinemas in Switzerland. Longer films were also made, such as the 40-minute *"Schulung zum Nahkampf* (Training in Close Combat)."[19] Swiss military attachés in foreign countries, particularly in the Axis countries, made the Swiss films available as part of the strategy of dissuasion.

The relationship between the army film service and civilian film organizations was regulated in a September 1941 directive stating that the *Armeefilmdienst* was to make films for actual military instruction, to strengthen trust in the army, and to communicate with the civilian population. This entailed cooperation with the *Wochenschau* in order to widen exposure to the civilian population.[20] The *Wochenschau* offered to make films with military themes that would be shown in the framework of the normal program. The *Wochenschau* composed military subjects, and its first 30 editions all included contributions to the national defense. Beginning with the production of the short films in July 1941, *Armeefilmdienst* productions were included in the *Wochenschau.*

A number of the editions of the *Wochenschau* and *Armeefilmdienst* productions have been reproduced in whole or part on videotape (see Videotape Bibliography), and many are summarized and analyzed below. The videotapes do not always identify and distinguish the source of specific footage, but it can be assumed generally that the *Wochenschau* produced the civilian themes and the *Armeefilmdienst* produced the military themes (particularly those of longer length). Reproduction of more editions on

---

[18] Ziegler, *Geschichte der Sektion Heer und Haus*, 50.

[19] Some representative films include: *Alarm! Einsatz leichter Truppen/Alerte! Mise en action des troupes légères* (18 min., premiered July 5, 1940), *Fest der Heimat/Fête du pays* (20 min., 1940), *Ausbildung und Kampf unserer Weissen Truppen/La Garde blanche* (1940), *Berge und Soldaten/Montagne et soldats* (1941), *Unsere Abwehrbereitschaft/Notre volonté de défense* (38 min., 1941), *Schulung zum Nahkampf/L'école du combat rapproché* (35 min., 1942), *Grenzwacht in den Bergen/Guet d'en haut* (1942), *Die Hochgebirgspatrouille/Patrouille de haute montagne* (12 min., 1944), *Ortskampf/Assaut d'un village* (22 min., 1944), *Pulver/Poudre* (23 min., 1945).

[20] *Aufklärung oder Indoktrination?*, 166.

videotape would contribute to a better understanding by both scholars and the public alike of Switzerland's role in World War II.

Mobilization

The Swiss military was mobilized at the end of August 1939, just before Hitler's attack on Poland. The *Wochenschau* edition flashes to the mobilization poster seen on walls throughout the country and then a church bell rings in a village. With beautiful Alps as background, a farmer and his wife or daughter in Heidi-like attire rush down the hill side. The man grabs one of four rifles on a rack and his helmet, dons a bayonet, and hurries in uniform from his house to the village.[21] This scene, with individual variations, must have been burned into the memory of every Swiss family. The film version exudes hope, duty, love of family and homeland.

Then it is down to business. Soldiers rush to a road. Covers are pulled up, revealing large square holes, into which are inserted armored-vehicle and tank obstacles. Mines are laid and carefully covered with sod. Cannon are brought up. Barbed wire is spread, and General Guisan is sworn in before Parliament. A further mobilization is announced. In the most labor-intensive, back-breaking work, soldiers move logs, stones, and fortifications into place.

There is footage of the period of the "Phoney War" in which winter soldiers trot on horseback through the snow. When spring comes, men practice gymnastics, jump over strands of barbed wire, box, somersault over large rocks, practice bayonet and knife fighting, throw hand grenades into trenches, and assault the trenches.[22]

With the Blitzkrieg against Western Europe, too much happened too fast. The *Wochenschau* depicts German fighter planes, General Guisan speaking, Swiss maneuvers with live ammunition, soldiers racing up vertical hills, pistol competitions, swim sprint races, horse obstacle courses, and practice with heavy artillery. Then there is the devastating scene of the French soldiers marching into Switzerland, laying down their arms, and being interned. A map shows Switzerland in white surrounded by black—an obvious contrast between good and evil.[23]

The September 1940 edition "Krieg" (War) said it all: the second great mobilization; a farmer hangs up a large scythe, grasps his rifle, and quickly

---

[21] **D**: KF 4.00, *Wehrhaft und frei*. Note: where the videotape does not show the film name or date, only the videotape is identified.

[22] **D**: KF 4.00, *Wehrhaft und frei*.

[23] **D**: KF 4.00, *Wehrhaft und frei*.

bids farewell to his family. Shops close. The soldiers take the oath. Then more building of fortifications and defenses. On steep mountain sides, near rivers, and city streets: up goes barbed wire, tank obstacles, and all manner of impediments. Air-raid alarms go off as women pull down shutters. Antiaircraft guns fire. The voice implores the importance of neutrality. Red Cross workers sort reams of papers. The scene shifts to war games-explosions, blazing machine guns, firing tanks. A soldier running through a trench is suddenly knifed from behind. Next it is General Guisan giving a speech on national defense. The film then flashes to some children and the voice admonishes viewers of the need to protect freedom and the Fatherland. Patriotic music ends the episode.[24] Once again the message is clear: the Swiss can and will resist attack, and the cost to Nazi Germany in blood will be heavy.

Industry, Agriculture, and Shortages

The *Wochenschau* had two overall messages regarding industry and agriculture. First, the situation was dangerous: cut off from her normal trading partners, Switzerland lacked fuel and natural resources, did not produce sufficient food, and was subject to shortages. Second, however, the combination of persistence, hard work, and science would make survival possible. These episodes, compared with the bombast of the German *Wochenschau*, may appear dry today, but they gave confidence that industrial and agricultural products would be available.

Segments on how the country would survive economically centered on specific topics. These topics included: the recycling of old tires and parts from junk cars (classic old cars by today's standards!),[25] the electric tramway takes over usual transportation, even for a wedding (!);[26] old tubes collected by school children are melted and used for soldering wire;[27] brown coal is mined with chisels and picks (no machine tools are shown);[28] the

---

[24] September 1940. "Krieg." Schweizer Filmwochenschau. Edition Cinégram S.A. Geneva.

[25] *Wiederverwertung alter Pneus* (Recycling Old Tires), February 1941. A: VR 384.00, *Schweizer Alltag 1939-1945*, 1 Teil.

[26] *Strassenbahn passt sich der Zeit an* (Electric Tramway Adapts to the Times), July 1941. A: VR 384.00, *Schweizer Alltag 1939-1945*, 1 Teil.

[27] *Alte Tuben für Lötdraht* (Old Household Tubes Used for Soldering Wire), August 1941. A: VR 384.00, *Schweizer Alltag 1939-1945*, 1 Teil.

[28] *Braunkohle wird gefördert* (Browncoal Is Mined), November 1941. A: VR 384.00, *Schweizer Alltag 1939-1945*, 1 Teil.

making of gas from wood,[29] the replacement of copper coins with zinc coins (pouring out of a stamping machine like water);[30] the harvesting of reed for the building industry;[31] and the scrapping of fences and household products for the metal industry.[32]

The children's harvest of cockchafer (a large scarab beetle) for processing as pig feed was the subject of a rather amusing episode. Children violently shake the branches of a tree, causing cockchafer to rain down onto a tarpaulin on the ground. They are poured into huge burlap sacks (watch out, they eat their way out!) and then transported to a machine, which processes huge quantities into feed. In the final scene, pigs eagerly devour the delicious delicacy![33] The serious lesson: the entire population works in the struggle for food.

Science in the service of cultivation was the subject of an episode about the application of the methods of the venerable Dr. F. T. Wahlen. Every man, woman, and child participated in this plan, which entailed growing potatoes and other crops in every available inch of land. Charts show that, in 1938, 83% of agricultural land was used for livestock and only 17% for crops, but by 1942 the numbers changed to 54% and 46% respectively. In 1934, 183,000 hectares (452,000 acres) of land were under cultivation, but that had now risen to 500,000 hectares (1,236,000 acres). The film shows scientists in laboratories conducting futuristic-looking experiments in agriculture.[34] Besides reporting news, this episode gave confidence to the population that an adequate, if Spartan, food supply would be available.

Several other episodes were devoted to the agricultural battle, emphasizing how famine had been averted by the hard work of all citizens, young and old.[35] Over a half century after the fact, Paul Ladame opined that

---

[29] *Holzgas als Benzinersatz* (Gas from Wood Replaces Gasoline), February 1942. **A**: VR 384.00, *Schweizer Alltag 1939-1945*, 1 Teil.

[30] *Räppler aus Zink* (Copper Money Replaced by Zinc Coins), March 1942. **A**: VR 384.00, *Schweizer Alltag 1939-1945*, 1 Teil.

[31] *Schilf für Bauindustrie* (Reed Harvest for the Building Industry), February 1943. **A**: VR 384.00, *Schweizer Alltag 1939-1945*, 1 Teil.

[32] *Alteisen für Metallindustrie* (Scrap Metal for the Metal Industry), June 1943. **A**: VR 384.00, *Schweizer Alltag 1939-1945*, 1 Teil.

[33] *Maikäfer als Schweinefutter* (Cockchafer as Pig Feed), March 1942. **A**: VR 384.00, *Schweizer Alltag 1939-1945*, 1 Teil.

[34] *Die Wissenschaft im Dienste des Mehranbaues* (Science in the Service of Cultivation), July 1942. **A**: VR 384.00, *Schweizer Alltag 1939-1945*, 1 Teil.

[35] Ladame, *Une Caméra contre Hitler*, 57-62. Other titles included *La bataille agricole*, *Notre pain quotidien*, and *Retour à la terre*.

the best *Wochenschau* films made were those on Dr. Whalen and the campaign to grow potatoes.[36]

Sometimes relief was needed from news about the war, hardship, and shortages. An episode featuring a ladies' fashion show depicts innovations of the textile industry. Beautiful models display the latest styles to a crowd of admiring women. The models then retire to lounge chairs, smoke cigarettes, laugh and chat. This must have functioned like therapeutic window shopping—a chance to forget the war and hope for a better future.[37]

Preparing tasty meals in the midst of shortages in a war economy was the theme of one episode. Help for the housewife was on the way in the form of a bulky tape recording outfit filled with food ideas and recipes. For the average person, the device itself was probably more scientific fantasy than actual reality.[38]

A 1944 episode devoted to food production and rationing depicted the war for cultivation with its most ubiquitous manifestation, two-day-old potato bread. A Swiss flagship on the high seas—a little known supplier of products from abroad—is shown. Land is cleared by animals or tractors pulling up roots and by rows of men with picks, and then the women do the final hoeing. The rationing plan for the month is explained, and the edition ends with the exhortation: "Zusammenhalten und Disziplin wahren (Hold together and keep discipline)!"[39]

Help is needed for our underprivileged citizens, admonished another episode. Flashes of a wheat harvest, people employed, a soccer game, healthy children, and show windows full of food and watches are contrasted with six somber people living in one room. A woman washes clothes on a scrub board, children have holes in their shoes and torn clothes, newspapers are used in a wood stove. They are down to the last potato, there is not enough bread, the ration cards are running out, the bills cannot be paid. Help arrives—suddenly there are plenty of potatoes, the children get new clothes, there is wood for the stove. The edition ends: "Wenn Du zögerst, frage Dein Herz (When you hesitate, ask your heart)."[40]

---

[36] Interview with Paul Alexis Ladame, Geneva, 29 May, 2000.

[37] *Neuerung in der Textilindustrie* (Innovations of the Textile Industry), March 1942. **B**: VR 384.00, *Schweizer Alltag 1939-1945*, 2.Teil.

[38] *Kriegswirtschafts-Aktualitäten* (Realities of the War Economy), June 1943. **A**: VR 384.00, *Schweizer Alltag 1939-1945*, 1 Teil.

[39] *Lebensmittel Versorgung und Rationierung* (Food Supply and Rationing), February 1944. **A**: VR 384.00, *Schweizer Alltag 1939-1945*, 1 Teil.

[40] *Bei uns geht die Armut nicht in Lumpen einher* (With Us, Poverty Does Not Walk Around in Rags), October 1944. **A**: VR 384.00, *Schweizer Alltag 1939-1945*, 1 Teil.

Episodes about shortages and hardship featured women and children, because they were frequently left to make it alone while the husband and father was away for military service. "The Woman in Our Time" flashes "Das Swing-Girl"—caricatures of sexy women—but quickly shifts to women in military service and in other walks of life. The housewife sees the basket of eggs shrink, she bundles hay, she runs low on ration coupons, and just when she is feeling low, the damned air raid alarm sounds. She checks on her precious child to sweet music. The alarm awakens her at 6:00 a.m. and she is on the run. She dons her apron, throws wood in the stove, feeds the children. Her daughter's shoe has a huge hole. She sends the children off to school and goes to the pharmacy, where a crowd competes to redeem ration coupons. Then it's back home for housework and more ration coupon clipping. While this episode superficially appears demoralizing, it was actually a tribute to the hard work, day in and day out, of women in Swiss society.[41]

Women in Service

Several episodes are devoted to women. Women contribute essential services in a wide variety of workplaces, including hospitals, factories, the military, farms, and the home. Women from all walks of life join the *Frauenhilfsdienst* (FHD), the Women's Auxiliary Service. FHD women awake in hotels or apartments turned into barracks, don their military uniforms, and march. They work for the General Staff, they search for and observe intrusions by foreign aircraft, and they serve all along the communications line for air defense.[42]

The FHD included contingents of dispatch-women on skis. In one episode, they are sleeping in a barn, awake, and rush outside to their skis. While delivering an important message from a soldier, one falls and is injured. Six women come to the rescue. The snow is deep and the scenery beautiful.[43] The adventure depicted here would entice young women to join the FHD.

---

[41] *Die Frau in unserer Zeit* (The Woman in Our Time), February 1945. A: VR 384.00, *Schweizer Alltag 1939-1945*, 1 Teil.

[42] FHD (Women's Auxiliary Service), April 1941. A: VR 384.00, *Schweizer Alltag 1939-1945*, 1 Teil.

[43] January 1942. C. Note: lack of citation to an episode title indicates that the title was not reproduced on the videotape.

The carrier pigeon service was another military assignment for FHD women.[44] They also prepared food services for soldiers who were mobilized.[45]

The 650th Anniversary of the Confederation

In 1941 the *Wochenschau* seized upon the opportunity of celebrating the 650th anniversary of the founding of the Swiss Confederation by creating productions depicting the medieval victories against the great powers.[46] Praising the production "Notre pain quotidien" (Our Daily Bread), Federal Councillor Philipp Etter wrote Ladame requesting an all out effort for the anniversary. He wrote:

> Switzerland must survive, as our ancestors wished. We will fight until the end so that the red flag with the white cross flies over the Gotthard. You made excellent movies so that our people do not die of hunger. You helped Dr. Wahlen to fill stomachs. For myself, I ask for you to help save the spirit, the courage, and the will to resist. Little Switzerland, curled up like a hedgehog, must draw strength through courage and confidence from its over six hundred year past, in order to support the soldiers who are feverishly working to further fortify the haven of last hope.[47]

Three short footages, whose scripts were approved by Etter, resulted. *Le Pacte à Rütli* (The Pact of the Rütli) concerned the founding events occurring around the lake of the first Cantons, Uri, Schwyz and Unterwald. Ladame remembered about making this film:

> Everywhere we went, people received us with joy and cooperated with zeal. I will always remember the mountaineers of the Muotathal interpreting, truer than nature, the pact of the three Waldstätten: Uri, Schwyz and Unterwalden. They believed in it. They relived it. 1291, for them, was like yesterday. The duke of Habsburg who wanted to invade their country was Hitler today.[48]

---

[44] January 1943. **C**: VP 380.00, *Schweizer Armee 1939-45.*

[45] December 1943. **C**: VR 380.00, *Schweizer Armee 1939-1945.*

[46] Ladame, *Une Caméra Contre Hitler*, 63-67. Unfortunately, none of the videotapes cited in this article include any footage from these films.

[47] Ibid., 63-64.

[48] Ibid., 65.

La Suisse héroique (Heroic Switzerland) depicted the battles of Morgarten, Sempach, and Morat, where small numbers of Swiss peasants defeated huge armies of knights. It featured the breast-plated cavaliers of the "Remonte fédérale", the best horsemen of Switzerland, with standards and pennants flowing, attacking the Habsburg cavalry. *La Suisse chrétienne* (Christian Switzerland) sought to show the hard-won tolerance of Swiss history, but the film satisfied no one.

There was also a successful documentary, *Le 650e anniversaire de la Confédération* (The 650th Anniversary of the Confederation), the anti-Nazi message of which could not have been clearer. By the end of the year, the above films would be shown to over 100,000 Swiss children. The films generally were met with spontaneous applause. General Guisan liked the films and asked Ladame to produce army films for the public, which was then undertaken by the *Wochenschau*.

Sports

A soccer match between Switzerland and Germany in Zürich shown in April 1941 had obvious symbolic value. Crowds swamp the stadium and citizens anxiously listen on the radio. The German players line up and give the *Heil Hitler* salute as a band plays. The members of the Swiss team, of course, cooly keep both arms down at their sides. The game is filled with exciting plays. The crowd is ecstatic as Switzerland wins 2 to 1.[49] Once again William Tell has defeated the haughty despot. The fans must have pondered more than a soccer match.

Another episode encouraged every Swiss, man or woman, to participate in sports and to earn the Swiss sport medal for general fitness. It contrasted group calisthenics on an athletic field with unhealthy factory work. The choices: gymnastics, 100 meter sprinting, swimming, biking, fencing, pistol shooting, wrestling, rowing, skiing, horseback riding, long distance racing with rifle on back, track and field.[50] Once again, participatory sports contributed to defense and the spirit of resistance.

The collapse of the tourism industry, which thrived before the war, resulted in massive unemployment in hotels throughout the country. One

---

[49] *Fussballmatch: Schweiz-Deutschland* (Soccer Match: Switzerland-Germany), April 1941. **B**: VR 384.00, *Schweizer Alltag 1939-1945*, 2 Teil.

[50] *Das schweizerische Sportsabzeichen* (The Swiss Sportsmedal), August 1941. **B**: VR 384.00, *Schweizer Alltag 1939-1945*, 2 Teil.

film encourages Swiss to take advantage of various outdoor recreational activities available at or near these hotels.[51]

Refugees and Humanitarianism

Helping refugees and humanitarianism were distinguishing characteristics of Switzerland for the entire war, and the *Wochenschau* created several episodes with these themes. One featured Switzerland's program to bring children into the country for three months of rest and recuperation. Trains arrive with the children, who are taken by nurses to a mess hall to eat what must have been their best meal since the war began. They are then gently split up and taken by individual families, who depart by horse-drawn wagons or taxis. Each child receives medical attention, attends educational classes, and helps out with household chores. They gain five kilograms in weight. There are tears when they must depart back home.[52] This film does not identify the country of origin of the children, but most came from France and Belgium.

Tragedy struck at home in 1944 when American airmen accidentally bombed Schaffhausen at the northern border. Parts of the city are in smoke and flames, and 37 are dead. Firemen, soldiers, Scouts, and citizens of all kinds are putting out fires and looking for loved ones. Many buildings are completely bombed out or gutted. The film barely mentions that it was American bombers and expresses no animosity. Three days later, a funeral service is held at a church. The people then march to a mass grave. It is a circular trench with coffins facing the center. A child's coffin is seen beside an adult one. The people crowd around and mourn.[53]

Refugees flowed into Switzerland as the war extended further into Europe. Visibly, Basel appears to be a city in peace and security, and without hunger. But, as shown in December 1944, the artillery and machine gun fire from across the border is deafening. The elderly, children, women, and the wounded—some 5,000 of them—are fleeing across the border. Swiss soldiers help them enter, and nurses then examine the babies.[54]

---

[51] *Arbeitslosigkeit im Gastgewerbe* (Unemployment in the Hotel Industry), July 1942. **B**: VR 384.00, *Schweizer Alltag 1939-1945*, 2 Teil.

[52] *Hilfe den kriegsgeschädigten Kindern* (Help for War-damaged Children), February 1942. **A**: VR 384.00, *Schweizer Alltag 1939-1945*, 1 Teil.

[53] *Schaffhausen bombardiert* (Schaffhausen Bombed), April 1944. **B**: VR 384.00, *Schweizer Alltag 1939-1945*, 2 Teil.

[54] *Menschen fliehen zu uns* (People Flee to Us), December 1944. **A**: VR 384.00, *Schweizer Alltag 1939-1945*, 1 Teil.

As a neutral country in the midst of the European battlefield, Switzerland became a safe place where severely wounded soldiers could be exchanged. Sponsored by the International Committee of the Red Cross, trains transported wounded Americans, English, Middle Easterners, Pakistanis, and Africans as well as Germans into Switzerland, where they were exchanged and put on other trains to be returned to areas under the control of the Allies and Axis respectively. Doctors and nurses treated those in immediate need.[55] Their facial expressions show the reality of war close up.

Just after the war in Europe ended, the *Wochenschau* featured Russian soldiers who were still interned in Switzerland. Located in Canton Wallis (Valais), the internees pick potatoes, sing, hear a harangue by a Bolshevik political commissar under a picture of Stalin, and then do the Russian step dance. After meeting with Swiss authorities, the Russian military delegate informs the assembled internees that they will be returning to Russia, which leads to wild applause. They leave over the border in trains, still singing.[56] This episode appears rather naive. It is now believed that these happy Russians were all executed on their return to the Soviet Union because they had observed freedom in Switzerland and could not be allowed to spread the poison.

Military Exercises

Military activities were the theme of *Armeefilmdienst* productions and were also featured in the *Wochenschau*. This was calculated to give the Swiss people confidence and to encourage participation, while at the same time sending the message to Germany that the Swiss military was prepared and would resist an attack at all costs.

Alpine snow scenes were highlighted in various military episodes. It was rugged land of high-altitude beauty where certain death awaited invaders. In one edition, soldiers in white camouflage sweep the terrain with binoculars. They spot something and take off on their skis, executing high jumps. The scene flashes to hard farm work with hand tools and plows

---

[55] *Austausch von Schwerverwundeten durch die Schweiz* (Exchange of the Severely Wounded Through Switzerland), March 1945. **B**: VR 384.00, *Schweizer Alltag 1939-1945*, 2 Teil.

[56] *Russische Internierte* (Russian Internees), August 1945. **B**: VR 384.00, *Schweizer Alltag 1939-1945*, 2 Teil.

pulled by animals.[57] In another, soldiers ascend snow-capped mountains using climbing picks and equipment.[58]

An episode showing snow maneuvers features live firing of rifles, machine guns, and mortars. Soldiers sprint out of small holes in the snow-laden mountain side, tumble and roll down, and attack. A mortar is loaded and fired onto a mountain side, causing an avalanche. Ski troops spring into action, jumping off a cliff wearing full gear (one can imagine a wipeout with a rifle on the back).[59] The creation of the avalanche is particularly intriguing. Avalanches were sometimes created to clear areas for reasons of safety but also had potential military use. Whatever the reality, this scene is suggestive that Swiss troops were ready to cause avalanches to bury any invaders alive.

An edition on the cavalry appears out of date in the age of blitzkrieg, although perhaps it would have been of special use in certain terrain. It shows classic horse training in various gaits, going down steep inclines, and other maneuvers. The grand finale is a troop of mounted soldiers with helmets, carbines on their backs, and swords hanging from their sides![60]

Even a militia army needs a band. A newsreel featured a performance in a large concert hall. The band members are ready for combat: they wear helmets. The music sounds every bit as determined as anything on the German *Wochenschau*.[61]

Some training exercises were public demonstrations for both military and civilian visitors—including possible German spies or informants. One such exercise, in which the audience of men, women, and children included General Guisan himself, was a "mini D-Day" conducted by pontoon troops. It begins with shock troops, in uniform with rifle and helmet, swimming across a river. From concealed locations along the wooded shore spring paddle boats with three soldiers in each and then progressively larger boats with more soldiers to assault positions on the other side. Gunfire and artillery fire punctuate the attack.[62]

"Shhhhh!" Spies. . .

---

[57] May 1941. **A**: VR 384.00, *Schweizer Alltag 1939-1945*, 1 Teil.

[58] September 1941. **C**: VP 380.00, *Schweizer Armee 1939-45*.

[59] **D**: KF 4.00, *Wehrhaft und frei.*

[60] *Das Eidgenössische Kavallerie-Remonten-Depot* (The Swiss Cavalry Remount Depot), February 1942. **C**: VR 380.00, *Schweizer Armee*, 1939-45.

[61] April 1942. **C**: VP 380.00, *Schweizer Armee 1939-45*.

[62] *Unsere Pontoniere* (Our Pontoniers), 1943. **C**: VP 380.00, *Schweizer Armee 1939-45*.

Wochenschau episodes did not tend to be overly dramatic and were matter of fact. One from 1941 began innocuously enough. Rugged Alps with glaciers and flashes to hard farm work with hand tools and plows pulled by animals were the usual fare. Suddenly the tone gets dramatic, with the sweep of a city over which was superimposed a phantom human skull, growing ever larger.[63] The scene was surreal, and its message was that there are hidden enemies everywhere.

"Wer nicht schweigen kann/Qui ne sait se taire (Whoever Cannot Be Silent)" was shown in May 1943,[64] just after the "March Alarm" in which a Wehrmacht invasion was expected. It was No. 145 of the *Wochenschau*, and the topic was ordered by General Guisan.[65] This episode is a masterpiece of drama, visualization, and contrast. Its story: Day and night, our army guards our borders and country for *"Verteidigen, Freiheit und Arbeit, Heim und Familie"* (defense, freedom and work, country and family). Soldiers march and sing patriotic songs; a mother tucks in a girl, who says a prayer; the father is standing guard on a dark, rainy night.

The guards are relieved, a train rushes through a tunnel, and the guards slosh to a dry building filled with soldiers. Look around: pictures of General Guisan, caricatured Swiss soldiers, girlies. The guards unchamber the rounds in their rifles and take off their soaked raincoats. A foxtrot tune plays. The camera sweeps across the room. Soldiers are sleeping or reading on their blankets in the straw, with pinups to keep them company. An American would call this picture: "Swiss GIs." The rifle rack shows 9 Model 1911 long rifles and carbines, and only 2 Model 1931 carbines—the issue rifle for several years now. The men smoke and listen to the radio news. Soup is brought in.

Next soldiers are at a train station mixing with the general public. A table of soldiers at a restaurant are laughing and talking. A man sits at the next table—is he suspicious? A soldier is getting a shave—what is he saying to the barber? Another soldier walks out of a store talking to a female clerk. Yet another walks by three enticing women. The city is being watched! There are spies! Men are playing cards. The music becomes ominous. Men and women are talking on the telephone laughing. Talking at a bowling alley. What are they saying?! A messenger reports to an officer, who plots on a map and tells the messenger too much. Next cards

---

[63] May 1941. **A:** VR 384.00, *Schweizer Alltag 1939-1945*, 1 Teil.

[64] *Wer nicht schweigen kann* (Whoever Cannot Be Silent), May 1943. **A:** VR 384.00, *Schweizer Alltag 1939-1945*, 1 Teil.

[65] Ladame, *Une Caméra contre Hitler*, 83-84.

are being played and the messenger is repeating every word to another soldier.

The scene flashes to the beginning where the mother was tucking in her daughter . . . to soldiers thinking . . . to grandmother and grandfather . . . to the soldiers quarters, where they are all asleep on the hay . . . a blacksmith pounds away at glowing metal . . . he is a soldier, and each one is dreaming now . . . one dreams of his loved ones, then the sergeant wakes him up. It is now time for the awakened soldiers to relieve other guards. A rendition of "My Fatherland" concludes the film, which must be one of the most dramatic and stimulating productions of the entire war.

The War for Europe

Dramatically changed security risks are depicted in newsreel episodes beginning with the Normandy invasion. A Swiss officer lectures his men about the new situation. Mountain troops with ropes and picks climb up massive vertical cliffs. A dozen ME 109 fighters fly over rugged mountains and shoot their machine guns at targets in the rocks. Assault troops fire rifles and cannon. Flame-throwers blaze away. As a tank speeds down a road, at a place where there are small hills on both sides, an explosion causes huge logs to roll downhill and pile up on the road to obstruct the tank. Medieval tactics still have value. The war is not over but is entering a new phase.[66] This film is designed to depict the Swiss as ready for a massive, brutal attack against any invader—i.e. Germany, which need not be named.

The army needs wireless operators, announced the newsreel, which proceeded to show potential recruits the adventures to be expected. Airmen sprint to their ME 109s and communicate with ground personnel, who are hidden in a barn, via Morse code on telegraph. (This demonstrates the lack of voice radio communication in the air.) The ground personnel give an urgent message to a soldier, who sprints away to another radio station, which transmits the message via Morse code to troops in the field. They hurry to positions, preparing for rifle and machine gun fire. A mock battle with live fire commences from a ridge as assault troops cross a shallow river. They signal another unit that they have crossed. Paper messages about enemy positions are then passed from one unit to another in the field. Maps are surveyed, calculations made, and shells loaded into heavy, camouflaged guns, which are aimed and fired. Infantrymen advance from trenches and foxholes covered by machine gun fire. They fire submachine guns and rifles

---

[66] June 1944. **D**: KF 4.00, *Wehrhaft und frei.*

and throw hand grenades. Flame-throwers are used and bombs placed in enemy positions. Riflemen advance with bayonets fixed through smoke and barbed wire.[67]

After all the excitement, in town a man hangs a poster notifying young men about recruit school. Then a class in Morse code is shown. "We need wireless transmitters, learn the Morse signals, they are essential." This film has plenty of action, but throughout is the theme of wireless telegraph to communicate threats and to counterattack. While the German newsreels showed promiscuous firing of all kinds of weapons from actual battles—always editing out the defeats—the Swiss counterpart would show that the Swiss could resist the Nazis through precision firing and informed tactics.

Another episode featured grenadiers. The army has made great strides in weapons and training since the first mobilization. A map shows a "V" with mountains and valleys. Enemies must move through the narrow gaps, where they are attacked from above. This is treacherous and steep landscape. Soldiers use ropes to climb down and cross the river. Live rifle fire hits around them in the water. Snipers hidden behind rocks on the mountain side shoot down. Lots of grenade throwing. Rubber floats are used to carry men and machine guns down stream. It turns into another mock battle, with explosions, automatic weapon fire, shock troops, flame throwers, and the feel of real battle. Soldiers sprint up to trenches surrounded by barbed wire and insert a long board with numerous rectangular explosives on it, then run away. The explosion covers a longer area rather than all at one point.[68]

Rope climbing, swimming with full gear in rocky gorges, scaling mountains. Ropes go across a gorge and the men rope their way and transport weapons and implements across. Long wooden frames are used to cover rocky and rugged terrain. Quickly artillery is in place in what looked to be inaccessible spots. This is a true Swiss blitz attack in the most rugged of terrain. Soldiers dash through the rocks and then a village as other soldiers shoot and throw grenades all around them. "Achtung! Panzer!" A small trench is dug across the dirt roadway, then the soldiers rush into ambush positions on each side of the road. As the tank appears, a soldier jumps up from the trench and throws a fire bomb right on the tank! Others

---

[67] *Die Armee braucht Funker* (The Army Needs Wireless Operators), July 1944. **C**: VP 380.00, *Schweizer Armee 1939-45.*

[68] *Die Grenadiere* (The Grenadiers), September 1944. **C**: VP 380.00, *Schweizer Armee 1939-45.*

suddenly appear and hurl more Molotov cocktails on the tank, which is ablaze.

The newsreels produced intriguing episodes concerning Swiss flak and the Swiss Air Force. It is night, and soldiers on duty hear aircraft, plot their course, and telephone the data to the antiaircraft center. The communication is received by one of perhaps twenty uniformed women auxiliaries talking on telephones all at once, in communication with different observers. Aircraft locations are then plotted on maps. The air raid alarm sounds in the city. An ashtray of cigarette butts is in front of the soldier on duty who is summoned by headquarters. "Alarm! Alarm!" he cries to the rows of soldiers sleeping in hay lofts. Soldiers swarm to the anti-aircraft guns. Gigantic spotlights search the skies. Aircraft is spotted! The observation and aiming instruments appear highly sophisticated. Fire! Shot after shot chases the aircraft.[69] This film depicts the ground defense; the next shows the air defense.

Pilots rev their motors while the control tower looks on. On the ground, they verbally communicate by radio—which was unavailable in the air. The scene shifts to pilot school, where students learn air acrobatics in biplanes. Then come ME 109s and a Swiss made and designed C-36, distinguished by its two vertical stabilizers with rudders. The fighters practice machine gun fire at targets in a lake. There is a sudden alarm. Pilots race to their planes while ground personnel plot the course. They pursue and apprehend a bomber. Fighters on each side of the bomber signal it to land by waggling their wings. The ground radios communicate that it is an American bomber and will land at Dübendorf. The Swiss fighters guide the US-marked bomber to make a clean landing, and ground crews rush to assist the damaged aircraft.[70]

Features concerning the military also depicted the human side. In one, it is the fifth Christmas of the war, General Guisan reminds the soldiers under torchlights. They still stand guard for neutrality, freedom, and national defense. The band plays a moving rendition of Silent Night. The mood is somber—the soldiers are not with their families—but confident. The scene is almost surreal: gifts are given out to soldiers with their helmets

---

[69] *Unsere Fliegerabwehr bei Nacht* (Our Aircraft Defense at Night), October 1944. **B:** VR 384.00, *Schweizer Alltag 1939-1945*, 2 Teil.

[70] *Flieger-Grenzverletzung* (Aircraft Border Violation), November 1944. **C:** VP 380.00, *Schweizer Armee 1939-45*.

on! Viewers would know that the militia army is ready for combat even during a Christmas ceremony.[71]

"Open your doors for soldiers when off duty" is a plea for solidarity at the local level. In a small town in the Jura, where Swiss troops are concentrated in early 1945 across from the battle zone, soldiers throw snowballs and flirt with women. Morale is boosted when they are taken into homes, served bread and wine, and invited to play board games with the children. The tone of voice is upbeat and happy. The snow begins to fall, and the soldiers again stand guard.[72]

The War Ends

The *Wochenschau* celebrated the end of the war along with the entire population. The capitulation of the Wehrmacht and the signing of the armistice meant the end of a long nightmare. Thousands of Swiss, American, British, and French flags are wildly waved by masses of rejoicing people in the streets. They sing the national anthems of the Allied countries, including "My Country 'Tis of Thee." A bell rings in the peace. There is a parade before the Parliament with General Guisan and the members of the Federal Council. The grande finale is a beautiful mountain scene with patriotic commentary—the Alpine democracy has survived.[73]

Europe remained a chaotic and potentially dangerous place, and active duty has not ended. A mid-summer 1945 episode featured a day with General Guisan at Schloss Jegenstorf. After a friendly "bonjour" to the guards, the General must decide the punishment for cases of misconduct. He grants amnesty in a minor case and refuses it for a traitor. After a horse ride through farm and forest, the General hears reports of a crisis at the Italian border and meets with Chief of the General Staff Huber. After a flash to the Rütli meeting of 1940 in which the General admonished all of the high officers to resist to the end, the episode shows Guisan observing war maneuvers, with explosions, machine gun fire, and assaulting troops. When night falls, the General plays cards with the General Staff and then is alone reviewing reports.[74]

---

[71] *Weihnachten mit dem General* (Christmas with the General), January 1944. **C**: VP 380.00, *Schweizer Armee 1939-45*.

[72] *Ein Städtchen im Jura* (A Small town in the Jura), January 1945. **A**: VR 384.00, *Schweizer Alltag 1939-1945*, 1 Teil.

[73] *Waffenstillstand* (The Armistice), May 1945. **A**: VR 384.00, *Schweizer Alltag 1939-1945*, 1 Teil.. See also untitled segments in **D**: KF 4.00, *Wehrhaft und frei*.

[74] *Ein Tag M. K. P. des Generals* (A Day with the General), July 1945. **C**: VP 380.00, *Schweizer Armee 1939-45*.

In August 1945 Japan surrendered, and at last "Der Krieg ist vorüber"—the war is over. The period of active service officially ended. The *Wochenschau* covered the vast celebration and parade in Bern.[75]

Without question, the newsreels of the *Wochenschau* and the *Armeefilmdienst* were significant ideological weapons that kept hope and the spirit of resistance alive and helped to dissuade a German attack. The ability of the Swiss people to maintain their freedom and independence during World War II, when most of the rest of Europe groaned under the Nazi heel, may be attributed in no small part to a fierce attitude of defiance against the New Order and to confidence in their capacity to survive. Over a half century after the fact, these newsreels are a testament to the courage of a free people of a small, neutral state right at the doorstep of Nazi Germany who successfully resisted what seemed at the time to be National Socialism's overwhelming power.

VIDEOTAPE BIBLIOGRAPHY

A = VP 384.00, *Schweizer Alltag 1939-1945*, 1. Teil. Bern: Armeefilmdienst.
B = VP 384.00, *Schweizer Alltag 1939-1945*, 2. Teil. Bern: Armeefilmdienst.
C = VP 380.00, *Schweizer Armee 1939-45*. Bern: Armeefilmdienst.
D = KF 4.00, *Wehrhaft und frei*. French version: *Être Fort pour Rester Libre*. Bern: Armeefilmdienst. Historical documentary made from various sources. Réalisation: Adolf Forter, Commentaire: Urs Schwarz.
VP 379.00, *Schweiz 1939-1945*. French version: *Suisse 1939-1945*. Film officiel Diamant. Historical documentary made from various sources.
Schweizer Alltag 1939-1945. Aus der Schweizer Film *Wochenschau*. Zürich: Rincovision.
Die Schweiz und der Zweite Weltkrieg. Zürich: Rincovision.
Le Général Guisan et son temps. General Guisan und seine Zeit. Il General Guisan e la sa epoca. Un film de Claude Champion. L'Association Film Général Guisan—Le Centre d'Histoire et de Prospective Militaires Pully.

---

[75] *Der Krieg ist vorüber* (The War Is Over), August 1945. **C**: VP 380.00, *Schweizer Armee 1939-45*.

Die Deutsche Wochenschau, Bundesarchiv, Koblenz, Germany. Videotape
    reproductions: *Through Enemy Eyes: A Newsreel History of the Third
    Reich at War* (Chicago: International Historic Films, various dates).
Polish Internment Camps in Switzerland, Professora Adama Vetulaniego
    (1941). Unpublished film made available by Zygmunt Prugar-Ketling.

EPILOGUE

Leo Schelbert

The eight essays of this work dealing with Switzerland in the Second World War intend to describe rather than to interpret, to present evidence rather than to engage in controversy. The borders between the transmission of data and the assessment of their meaning, of course, are fluid since, as Ludwik Fleck observed, 'thought styles' and 'thought collectives' guide authors as to which evidence to use and which to omit and, within the data selected, which to make central and which to marginalize.[1] It may be useful, therefore, to present the interpretative stance of this collection of essays in the form of eight theses, although this might do less than justice to the nuanced understanding of the various authors. The eight claims are:

One: The military threat to Switzerland posed by the Axis powers was real and serious, but was met by the Swiss military leadership with strategic skill, an intensive mobilization of resources, and an unconditional determination to resist invasion at any cost.
(H. Senn)

Two: Switzerland's response to the threats it faced must be set into the context of the German National Socialist, the Italian Fascist, and the Soviet Russian totalitarianisms, each with the intent sooner or later of liquidating the Swiss nation by military conquest, ideological control, and political dominance.
(J. Stüssi-Lauterburg)

Three: Swiss women played an integral and decisive role in the mobilization of the nation on the economic, military, and ideological front, and their experience in time of war prepared

---

[1] Ludwik Fleck, *Genesis and Development of a Scientific Fact.* Edited by Thaddeus J. Trenn and Robert K. Merton. Translated by Fred Bradley and Thaddeus J. Trenn. Foreword by Thomas S. Kuhn. Chicago: The University of Chicago Press, 1979.

the ground for the eventual equality of Swiss women also in the public realm.
(Th. Maissen)

Four: Allied violations of Swiss air space and bombing of Swiss territory were not a retaliation for its neutral stance, but genuine errors caused by weather conditions and a still untested radar technology, and the Swiss generally responded to the events officially as well as publicly with calm, moderation, and an appreciation of the United States as a 'Sister Republic'.
(J. Hutson)

Five: Swiss unconditional neutrality as observed in both world wars derived from its historical tradition, conformed to its definition in international law, and was the foundation that allowed Switzerland to help mitigate the vast suffering inflicted by total war.
(E. Bonjour)

Six: The need for raw materials crucial to armed resistance as well as the survival of its people put Switzerland between the 'hammer' of the Axis and the 'anvil' of the Allies, a predicament met by the Swiss leadership with ingenuity, patient negotiating, rationing, and an intensive program of mandated food production.
(H. K. Meier)

Seven: Chosen as a 'Protecting Power' by many nations and assisted by the semi-official activities of the Geneva-based private Swiss institution called the International Committee of the Red Cross, Swiss officials contributed significantly to the mitigation of suffering and to the observance of the various international conventions designed to protect and assist the victims of war and persecution.
(L. Schelbert)

Eight: The Swiss *Wochenschau*, a 'week in review' program, and the *Armeefilmdienst,* the army's film service, were a potent force in Swiss life during the war years. They boldly counteracted Axis propaganda, strengthened the will to armed resistance, promoted

unflagging vigilance, and offered encouragement when things
looked hopelessly bleak.
(S. Halbrook)

This then is not to claim that the Swiss were saints or heroes in facing
the calamities of war and the indescribable violence and destruction that
surrounded them. Yet the essays do show that one may not minimize or
ignore what were then perceived as mortal threats to the nation's very
existence, that one may not portray measures then taken as mere ploys of
a selfish elite intent on enriching itself and on maintaining ideological
control, and that one may not reduce the response of the Swiss people to a
callously xenophobic posture. The essays of this book view such
interpretations as improperly reductionist and as claims that fail validly to
consider the nation's efforts to balance the contradictory demands of
national survival and of an internationally sanctioned neutrality with the
pursuit of international peace and the promotion of a genuine and inclusive
humanitarianism.

APPENDICES

1. Selected Documents

[1] *Against Demoralization: Defense Letter [Wehrbrief] No. 9, 1940*
(Third Quarter, 1940. Issued by the Army Command, Section 5, "Army and Home")

> This text serves as an example of how the Swiss leadership tried to encourage the people at large during trying times. (Ed.)

Although you make heavy sacrifices, don't lose courage!
Certainly there is no doubt that at present hundreds of thousands have cause to be dissatisfied.
Dissatisfied
    because they have been torn from their civilian activities—
    because they, instead of being able to pursue their career at home and
        to look after their families, must do their military service—
    because they have not been given leave, yet others have—
    those on leave, because they have lost clients during their absence or
        their business is doing badly because of the war—
    because they cannot resume their former position but must look anew
        for work—
    the women, because the husband has not been home for months and
        does not help in the education of the children—
    because the cost of living becomes daily higher, yet the household
        expenses steadily sparser—
    because the emergency support or the compensation for the loss of
        earnings does not suffice.
All these reasons for dissatisfaction are undoubtedly not taken from thin air, but are only all too real. That there is no possibility to solve these difficulties as long as the war in Europe continues and that there is no prospect for a better future, can only add to discouragement.

To all who are dissatisfied, may they be soldiers at the frontier or pursuing work in the hinterland, I would like to put a friend at their side who each day talks with them and repeats to them the following each day:
    I know that your dissatisfaction has its good reasons—
    I know that your existence is at stake—
    I know that your family lives in financial worries and has only the
        minimum to live on—

I know that the long military service is often burdensome and makes
>   you impatient and ill humored—

I know that much in the service is not as it could and should be -

but

I advise you as a good friend to keep your head high and to realize
each day that despite everything you have reason to be glad and
encouraged,

>   because the horrors of war have been spared our country whereas all
>   countries around us have been in their grip—

>   because your family is still well ordered together and knows its
>   provider to be healthy and safe at the frontier—

>   because there are still many opportunities to restore your career or to
>   build it anew—

>   because it is ungrateful not to acknowledge that all Swiss, poor or rich,
>   are numbered among the privileged because they possess the
>   highest good a person can own—freedom.

Repeat every morning:

>   as long as your country remains spared war,

>   as long as you keep your bodily and mental strength and your family
>   stays healthy consider yourself lucky.

Away with dissatisfaction, consider the whole. More than ever your
personal well-being is tied to the well being of your country.

Translated from the German by L. Schelbert

[2] *Swiss Neutrality Defined: The View of Edgar Bonjour*

> Given the critique Swiss neutrality has been subjected to, the view of
> Edgar Bonjour, the most learned scholar on this subject, which he had
> formulated during the war, provides an impressive defense of
> Switzerland's neutral stance during the Second World War. (Ed.)

Hostile Criticism of Neutrality
. . . [A] historical survey of Swiss neutrality clearly shows how the
principle of neutrality in foreign relations has grown by natural necessity
out of the national existence of the [Swiss] Confederation, its geographical
situation, its federal structure, its position as a minor state, its religious
cleavage, its multi-racial character and its democratic organization. These
constants of Swiss life are all interrelated and interdependent. With them,
neutrality forms one organic whole, no element of which can be torn out
without grievous harm to the rest. It is the axiom of Swiss sovereignty

which has borne the test of centuries of foreign relations. For the experience of Swiss history yields one perfectly unambiguous result—without neutrality, no national sovereignty. But without neutrality also, no Swiss freedom, which freedom must be taken to cover the manifold institutions of liberty which are regarded by the world as being of the very essence of Swiss policy. Only under the shield of neutrality could they thrive and bloom. It was only the subjection of foreign to home policy which permitted Switzerland to give permanence to her free institutions. In the same way, in England it was the long peace due to her insular position which enabled her free institutions to develop, a blessing which rarely falls to the lot of the great power. For the great power generally makes its home policy the handmaid of its foreign policy, and often, to assert its power, must order its internal organization to meet the needs of foreign policy.

The insight into the high function of neutrality as the foundation on which the Swiss body politic rests should be sufficient to silence any doubts as to the worth or worthlessness of the Swiss principle of foreign relations. Yet questions born of these doubts are constantly and passionately raised, and neutrality is violently attacked from within by the Swiss themselves. Even in the 19th century, in the infancy of the policy, members of one religious party advocated the surrender of neutrality in order that they might go to the help of their brothers in the faith abroad. In Zürich the head of the clergy preached on the text in Revelations: "So then because thou art lukewarm, and neither cold nor hot, I will spue thee out of my mouth." And a broadside of the period poured scorn on the "mad folly of this shameful and horrible neutrality. The middle or neutral way is not that of the good Christian, but the most wretched of all." In the middle of the nineteenth century, prominent politicians demanded that Switzerland should help neighbour peoples struggling for their freedom, raising the slogan of the solidarity of the people. This idea of Switzerland's liberating mission, actually mooted in the central governing body of the Confederation, is an hallucination which carried away enthusiastic spirits at the time, and has infected the usually somewhat unimaginative and rationally minded Swiss at other times too. We have only to think of the high Helvetic mood which reigned at the foundation of the League of Nations. In the recent Spanish civil war, and again in the present war [Bonjour, writing in 1946], Switzerland has been called upon to take sides in the conflict of principle between two opposing political systems.

All these demands for an occasional surrender of Swiss neutrality in favour of some high human ideal show a complete lack of understanding for the vital conditions of Swiss life, and further testify to the absence of a nice appreciation of the power ratio in Europe. The political wisdom of official

Switzerland has always clung to traditional neutrality in the teeth of such dubious tendencies, even when they made themselves felt in great force. Today the proposals for an organization of international security after the present war [Bonjour, writing in 1946] once more raises the question of the justification of a neutral Switzerland in a Europe united against all law and peace breakers. But even in League of Nations circles it is recognized that Switzerland must retain the right of making no kind of sacrifice of her neutrality until the new system of collective security has proved itself to be a really super-national institution of law. At present it certainly does not look as if a condition could be arrived at in anything like the near future which could make even a differential neutrality such as existed between 1920 and 1938 a question of practical politics.

Swiss neutrality has also, or even mainly, been called in question outside of the country. We can understand that every belligerent should try to persuade Switzerland to take sides. The moral and legal invective, however, only gained strength at the beginning of last century during the German wars of liberation. . . . From the standpoint of a European legal order mainly directed by Prussia and Austria, Swiss neutrality was the object of severe criticism, the polemical intentions of which were not difficult to discern. Space forbids the quotation of more than a few of the voices then raised in chorus, but it was said, for instance that "no belligerent power should suffer the egoism which looks on, furtively spying out its own advantage", for that meant graver dangers than open violence. In Germany it was noted with satisfaction that the idea of neutrality, condemned as weakness, could be rendered by no native word. Finally, neutrality was seen to be unlawful since it stood in contradiction to the natural law of nations. Switzerland was asked whether she would abandon her unnatural neutrality and return to the Germanic Central European state.

The Confederation resisted these blandishments, just as it resisted the torrent of propagandist literature which poured over the country in 1914-1918. At that time Swiss neutrality stood low in the world's esteem, for it will always be difficult to make other countries realize the intrinsic nature of the Swiss attitude in foreign relations. For a country fighting desperately for its life in the sincere belief that it is staking all for the highest aims of humanity, the quietude, the aloofness, the apparent insensitiveness of a third party always awakes suspicion and breeds contempt. Should the neutrals be better off than the belligerents, they are soon accused of exploiting their neutrality for purposes of economic welfare, a reproach which has been unjustly brought against Switzerland in every European war for more than two hundred years.

The Swiss writer Heinrich Federer has taken the state of mind just described as the subject of one of his most touching stories: *Unser Herrgott und die Schweizer [Our Lord God and the Swiss]*. Wounded soldiers of all nations involved in the international struggle call the Swiss to account for themselves before the throne of God. "Neutral—what does that mean?" cries a bleeding sargeant. "Day is not neutral, nor is night. Nothing wholesome or hearty on earth is neutral; only the bat is neutral. And the Swiss is terribly like the bat, fluttering about between light and dark, neither fish nor bird—just neutral. Lord God, Thou hast said Thyself in St. John or St. Luke that neutrality is a grievous sin. Punish it then!" God then listens to the bungling defence of the Swiss and exhorts him to humility and to active philanthropy. Then, turning to the soldiers, He takes up the defence of Swiss neutrality: "Who would be so foolish as to drag into the general filth and strife this tiny spot of earth where men and women may still hold out in fellowship hands not stained with blood? Leave the Swiss alone. And believe Me, it does not only take courage to be the storm: it takes courage to be the island in the storm."

After the first world war, the onslaughts on Swiss neutrality died down, only to set in again in the 1930s with unprecedented force. In a pseudo-scientific treatise incorporating the dawning doctrine of race and the totalitarian ideal of the state, the neutrality of Switzerland was viciously distorted and slandered and branded as a weakness of will, as a moral defect, as senility, as disease. Neutrality, it was said, was the symptom of a European sickness, the negation of all politics, was sterility, rootlessness, scepticism, in fact the refusal of a destiny (Christoph Steding, *Das Reich und die Krankheit der europäischen Kultur*. Hamburg 1938). A famous international lawyer from the opposing camp of partisans of the League of Nations proclaimed the decay of the idea of neutrality as a scientific fact. The author claims to have proved: "que la neutralité apparait aujourd'hui comme une véritable anachronisme; n'étant plus en harmonie avec l'état du droit des gens ni avec les nécessités économiques et les aspirations des peoples, elle est irrémédiablement condamnée comme institution; elle a destinée à disparaître [that today neutrality appears as a veritable anachronism; being out of harmony with the state of international law as well as the economic necessities and the aspirations of people, it is irreparably condemned as an institution; it is destined to disappear]." (Nicolas Politis, *La Neutralité et la Paix*. Paris 1935). And only recently [Bonjour, writing in 1946] a widely read book by an English writer expressed the view: "Neutrality is finished as a political concept", that the minor states of Europe "must henceforth surrender their sovereign rights of neutrality" (Julian Huxley, *Democracy Marches*. New York 1941).

In Switzerland these calumnies and prophecies of woe are taken quite coolly, and native equanimity remains unshaken. Either they are disproved by present political conditions, or they stand self-condemned by their own tendentiousness. That Swiss neutrality is no bed of roses on which the Swiss, heedless of the way of the world, lose the habit of effort is proved by their labours in the military and economic spheres. And that neutrality alone is no guarantee against attack from the outside, but demands extreme vigilance from every citizen, has been shown by the most recent past. The ridiculous assumption that neutrality is the necessary attribute of an ageing people is disproved precisely by the early history of Prussia-Brandenburg. Further, the assertion that Europe granted Switzerland her neutrality, and therefore can take it back again, is countered by the Swiss with the historical fact that their neutrality is no charitable gift of the great Powers, but was—though not arbitrarily—chosen and desired by them within definite laws dictated by the necessities of their political existence. It is just because they have declared their neutrality permanent, and therefore do not change their views of foreign affairs in the vicissitudes of international relations, that they are proof against the charge of time-serving. The Swiss bear the heavy burden of their armed neutrality without any intention of exploiting changed political constellations for the acquisition of power, in sharp contrast to the occasional neutrals or "non-belligerents." As long as there is no really super-national court of arbitration in international relations, the neutral Swiss have every right to decline to shed their blood in the interest of a system of great Powers.

The misgivings that arise at home, however, are far more serious and dangerous than foreign invective. For is not neutrality an inglorious and paltry ideal at a time which demands the supreme sacrifice from every man? What ardour or energy can it inspire? Is it not too cool for hot-blooded youth, too many-facetted for an age which loves clear-cut issues? What enthusiasm can be felt for an attitude which aims at a general insurance against danger? Is this aloofness not a bare betrayal of what others are giving their lives for? There is real spiritual distress when a man's general outlook on life is incompatible with the neutral attitude required of him, and when, as a human being, he is at odds with himself as a citizen. Does neutrality not lead to a deadening of moral feeling, does it not, when consistently maintained, end in the abominable condition of a resigned and cowardly indifference? Or does it not make bigots of men because, not being in the heat and tumult of the battle, they imagine they are above it?

Clear definitions soon dispel confusions of this kind. Neutrality is a principle of foreign policy, not of ethics. It presents a program of foreign relations, not a moral ideal. For the Swiss it is a method of political diplomacy, not their goal of their being as a nation. Switzerland is not there for neutrality, but neutrality for Switzerland. In neutrality, the Swiss see a product of the reason of state which aims at the welfare of the state and of the community of the people it embraces, but not a fundamental spiritual attitude. That is, the Swiss regard their neutrality solely as an affair of the state and not of the private individual. Their neutrality is the fruit of practical experience, not of theoretical speculation, of cool rationalism, not of elemental instinct. In the moral domain Swiss know no neutrality. They have to decide between good and evil, right and wrong. Any man refusing to take sides in that conflict and striving to achieve a so-called neutral attitude would prove himself guilty of a lack of logical discrimination, and still more, of a strange moral callousness.

> From Edgar Bonjour, *Swiss Neutrality. Its History and Its Meaning.* Translated by Mary Hottinger (London: George Allen & Unwin, 1946):119-125. Reprinted by permission.

[3] *Switzerland's 'Benevolent Neutrality' in World War II: The View of Allen Dulles*

> Allen Dulles was in charge of American espionage in Bern, Switzerland from 1942 to 1945. He thus experienced the workings of Swiss neutrality first-hand and assessed it in the selection given below. (Ed.)

In World War II Swiss neutrality meant that Switzerland would not willingly engage in the conflict on either side or support either side in any military or nonmilitary endeavor. It did not mean that Switzerland would not defend itself if attacked or that it had committed itself to be neutral in spirit where Nazism was at issue. It was clear from the beginning that the Swiss had nothing to fear from the Western Allies and everything to fear from Nazi Germany which on at least two occasions had considered the possibility of invading Switzerland, once in 1940 before the fall of France opened the door to the West, and again in 1943 during the crucial days in the battle for North Africa.

At the peak of its mobilization Switzerland had 850,000 men under arms or standing in reserve, a fifth of the total population. The commander of this force was General Henri Guisan, an outstanding patriot. That Switzerland did not have to fight was thanks to its will to resist and its large investment in its own defense. The cost to Germany of an invasion of Switzerland would certainly have been very high.

After the country had been completely surrounded by the Axis, the defense of Switzerland was based on the strategic assumption that the areas in which major cities and industries lay, could not be defended against German attack. The concentrated defense would therefore take place in the Alpine fastnesses into which the major portion of the Swiss Army would withdraw. A system of fortifications, tunnels, underground supply depots would have made it very difficult for any opponent to root out the Swiss defenders from this stronghold. Furthermore, the railroad tunnels under the Alps which the Germans needed for shipping supplies to Italy would be destroyed by the Swiss themselves. This was announced publicly and the Germans were thus given notice that, if they invaded Switzerland, they would lose rather than gain by an attack.

In the desperate days of 1940, when Switzerland became encircled by the Axis, some elements of the Swiss government were inclined to look for compromises to avoid open conflict with the Germans. In the Swiss Army, however, there was a group of patriotic officers who stood firmly for the idea of resisting the Germans at any cost. Among them were some of the top military intelligence personnel of the Army who were well informed about German intentions toward Switzerland.

Under the leadership of Captains Max Waibel and Hans Hausamann an intelligence unit known as "Bureau Ha" (after the first two letters of Hausamann's name) had reason to believe that German agents were prepared, by the use of physical force, to prevent General Guisan from issuing orders to the Swiss Army to defend the country. Hausamann and other officers, including Max Waibel, who will later play a prominent role in our story, went so far as to make a secret agreement among themselves that they would take the higher commands if their senior officers showed any reluctance to oppose a German move into Switzerland. For this patriotic act of insubordination some of them were sentenced to short terms of arrest, a small price to pay for the strengthening of the Swiss will to resist which resulted from their firm stand.[2]

The official Swiss position in regard to my mission observed the proper decorum of neutrality, but it was a benevolent neutrality.

The Swiss had to be assured, of course, of my discretion and good sense, and my full understanding of their position. For example, the Swiss desired to forestall any action on our part which, if it came to the attention of the Germans, could be thrown up to the Swiss as an instance of favoring

---

[2] A fair account of these events can be found in an excellent book by Alice Meyer, *Anpassung oder Widerstand* (Compromise or Resistance) (Frauenfeld, Switzerland: Huber, 1965). [Footnote of A. W. Dulles]

one belligerent over the other. There was fear that any blatant breach of neutrality would be taken by the Germans as an excuse for reprisals. I cooperated to the utmost, by making it clear to the Swiss that I had no interest in spying on any Swiss measures of defense. The stronger they were in their preparations against a German attack, the better we liked it. The Germans, on the other hand, had agents and saboteurs in Switzerland spying out Swiss defense secrets. Scores of German agents were arrested, and a few were shot.

We realized, of course, that the Swiss Intelligence Service, in the normal course of business, had contact with both German and Allied intelligence. Since the Swiss were neutral, they could maintain such connections with each group of belligerents, and in their own defense interest they were wholly justified in doing so. Misunderstandings were minimized by the fact that one set of intelligence officers worked chiefly with the Germans, and another with the Allies. Colonel Roger Masson, of the Swiss General Staff, had contact with Walter Schellenberg, the head of Himmler's intelligence service, and Max Waibel and his close associates consulted with us. What went on between Masson and Waibel, both of whom reported to General Guisan, I do not know to this day. I put my confidence in Waibel and never had any reason to regret it. As we later proceeded to develop our secret and precarious relations with the German generals early in 1945, we would have been thwarted at every step if we had not had the help of Waibel in facilitating contacts and communications and in arranging the delicate frontier crossings which had to be carried out under conditions of complete secrecy. In all his actions Waibel was serving the interests of peace.

In any discussion of Swiss neutrality in World War II, it would be seriously remiss to omit the humanitarian role of Switzerland. It was a refuge and an island of humane and charitable undertakings for the persecuted, the homeless and the displaced. As the site of peace organizations and international institutions devoted to cooperation among nations, it was one place where both Allies and Germans could hope to find competent and constructive helpers in the quest for peace.

Source: Allen Dulles, *The Secret Surrender* (New York: Harper & Row, 1966): 25-27. Reprinted by the kind permission of HarperCollins.

2. A Chronology, 1938–1945

(Entries in italics refer to actions relating to Switzerland)

1938

March 11	German Invasion of Austria
May 14	*Return of Switzerland to Unlimited Neutrality*
September 29	Munich Conference between Hitler, Mussolini, Daladier, and Chamberlain
October 1	German Annexation of the Sudetenland
December 12	*Federal Council Announces Economic Reorganization Intensified Build-up of the Swiss Armed Forces*

1939

March 15	German Invasion of Czechoslovakia
May 22	Military Alliance between Germany and Italy
August 23	German-Soviet Non-aggression Pact
August 25	English-Polish Pact of Alliance
August 29	*Mobilization of the Swiss Frontier Guard*
August 30	*Selection of Henri Guisan as Commander-in-Chief of the Swiss Army*
August 31	*Declaration of Armed Neutrality by Switzerland*
September 1	German Invasion of Poland
	General Mobilization of the Swiss Army [430,000 soldiers; 200,00 reservists]
	Order for Intensified Agricultural Production [Anbauschlacht]
September 3	Declaration of War against Germany by France and Great Britain
September/ October	*Secret Swiss Military Alliance with France and Secret Agreement with Great Britain for Airstrips in Case of German Attack on Switzerland*
September 4	*Swiss Rationing Order for Food, Textiles, Clothing, and Shoes*
September 17	Russian Invasion of Poland
September 27	Capitulation of Warsaw

223

September 28 Partition of Poland between Hitler and Stalin
September 30 Beginning of Hostilities of Soviet Russia against Finland

1940
March 12		Finnish-Soviet Peace Treaty
April 9		German Invasion of Denmark and Norway
April 18		*Declaration of Federal Council and the Commander-in-Chief to Defend Switzerland "to the utmost with all available means against any aggressor"*
May 10		German Invasion of Belgium, Holland, and Luxembourg German Invasion of France
			Second General Mobilization of the Swiss Army
May 15		Surrender of Holland
May 28		Surrender of Belgium
June 4		German Troops' Seizure of Dunkirk
June 10		Italy enters the War
June		*Battles between German and Swiss Air Force*
June 14		Fall of Paris
June 17		Surrender of France
			Massing of German Tank Divisions on the Western Borders of Switzerland
			French and Polish Troops Take Refuge in Switzerland
June 22		The Vichy Government Controls Middle and Southern France German Occupation of Northern and Western France
June 25		Armistice between Germany, Italy, and France
			Accommodationist Radio Address of Pilet-Golaz, President of Switzerland
July 7		*Partial Demobilization of the Swiss Army*
July 25		*General Guisan Assembles the Officer Corps on the Rütli and Calls for Unconditional Armed Resistance and a Determined Ideological Defense Against National Socialist Propaganda*
			Development of the 'Reduit' Concept of the Military Defense of Switzerland
			Switzerland Assumes Diplomatic Representation for the Belligerents
July/August	Incorporation of the Baltic States into the Soviet Union
August 6		Advance of Italian Troops into Greece
September 13	Italian Invasion of Egypt via Libya

| September 29 | Pact between Germany, Italy, and Japan |
| October 28 | Italy Attacks Greece |

1941

January	War in North Africa, Fall of Tobruk
February-March	German Invasion of Bulgaria and Romania
April 6	German Invasion of Yugoslavia
April 12	Move of Rommel's Africa Corps towards Egypt's Frontiers
April 16	German Occupation of Greece
May 18	Surrender of Italian Troops in Abyssinia
June 14	*The United States Freezes the Assets of All Continental European Countries, Including Switzerland*
June 22	German Attack of the Soviet Union
July	*Partial Demobilization of the Swiss Army* *Introduction of Relief Military Service in Switzerland*
July 18	*Economic Agreement between Germany and Switzerland*
November	German Troops before Moscow
November 30	Russian Counteroffensive
December 7	Japanese Attack on Pearl Harbor
December 8	Great Britain and the United States Declare War against Japan Japanese Attack on the Philippines
December 11	Germany and Italy Declare War against the United States

1942

January 31-February 2	Surrender of German 6. Army Commanded by F. Paulus and W. von Seydlitz
March 28	*Start of Negotiations between the Allies and Switzerland Concerning Limiting Trade with Germany*
June 20	German Advance against El Alamein
September 29	Russian Counter Offensive on the Eastern Front
October	Allied Bombardment of North Italian Cities
October 10	Battle of El Alamein between German and Allied Troops
November 8	Landing of British and American Troops in French North Africa
November 11	German Occupation of All of France

1943

January 26	Casablanca Conference
January 27	First Bombing Attacks against German Cities
February 2	Retreat of German Forces from Stalingrad
February 18	Total War against Germany
April 27	*American Suspension of Navicerts and Export Licenses for Imports to Switzerland, Resumption of Allied Blacklisting of Swiss Firms*
May 18	Surrender of the German and Italian Troops in North Africa
July 10	Landing of Allied Troops in Sicily
July 25	Overthrow of Mussolini and Collapse of Italian Fascism
September 3	Allied Landing in Southern Italy
September 8	Surrender of Italy
September 28	Teheran Conference of Roosevelt, Churchill, and Stalin
October 13	Italy Declares War on Germany
December 19	*New Economic Agreement between the Allies and Switzerland Concerning Trade with Germany*

1944

January 3	Russian Troops Reach Poland's Frontier
March 19	German Troops Occupy Budapest
	Swiss Consul General Charles Lutz Begins Issuing Protection Papers to Some 50,000 Hungarian Jews
April 4	*American Bombardment of Schaffhausen*
June 4	Allied Troops Occupy Rome
June 6	Allied Invasion of Normandy
July 20	Assassination Attempt on Hitler Fails
August 25	Liberation of Paris and Entry of De Gaulle in Paris
August 26	*American Troops Reach the Swiss Frontier*
August-September	*Partial Remobilization and Regrouping of the Swiss Army* French Troops Advance into Southern Germany
September 1	Liberation of Bucharest
September 2	American Troops Reach the Rhine
September 3	Liberation of Brussels and Antwerp
September 15	Russian Occupation of Sofia
October 20	Russian Occupation of Belgrade
November	Russian Troops Enter Germany

1945

January	Russian Occupation of Budapest
January 12	Russian Occupation of Warsaw
March 4	*Allied Bombing of Zürich and Basel*
March 8	*General Spaatz Announces New Measures of the Allied High Command to Prevent Further Bombing Errors of the Allied Air Force in Bern*
March 24	Allied Troops Cross the Rhine
April 15	Russian Occupation of Vienna
April 24	Russian Enter Berlin
April 28	Execution of Mussolini
April 29	Surrender of German Troops in Upper Italy
April 30	Suicide of Hitler
May 2	Cease-fire in Italy, Surrender of Berlin
May 7	Russian Occupation of Prague Total Surrender of Germany
May 8	Cease-fire in Europe
June 26	Founding of the United Nations
July 12	Partition of Germany into four Zones of Occupation
August 6, 9	American Atom Bombing of Hiroshima and Nagasaki
August 20	*Demobilization of Swiss Army* *Resignation of General Guisan, Commander-in-Chief of Swiss Army*
September 9	Surrender of Japan

BIBLIOGRAPHY

Åkerrén, Bengt. "Schweden als Schutzmacht", in: *Schwedische und schweizerische Neutralität im Zweiten Weltkrieg.* Herausgegeben von Rudolf L. Bindschedler et al. (Basel: Helbing & Lichtenhahn, 1985): 111-119.

Anger, Per. *With Raoul Wallenberg in Budapest. Memories of the War Years in Hungary.* Preface by Elie Wiesel. Translated from the Swedish by David Mel Paul and Margareta Paul. New York: Holocaust Library, 1981.

Barth, Karl. *Eine Schweizer Stimme 1938–1945.* Zollikon-Zürich: Evangelischer Verlag, 1945.

Bayac, J. Delperrie de. *Histoire de la Milice, 1918-1945.* 2 vols. Collection marabout université. [Verviers?]: Arthème Fayard, 1969.

Bendel, Max. *Zerstörter Schaffhauser Kunstbesitz aus dem Museum zu Allerheiligen.* Herausgegeben vom Kunstverein Schaffhausen und der Vereinigung Schaffhauser Kunstfreunde. Zürich: Atlantis Verlag, 1944.

Ben-Tov, Arieh. *Facing the Holocaust in Budapest. The International Committee of the Red Cross and the Jews in Hungary, 1943–1945.* Henri Dunant Institute, Geneva. Dordrecht: Martinus Nijhoff, 1988.

Besymenski, Lew. *Sonderakte Barbarossa. Dokumentarbericht zur Vorgeschichte des deutschen Überfalls auf die Sowjetunion aus sowjetischer Sicht.* Reinbeck bei Hamburg: Rowohlt, 1973.

Biagini, Antonello and Fernando Fratolillo. *Diario Storico del Commando Supremo.* Vol. 4, tome 2. Roma: Ufficio Storico, Stato maggiore dell' esercito, 1992.

Bindschedler, Rudolf L. et al., eds. *Schwedische und schweizerische Neutralität im zweiten Weltkrieg.* Basel: Helbing und Lichtenhahn, 1985.

Bindschedler-Robert, Denise. "Les bons Offices dans la Politique étrangère de la Suisse", in: *Handbuch der schweizerischen Aussenpolitik.* Hrsg. von Alois Riklin et al. (Bern: Paul Haupt, 1975): 679-691.

Blum, John Morton, ed. *Years of Urgency 1938–1941. From the Morgenthau Diaries.* Boston: Houghton Mifflin, 1965.

Bolli, Jean Jacques. *L'aspect horloger des relations commerciales américano-suisses de 1929 à 1950.* La Chaux-de-Fonds: La Suisse horlogère, 1956.

Bonjour, Edgar. *Swiss Neutrality. Its History and Meaning.* Translated by Mary Hottinger. London: Allen & Unwin, 1946.

_____. *Geschichte der schweizerischen Neutralität. Vier Jahrhunderte eidgenössischer Aussenpolitik.* 6. Auflage. 9 vols. Basel: Helbing & Lichtenhahn, 1970-1976.

Braham, Randolph L. *The Hungarian Jewish Catastrophe. A Selected and Annotated Bibliography.* Second edition. Revised and enlarged. New York: The City University of New York, distributed by Columbia University Press, 1984.

Brand, Urs. "Der französische Sozialistenführer Jean Jaurès und das schweizerische Milizsystem", in *Allgemeine schweizerische Militärzeitschrift* 139 (October 1973): 510-517.

Braunschweig, Pierre-Theodore. *Geheimer Draht nach Berlin. Die Nachrichtenlinie Masson-Schellenberg und der schweizerische Nachrichtendienst im Zweiten Weltkrieg.* Zürich: Verlag Neue Zürcher Zeitung, 1989.

Bringolf, Walther. *Mein Leben. Weg und Umweg eines Schweizer Sozialdemokraten.* Bern: Scherz, 1965.

Brunner, Edouard et al., eds. *Einblick in die schweizerische Aussenpolitik. Zum 65. Geburtstag von Staatssekretär Raymond Probst.* Zürich: Verlag Neue Zürcher Zeitung, 1984.

Brunner, Hanspeter. *10 Jahre schweizerisch-amerikanische Handelsbeziehungen 1936–1945. Zwei Vorträge.* Zürich: Schulthess, 1946.

Bucher, Erwin. *Zwischen Bundesrat und General. Schweizer Politik und Armee im Zweiten Weltkrieg.* Zürich: Orell Füssli, 1993.

Burckhardt, Carl J. *Meine Danziger Mission 1937–1939.* Zürich: Fretz & Wasmuth, 1960.

Bütler, Heinz. *"Wach auf, Schweizervolk!" Die Schweiz zwischen Frontismus, Verrat und Selbstbehauptung, 1914–1940.* 2. Auflage. Gümligen, Bern: Zytglogge, 1980.

Carlgren, Wilhelm. "Die Mediationstätigkeit in der Aussenpolitik Schwedens während des Zweiten Weltkrieges", in: *Schwedische und schweizerische Neutralität im Zweiten Weltkrieg.* Herausgegeben von Rudolf Bindschedler et al. (Basel: Helbing & Lichtenhahn, 1985): 97-110.

Carnegie Endowment for International Peace, Division of International Law. Pamphlet No.4. *The Hague Conventions of 1899 (I) and 1907 (I) for the Pacific Settlement of International Disputes.* Washington, DC: Published by the Endowment, 1915.

Cassin, René. "Vichy or France?", in *Foreign Affairs* 20 (October 1941): 102-112.

Cesarani, David, ed. *Genocide and Rescue. The Holocaust in Hungary 1944.* Oxford: Berg, 1997.

Churchill, Winston. *The Second World War.* Vol. 6: *Triumph and Tragedy.* London: Cassell, 1954.

Cointet, Michèle. *Vichy capitale 1940–1944.* Collection Vérités et Légendes. Paris: Perrin, 1993.

Commission nationale pour la publication de documents diplomatiques suisses. *Diplomatische Dokumente der Schweiz 1848–1945.* Vol. 15. Bern: Benteli, 1992.

Daniels, Roger. "American Refugee Policy in Historical Perspective", in: *The Muses Flee Hitler. Cultural Transfer and Adaptation 1930–1945.* Edited by Jarrell C. Jackman and Carla M. Borden (Washington, DC: Smithsonian Institution Press, 1983): 61-77.

_____. *Coming to America. A History of Immigration and Ethnicity in American Life.* New York: HarperCollins, 1990.

Darwin, H. G. "Mediation and Good Offices", in: *International Disputes. The Legal Aspects.* David Davies Memorial Institute of International Studies. (London: Europa Publications, 1972): 83-92.

DellaPergola, Sergio. "Between Science and Fiction: Notes on the Demography of the Holocaust", in *Holocaust and Genocide Studies* 10, 1 (1996): 34-51.

Documents on German Foreign Policy, 1918–1945. From the Archives of the German Foreign Ministry. Series D, XIII: *The War Years 1941.* London: H. M. Stationary Office, 1941.

Douglas, Roy. *The World War 1939–1945. The Cartoonist's View.* London: Routledge, 1991.

Dulles, Allen. *The Secret Surrender.* New York: Harper & Row, 1966.

Duttwyler, Herbert E. *Der Seekrieg und die Wirtschaftspolitik des neutralen Staates.* Zürich: Polygraphischer Verlag, 1945.

Erdman, Paul. *Swiss-American Economic Relations. Their Evolution in an Era of Crises.* Basel: Kyklos, 1959.

Ernst, Alfred. *Neutrale Staaten im Zweiten Weltkrieg.* Münsingen: Tages-Nachrichten, 1973.

Ernst, Rudolf J. *Die schweizerischen Kapitalanlagen in den Vereinigten Staaten.* Zürich, 1943.

Etter, Philipp. *Reden an das Schweizervolk, gehalten im Jahre 1939.* Zürich: Atlantis, 1939.

Fink, Jürg. *Die Schweiz aus der Sicht des Dritten Reiches 1933–1945.* Zürich: Schulthess Polygraphischer Verlag, 1985.

Fleck, Ludwik. *Genesis and Development of a Scientific Fact.* Edited by Thaddeus J. Trenn and Robert K. Merton. Translated by Fred Bradley and Thaddeus Trenn. Foreword by Thomas S. Kuhn. Chicago: The University of Chicago Press, 1979.

Foreign Relations of the United States. *Diplomatic Papers. 1945.* Vol. II: *General: Political and Economic Matters* (Washington, DC: United States Printing Office, 1967): 1133-1134.

Forsythe, David P. *Humanitarian Politics. The International Committee of the Red Cross.* Baltimore: Johns Hopkins University Press, 1977.

Fox, Annette Baker. *The Power of Small States: Diplomacy in World War II.* Chicago: The University of Chicago Press, 1959.

Fritschi, Oskar Felix. *Geistige Landesverteidigung während des Zweiten Weltkrieges.* Winterthur: Fabag und Druckerei Winterthur, 1971.

Fuhrer, Hans Rudolf. "Die Schweiz im Nachrichtendienst", in: *Schwedische und schweizerische Neutralität im Zweiten Weltkrieg.* Herausgegeben von Rudolf L. Bindschedler et al. (Basel: Helbing & Lichtenhahn, 1985): 405-426.

Gautschi, Willi. *General Henri Guisan.* Zürich: Verlag Neue Zürcher Zeitung, 1989.

Gehrig-Straube, Christine. *Beziehungslose Zeiten. Das schweizerische-sowjetische Verhältnis zwischen Abbruch und Wiederaufnahme der Beziehungen (1918–1946) aufgrund schweizerischer Akten.* Zürich: Hans Rohr, 1997.

Gelber, Yoav. "Moralist and Realistic Approaches in the Study of the Allies' Attitude to the Holocaust", in: *Comprehending the Holocaust. Historical and Literary Research*. Edited by Asher Cohen, Yoav Gelber, and Charlotte Wardi (Frankfurt am Main: Peter Lang, 1988): 107-123.

Generaladjudantur der Schweizer Armee, Division Heer und Haus. *Wehrbrief 25*, May 25, 1943.

Gordon, David L. and Royden Dangerfield. *The Hidden Weapon. The Story of Economic Warfare*. New York: Harper, 1947.

Gruner, Erich. *Die Parteien in der Schweiz*. Zweite Auflage. Bern: Francke, 1977.

Gwerder, Josef. *Dampfschiff 'Stadt Luzern'. Bordbuch*. Luzern: Keller, 1989.

Halbrook, Stephen P. *Target Switzerland*. Rockville Centre, NY: Sarpedon, 1998.

Halder, Franz. *Kriegstagebuch. Tägliche Aufzeichnungen des Chefs des Generalstabes des Heeres*. 3 vols. Hrsg. vom Arbeitkreis für Wehrforschung. Stuttgart: W. Kohlhammer, 1962.

"Hands Across the Sea", in *Fortune* 29 (February 1944): 46-47.

Harvel, Ursel P. *Liberators over Europe. 44th Bombardment Group*. San Angelo, TX:

Hediger, Ernest S. "Switzerland in Wartime", in *Foreign Policy Reports*, 18, No. 20 (January 1, 1943): 262-271.

Heer, Hannes und Klaus Naumann, eds. *Vernichtungskrieg. Verbrechen der Wehrmacht 1941–1944*. Hamburg: Hamburger Edition HIS Verlagsgesellschaft, 1995.

Helmreich, Jonathan. "The Diplomacy of Apology. United States Bombings of Switzerland During World War II", in *Air University Review* 28 (May-June 1977): 20-37.

Hillgruber, Andreas, comp. *Staatsmänner und Diplomaten bei Hitler. Vertrauliche Aufzeichnungen über Unterredungen mit Vertretern des Auslandes*. 2 vols. München: Deutscher Taschenbuch Verlag, 1969.

Hofer, Walther. "Neutralität im totalen Krieg", in: *Einblick in die schweizerische Aussenpolitik. Zum 65. Geburtstag von Staatssekretär Raymond Probst*. Herausgegeben von Edouard Brunner et al. (Zürich: Verlag Neue Zürcher Zeitung, 1984): 171-200.

Homberger, Heinrich. "Minister Dr. Hans Sulzer zum Gedächtnis", in *Schweizerische Monatshefte* 39 (January 1960): Sonderbeilage.

House Reports. 79th [US] Congress, 1st Session (January 3–December 21, 1945): No. 728: "Investigations of the National War Effort", June 12, 1945.

Huber, Peter. "Schweizer Spanienkämpfer in den Fängen des NKWD", in *Schweizerische Zeitschrift für Geschichte* 41 (1991): 335-353.

Hull, Cordell. *The Memoirs of Cordell Hull*. 2 vols. New York: Macmillan, 1948.

Hutson, James H. *The Sister Republics. Switzerland and the United States from 1776 to the Present*. Washington, DC: Library of Congress, 1991. Expanded second edition, 1992.

Janner, Antonino. *La Puissance protectrice en Droit internationale d'après les expériences par la Suisse pendant la seconde guerre mondiale*. Juristische Fakultät der Universität Basel. Institut für internationales Recht und internationale Beziehungen. Schriftenreihe Heft 7. Basel: Helbing & Lichtenhahn, 1948.

Jochmann, Werner, ed. *Adolf Hitler Monologe im Führer-Hauptquartier, 1941–1944. Die Aufzeichnungen Heinrich Heims.* Hamburg: Albrecht Knaus, 1980.

Jost, Hans U. *Politik und Wirtschaft im Krieg. Die Schweiz 1938–1948.* Zürich: Chronos, 1998.

Kimche, Jon. *General Guisans Zweifrontenkrieg. Die Schweiz zwischen 1939 und 1945.* Berlin: Ullstein, 1962.

Koch, Peter F. *Geheim-Depot Schweiz. Wie Banken am Holocaust verdienen.* Mit einem Kapitel von Richard Chaim Schneider. München: List Verlag, 1997.

Kreis, Georg. "Neue Forschungen zum Zweiten Weltkrieg in der Schweiz", in: *Neue Forschungen zum Zweiten Weltkrieg. Literaturberichte und Bibliographien.* Herausgegeben von Jürgen Rohwer und Hildegard Müller (Koblenz: Bernard & Graefe, 1990): 418-426.

_____. "Vier Debatten und wenig Dissens", in *Schweizerische Zeitschrift für Geschichte* 47 (1997):451-476.

_____. "Die schweizerische Flüchtlingspolitik der Jahre 1933–1945", *Schweizerische Zeitschrift für Geschichte* 47 (1997): 552-579.

Kurz, Hans Rudolf, ed. *Dokumente des Aktivdienstes.* Frauenfeld: Huber, 1965.

_____. *Nachrichtenzentrum Schweiz. Die Schweiz im Nachrichtendienst des Zweiten Weltkriegs.* Frauenfeld: Huber, 1972.

_____. *Hundert Jahre Schweizer Armee.* Thun: Ott, 1978.

Ladame, Paul Alexis. *Une caméra contre Hitler.* Genève: Editions Slatkine, 1997.

_____. *Defending Switzerland.* Delmar, NY: Caravan Books, 1999.

Laemmel, Hans. "Missverständnisse um die Filmwochenschau", in *Neue Zürcher Zeitung* (December 1999):

Langer, William L. und S. Everett Gleason. *The Undeclared War 1940–1941.* New York: Harper, Published for the Council of Foreign Relations, 1953.

Latham, Earl. *The Communist Controversy in Washington: From the New Deal to McCarthy.* Cambridge, MA: Harvard University Press, 1966.

Lester Elenore. "Raoul Wallenberg: The Righteous Gentile from Sweden", in: *The Holocaust in Hungary. Forty Years Later.* Edited by Randolph L. Braham and Bela Vago (New York: The City University of New York, distributed by Columbia University Press, 1985): 147-160.

Levai, Jenö, ed. *Eichmann in Ungarn. Dokumente.* Budapest: Pannonia Verlag, 1961.

_____. *Hungarian Jewry and the Papacy. Pope Pius Did Not Remain Silent.* Translated by J. R. Foster. London: SANDS, 1968.

Levine, Herbert S. "The Mediator: Carl J. Burckhardt's Efforts to Avert a Second World War", in *The Journal of Modern History* 45 (September 1973): 439-455.

Lezzi, Otto. *Sozialdemokratie und Militärfrage in der Schweiz.* Frauenfeld: Huber, 1996.

Lossberg, Bernhard von. *Im Wehrmachtsführungsstab. Bericht eines Generalstabsoffiziers.* Hamburg: H. H. Nölke, 1949.

Luck, Murray, ed. *Modern Switzerland*. Palo Alto: SPOSS, 1978.

Ludwig, Carl. *Die Flüchtlingspolitik der Schweiz seit 1933 bis zur Gegenwart (1957). Bericht.* Bern: Herbert Lang, 1966.

Lüem, Walter und Andreas Steigmeier, eds. *Die Limmatstellung im Zweiten Weltkrieg.* Baden [Schweiz]: Baden Verlag, 1997.

Lunn, Arnold. *Mountain Jubilee*. London: Eyre & Spottiswoode, 1943.

McBride, Charles. *Mission Failure and Survival*. Manhattan, KS: Sunflower University Press, 1989.

Medlicott, W. N. *The Economic Blockade*. 2 vols. London: H. M. Stationary Office, 1952-1959.

Meier, Heinz K. *Friendship under Stress. U. S.–Swiss Relations 1900–1950.* Bern: Herbert Lang, 1970.

Meurant, Jacques. *La presse et l'opinion de la Suisse romande face à l'Europe en guerre, 1939–1941.* Neuchâtel: Editions de la Baconnière, 1976.

_____. "Le Comité internationale de la Croix-Rouge et la protection des civils", in *Revue d'histoire de la deuxième guerre mondiale* 31, No. 121 (Janvier 1981): 129-138.

Meyer, Alice. *Anpassung oder Widerstand. Die Schweiz zur Zeit des deutschen Nationalsozialismus.* Frauenfeld: Huber, 1965.

Moltmann, Günter. "Die Genese der Unconditional-Surrender-Forderung", in: *Probleme des Zweiten Weltkrieges.* Herausgegeben von Andreas Hillgruber (Köln: Kiepenheuer & Witsch, 1967): 171-198.

Morel, Yves-Alain. *Aufklärung oder Indoktrination? Truppeninformation in der Schweizer Armee.* Zürich: Thesis Verlag, 1996.

Muggeridge, Malcolm, ed. *Ciano's Diary 1939–1943*. London: Heinemann, 1947.

Newsom, David D. *Diplomacy under a Foreign Flag. When Nations Break Relations.* An Institute for the Study of Diplomacy Book. New York: St. Martin's Press, 1990.

Novick, Peter. *The Holocaust in American Life*. Boston: Houghton Mifflin, 1999.

Oertle, Vinzenz. "Sollte ich aus Russland nicht zurückkehren . . . ." Thesis. History, University of Zürich, 1998.

Patai, Raphael. *The Jews of Hungary. History, Culture, Psychology.* Detroit: Wayne State University Press, 1996.

Pedrazzi, Dominic, Jürg Stüssi-Lauterburg, and Anne-Marie Volery, eds. *"En toute confiance." Correspondance du Général et de Madame Henri Guisan avec le Major Albert R. Mayer, 1940–1959.* Brugg: Effingerhof, 1995.

Pfanner, Helmut F. "The Role of Switzerland for the Refugees", in: *The Muses Flee Hitler. Cultural Transfer and Adaptation 1930–1945.* Edited by Jarrell C. Jackman and Carla M. Borden (Washington, DC: Smithsonian Institution Press, 1983): 235-248.

Pipes, Richard, ed. *The Unknown Lenin. From the Secret Archive.* New Haven: Yale University Press, 1996.

Polk, Judd. "Freezing Dollars Against the Axis", in *Foreign Affairs* 20 (October 1941): 113-130.

Probst, Raymond R.. *'Good Offices' in the Light of Swiss International Practice and Experience*. Dordrecht: Martinus Nijhoff Publishers, 1989.

Rings, Werner. *Advokaten des Feindes. Das Abenteuer der politischen Neutralität.* Wien: Econ-Verlag, 1966.

_____. *Schweiz im Krieg 1933–1945. Ein Bericht.* 2. Auflage. Zürich: Ex Libris, 1974.

_____. *Life with the Enemy. Collaboration and Resistance in Hitler's Europe 1939–1945.* Translated by J. Maxwell Brownjohn. Garden City, NY: Doubleday, 1982.

Rosen, Josef. *Wartime Food Development in Switzerland.* War-Peace Pamphlet, No. 9. Stanford, CA:, Stanford University, Food Research Institute 1947.

Rosenberg, Martin. *Was war Anpassung, wo war Widerstand?* Bern: Generalsekretariat der Konservativen Christlichsozialen Volkspartei, 1966.

Rovighi, Alberto. *Un secolo di relazioni militari tra Italia e Svizzera 1861–1961.* Roma: Ufficio Storico, Stato Maggiore dell' Esercito, 1987.

Rozett, Robert. "Child Rescue in Budapest, 1944–5", *Holocaust and Genocide Studies* 2,1 (1987): 49-59.

Rubinstein, William D. *The Myth of Rescue. Why the Democracies Could Not Have Saved More Jews from the Nazis.* London: Routledge, 1997.

Sallaz, Kurt und Peter Rilkin. *Panzer und Panzerabwehr.* Dietikon-Zürich: Stocker und Schmid, 1982.

Schaffer, Ronald. "American Military Ethics in World War II: The Bombing of German Civilians", in *Journal of American History* 67 (June 1980): 327-330.

Schärer, Martin. "L'activité de la Suisse comme puissance protectrice durant la seconde guerre mondiale", in *Revue d'histoire de la deuxième guerre mondiale* 31, No. 121 (January 1981): 121-128.

Schönmann, Otto. *Die ausserordentlichen Militär- und Kriegskredite im schweizerischen Bundeshaushalt.* Dissertation Basel. Basel: Druck Theodor Kestenholz, 1942.

Schwarz, Urs. *Die schweizerische Kriegsfinanzierung 1939–1945 und ihre Ausstrahlungen in der Nachkriegszeit.* Winterthur: P. G. Keller, 1953.

_____. *The Eye of the Hurricane. Switzerland in World War Two.* Boulder, CO: Westview Press, 1980.

Senn, Hans. *Basel und das Gempenplateau im Zweiten Weltkrieg.* Frauenfeld: Huber, 1996.

Sherry, Michael S. *The Rise of American Air Power. The Creation of Armageddon.* New Haven: Yale University Press, 1987.

Somary, Felix. *Raven of Zurich. The Memoirs of Felix Somary.* Translated from the German by A. J. Sherman. Foreword by Otto von Habsburg. New York: St. Martin's Press, 1986.

Sprecher, Thomas, *Thomas Mann in Zürich.* Zürich: Verlag Neue Zürcher Zeitung, 1969.

Stamm, Konrad Walter. *Die guten Dienste der Schweiz. Aktive Neutralitätspolitik zwischen Tradition, Diskussion und Integration.* Bern: Herbert Lang, 1974.

Statistisches Jahrbuch der Schweiz, 1970. Basel: Birkhäuser, 1970.

Stauffer, Paul. "Friedenserkundungen in der Anfangsphase des zweiten Weltkrieges: Carl J. Burckhardt und Birger Dahlerus", in: *Einblick in die schweizerische Aussenpolitik. Zum 65. Geburtstag von Staatssekretär Raymond Probst.* Herausgegeben von Edouard Brunner et al. (Zürich: Verlag Neue Zürcher Zeitung, 1984): 375-399.

_____. *Zwischen Hoffmannsthal und Hitler: Facetten einer aussergewöhnlichen Existenz.* Zürich: 1991.

Stucki, Walter. *La fin du régime de Vichy.* Neuchâtel: Editions de la Baconnière, [1947].

Szöllösi-Janze, Margit. *Die Pfeilkreuzler Bewegung in Ungarn. Historischer Kontext, Entwicklung und Herrschaft.* München: R. Oldenbourg, 1989.

Tomasevich, Jozo. *The Chetniks. War and Revolution in Yugoslavia 1941-1945.* Stanford, CA: Stanford University Press, 1975.

Toynbee, Arnold and Veronica M. Toynbee, eds. *The War and the Neutrals. Survey of International Affairs 1939–1946.* London: Oxford University Press, 1956.

Tschuy, Theo. *Carl Lutz und die Juden von Budapest.* Vorwort von Simon Wiesenthal. Zürich: Verlag Neue Zürcher Zeitung, 1995.

Urner, Klaus. *Die Schweiz muss noch geschluckt werden. Hitler's Aktionpläne gegen die Schweiz.* Zürich: Verlag Neue Zürcher Zeitung, 1990. Überarbeitete und aktualisierte Neuausgabe [Taschenbuch]. Zürich: Pendo, 1998.

US Bureau of the Census. *Historical Statistics of the United States. Colonial Times to 1970.* Bicentennial Edition. Part 1. Washington, DC: Government Printing Office, 1975.

Vaudaux, Adolphe. *Blockade und Gegenblockade. Handelspolitische Sicherung der schweizerischen Ein- und Ausfuhr im Zweiten Weltkrieg.* Zürcher Studien zum internationalen Recht, 14. Zürich: Schulthess Polygraphischer Verlag, 1949.

Vogler, Albert. *Die schweizerischen Militärausgaben von 1860–1963 und ihre Auswirkungen auf die wirtschaftliche Entwicklung der Schweiz.* Dissertation Freiburg. Lungern: Druck Burch & Cie., 1965.

Waeger, Gerhart. *Die Sündenböcke der Schweiz. Die Zweihundert im Urteil der geschichtlichen Dokumente.* Olten: Walter-Verlag, 1971.

Wahlen, Friedrich T. *Politik aus Verantwortung. Reden und Aufsätze.* Herausgegeben und eingeleitet von Alfred A. Häsler. Basel: Friedrich Reinhardt Verlag, 1974.

Wahlen, Hermann, ed. *Rudolf Minger spricht. 24 Reden.* Bern: Francke, 1967.

Wehrli, Edmund. *Schweiz ohne Armee–eine Friedensinsel?* Zürich: Gesellschaft für militärhistorische Studienreisen, 1985.

Werenfels, Samuel. "Die schweizerische Praxis in der Behandlung von Flüchtlingen, Internierten und entwichenen Kriegsgefangenen im Zweiten Weltkrieg, " in: *Schwedische und schweizerische Neutralität.* Herausgegeben von Rudolf L. Bindschedler et al. (Basel: Helbing & Lichtenhahn, 1985): 377-404.

Wetter, Ernst. *Das Duell der Flieger und der Diplomaten.* Frauenfeld: Huber, 1987.

Willemin, Georges and Roger Heacock, under the Direction of Jacques Freymond. *The International Committee of the Red Cross.* International Organization and the Evolution of World Society, Vol. 2. The Graduate Institute of International Studies, Geneva. Boston: Martinus Nijhoff Publishers, 1984.

World Peace Foundation. *Documents on American Foreign Relations, 1941–1942.* New York: Simon & Schuster, 1939-1970.

Wylie, Neville. "Pilet-Golaz and the Making of Swiss Foreign Policy: Some Remarks", in *Schweizerische Zeitschrift für Geschichte* 47 (1997): 608-620.

Zaugg-Prato, Rolf. *Die Schweiz im Kampf gegen den Anschluss Oesterreichs an das deutsche Reich, 1918–1938.* Bern: Peter Lang, 1982.

Ziegler, Jean. *The Swiss, the Gold, and the Dead.* Translated by John Brownjohn. New York: Harcourt Brace, 1997.

Ziegler, Roland. *Geschichte der Sektion Heer und Haus.* Bern: AHQ, 1945.

──────────. *"Heer und Haus." Die Schweiz in Waffen.* Murten: Vaterländischer Verlag, 1945.

Zschokke, Helmut. *Die Schweiz und der spanische Bürgerkrieg.* Zürich: Limmat-Verlag, 1976.

LIST OF CONTRIBUTORS

Edgar Bonjour (1898-1991) was Professor of History at the University of Basel. He published a number of books, among them a nine volume work on Swiss neutrality, titled *Geschichte der schweizerischen Neutralität. Vier Jahrhunderte eidgenössischer Aussenpolitik.* 6th edition. Basel: Helbing & Lichtenhahn, 1970-1976. His articles and addresses have been published in seven volumes under the title *Die Schweiz und Europa. Ausgewählte Reden und Aufsätze.* Basel: Helbing & Lichtenhahn, 1958-1981.

Stephen P. Halbrook is an attorney, constitutional lawyer, and professor of history at Florida State University. He has published several works, among them *That Everyman Be Armed. The Evolution of a Constitutional Right.* 2nd edition. Oakland, CA: Independent Institute, 1994. His recent study is titled *Target Switzerland. Swiss Armed Neutrality in World War II.* Rockville Center, NY: Sarpedon Publishers, 1998. The book appeared in German as *Die Schweiz im Visier. Die bewaffnete Neutralität der Schweiz im Zweiten Weltkrieg* Schaffhausen: Verlag Novalis; 1999. In May 2000 he received a prize from the Max Geilinger Stiftung in recognition of his scholarly achievements. He is now engaged in a study that explores the experiences of individual Swiss during World War II.

James H. Hutson received his Ph.D. in history from Yale University in 1964, where he taught from 1964 to 1969. He then took a position at the Library of Congress and since 1982 has been Chief of its Manuscript Division. He is the author of several books, among them *The Sister Republics. Switzerland and the United States from 1776 to the Present.* Washington, D.C.: Library of Congress, 1991; expanded second edition 1992. French and German editions were published by the Stämpfli Verlag in Bern. Dr. Hutson also published *Religion and the Founding of the American Republic.* Washington, D.C.: Library of Congress, 1998.

Thomas Maissen studied history, Latin, and philosophy in Basel and Rome and did post-graduate work in Naples and Paris. He earned his doctorate in 1993 with a dissertation dealing with Renaissance historiography and political thought. He has published several books and numerous articles on Swiss and Renaissance history and is responsible for historical analysis at the *Neue Zürcher Zeitung.* In 1998 he published with Katri Burri *Bilder aus der Schweiz, 1939–1945.* Second edition, in the Verlag Neue Zürcher Zeitung.

Heinz K. Meier (1929-1989) was Louis I. Jaffé Professor of History at Old Dominion University in Norfolk, Virginia, from 1968 to 1975, when he became Dean of the School of Arts and Letters, a position he held until 1985. His work *Friendship Under Stress. U. S.—Swiss Relations 1900-1950* (Bern: Herbert Lang, 1970) offers an incisive and empathetic portrait of the shifting relationship between the two nations. In 1963 he was also instrumental in re-activating the Swiss American Historical Society and served as editor of its publications and two terms as its President.

Leo Schelbert received his Ph.D. in American History in 1966 from Columbia University in New York City. From 1963 to 1969 he taught at Rutgers University in Newark, NJ. From 1969 to 1971 he was on research leave in Switzerland, then took a position at the University of Illinois at Chicago with specialization in the history of American immigration. His published work includes several books and some fifty articles that deal mainly with the history of migration, especially of Swiss to the territory of the present United States. His critically edited documentary titled *America Experienced. Eighteenth and Nineteenth Century Accounts of Swiss Immigrants* was published by Picton Press in 1997.

Hans Senn studied history at the Universities of Zürich and Bern, Switzerland. After earning his Ph.D. in History he pursued a professional military career, attending for two years the École Supérieur de Guerre in Paris. He then joined the General Staff of the Swiss Army, in which he served as Chief of Operations, then as Vice Chief of Planning, and finally as Chief of the General Staff of the Swiss Armed Forces. After his retirement from the army he has been teaching military history and science at the University of Bern. He has published several articles and is engaged in historical research.

Jürg Stüssi-Lauterburg is a Swiss historian specializing in military history. He has featured the story of women in the Swiss military and is the author of *Föderalismus und Freiheit: Der Aufstand von 1802. Ein in der Schweiz geschriebenes Kapitel Weltgeschichte.* Brugg: Effingerhof, 1994. He has authored several articles and in 1999 published his latest book, titled *Weltgeschichte im Hochgebirge*, which explores the Swiss dimension of the European war of 1799.

Faith Ryan Whittlesey received her J. D. from the University of Pennsylvania in 1963 and did post-graduate work at the Academy of International Law at the Hague, Netherlands. She was a member of the Pennsylvania House of Representatives from 1972 to 1976. From 1981 to 1983 and again from 1985 to 1988 she served as ambassador of the United States to Switzerland. From 1983 to 1985 she was a member of the senior staff of the White House and served as an assistant to the President of the United States for public liaison. As President of the American Swiss Foundation she has been instrumental in promoting understanding between the United States and Switzerland.

INDEX

prepared by Picton Press